D0073170

Bankers to the Crown

Bankers to the Crown

The Riccardi of Lucca and Edward I

Richard W. Kaeuper

PRINCETON UNIVERSITY PRESS PRINCETON, NEW JERSEY

Publication of this book has been aided by the Whitney Darrow Publication Reserve Fund of Princeton University Press.

L. C. Card: 77-39788
ISBN: 0-691-05204-2
This book has been composed in IBM Press Roman by Science Press.
Printed in the United States of America by Princeton University Press, Princeton, New Jersey
A shorter version of chapter four appears in the winter 1972 issue of the *Welsh History Review*.

To Margaret

Preface

The name of Edward I (1272–1307) must be placed near the top of any list of outstanding Medieval English kings, ranking him in the select company of such rulers as William I, Henry I, and Henry II. His reign, and especially the productive first two decades before the troubled years beginning in 1294, represents a high point for the development of monarchy. From the unity forged by the House of Wessex, through the massive power increments in the fields of law, finance, and the military achieved by the Normans and early Plantagenets, the monarchy played an increasingly significant role in the ordering of English society. These kings added to the ancient sanctity of kingship a mastery of the new and vital forces of their age: the growing money economy, a feudal structure with the king at its apex, the striking increase in the numbers of educated men. Yet if monarchical power was increasing, it is also true that the reaction to that power was taking more effective and sophisticated forms. Having learned their lessons in a hard school of experience, the politically important groups in England were capable, by the thirteenth century, of checking the royal power, as they demonstrated most clearly on the field at Runnymede. After this reaction against King John and the struggles of crown and baronage while Henry III was king, the reign of Edward I presents a strong contrast.

Edward's success rested, in part, on personal qualities that differed sharply from those of King John, his grandfather, and Henry III, his father: a capacity to command obedience and earn respect. But it is also evident that power and prestige require a sound financial system that provides needed funds without provoking widespread or violent reaction. A company of Italian merchant-bankers, the *Societas Riccardorum de Luka*, was essential to such a system—and thus essential to Edward's success—between 1272 and 1294. The Riccardi of Lucca were the first in a procession of Italian companies that were to serve as invaluable financiers to the crown; the Frescobaldi, Bardi, and Peruzzi would follow in their footsteps. Although they were invaluable to the crown, the path led in all cases to ruin for the bankers.

An explanation of this first close relationship between an Italian *societas* and the English government necessarily involves analyzing many accounts between king and banker. The sums of money which give the quantitative measure of Riccardi importance in royal finance will have small meaning without some sense of the value of English money in the thirteenth century.[1] A rough scale of incomes and wages is more reliable and useful than a set of price lists.

At the top of the social scale the richest earls (Edmund, Earl of Cornwall; Thomas, Earl of Lancaster; the Clare Earls of Gloucester) could count on a landed income in the range of £6,000 to £8,000 a year, lesser comital families enjoying incomes of £2,000 to £5,000 a year.[2] A rich

[1]The most common coin was the penny, although halfpennies, farthings (quarter-pennies) and a few groats (fourpence) were struck in the 1279 recoinage. Sir John Craig, *The Mint*, p. 45. The pound (*librum*) was divided into twenty shillings (*solidi*), each of which was divided into twelve pennies (*denarii*). The mark was a unit of account equal to two-thirds of a pound (13s. 4d.).

[2]Michael Altschul, *A Baronial Family in Medieval England: the Clares, 1217-1314*, pp. 202-206, cites the following figures: Thomas, Earl of Lancaster, £8,000 in 1313-1314; Edmund, Earl of Cornwall, £5,000 to £6,000; the Clare Earls of Gloucester, £5,000 to £6,000; Roger Bigod, Earl of Norfolk, £4,000 in 1306; Isabella de Fortibus, Countess of Devon and Aumale, £2,500; the Warennes, Earls of Surrey, the Lacies, Earls of Lincoln,

bishopric might similarly bring more than £2,000.[3] Many barons had to be satisfied with sums of several hundred pounds.[4] But one could evidently live in some state on as little as £20 a year. Landed income of this amount was chosen as the level of wealth suitable for knighthood in the 1278 Distraint of Knighthood and the General Levy for France in 1297.[5] Mounted soldiers earned wages of 6d. to 2s. a day, depending on the quality of their arms and mounts, and the common footmen drew only 2d. a day.[6] Skilled workers had to be content with much less than the knights. The masons who built the king's massive castles in Wales drew a weekly wage ranging from 1s. 2d. to 3s., smiths and carpenters generally doing slightly less well. Minor workmen might collect only 1½d. a day.[7] At 3s. a week a man would earn less than £8 a year if he worked every week; at 1½d. a day the figure is about £2, working six-day weeks all year.

Some sense of the range of incomes helps to place the

---

and Beauchamps, Earls of Warwick, the Bohuns, Earls of Hereford and Essex, the Valences, Earls of Pembroke, all probably more than £2,000, although precise figures are not available.

[3]Winchester, Durham, Canterbury, and Ely all fall into this category. See J.R.H. Moorman, *Church Life in England in the Thirteenth Century*, p. 169. In *The Abbey and Bishopric of Ely* (1951), p. 94, Edward Miller has shown that the total gross income of Ely in 1298–99 was £3,500. J. Z. Titow has similarly shown that the thirteenth century income of Winchester fluctuated between £3,000 and £5,350 between 1221 and 1270. His work is cited by Edward Miller in *Past and Present* 28 (1964).

[4]Sidney Painter, "Studies in the History of the English Feudal Barony," *The Johns Hopkins University Studies in History and Political Science* LXI no. 3, pp. 173–174.

[5]Carl Stephenson and H. G. Marcham, *Sources of English Constitutional History*, nos. 50 (A) and 50 (D). William Stubbs, *Select Charters*, pp. 463–466.

[6]John E. Morris, *The Welsh Wars of Edward I*, pp. 49–54, 92–93. F. M. Powicke, *The Thirteenth Century*, p. 411.

[7]See the wage-scales in H. M. Colvin, ed., *The History of the King's Works*, vol. I, Chapter VI (by A. J. Taylor) and especially the table in vol. II, pp. 1030–1031.

figures in Riccardi accounts in better perspective. These accounts are of several types.[8] General reckonings of the merchants' receipts and expenses for the crown over a period of several years might be placed on the pipe rolls,[9] the massive yearly exchequer records, but they were occasionally drawn up as separate documents which fall under the modern rubric of Exchequer Accounts Various[10] (a class which may contain virtually any document of financial interest). To supplement these highly condensed statements, or to replace them where none are extant, we must turn to the records of specific royal revenues and particular government departments or officials. The customs proceeds and Riccardi loans charged on them appear in separate accounts for the periods not covered by general accountings.[11] *Liberate* rolls record warrants sent to the exchequer under the great seal to authorize payments, and issue rolls testify to payments made out of the treasury.[12] Since the Riccardi were intimately associated with the wardrobe, the financial department of the king's household, the accounts of the keeper of the wardrobe (for one or more regnal years) provide further substantial information.[13] The merchants also appear frequently in the two series of exchequer memoranda, the rolls kept by the lord treasurer's remembrancer and the king's remembrancer, which are similar but not

[8] On the Medieval English governmental records in general see the *Guide to the Contents of the Public Record Office* (1963) and V. H. Galbraith's studies: *An Introduction to the Use of the Public Records*, and *Studies in the Public Records*.

[9] An example is E 372/143 m. 35d. For the late pipe rolls see the introduction by Mabel H. Mills to *The Pipe Roll for 1295, Surrey Membrane* (Surrey Record Society, vol. VII, 1924).

[10] An example is E 101/126/1.

[11] See Table I at the end of Chapter III, below.

[12] On these rolls see Hilary Jenkinson, *A Manual of Archive Administration*, Appendix V, "Archive History of the Exchequer of Receipt."

[13] See Charles Johnson, "The System of Account in the Wardrobe of Edward I," *T.R.H.S.*, 4th series, VI (1923).

identical.[14] Financial business of every variety appears, but one particularly useful section of these rolls lists recognizances for debt in which private individuals formally registered their obligations to creditors. Almost without exception the documents mentioned so far have not been indexed and we find a particular individual or transaction only by scanning. But the invaluable Patent and Close rolls, the "out-letters" issued from Chancery,[15] and the Fine rolls have been indexed as well as calendared. All these sources (and many more) must be coordinated in order to evaluate the system of finance based on the Riccardi.

The problems presented by medieval financial documents are notorious. Tout mentions "the bewildering and varying number of accounts, the feeling that you have never got even all the recorded facts before you;" he warns that at best the wardrobe or exchequer accounts vaguely represent "turnover" in that department for the year. The "complicated system of constant short loans and their continued renewal and occasional repayment" militate against "facile generalizations" amid the "confusion and intricacies of medieval finance" in which calculations must be based upon "huge masses of ill-arranged, technical manuscript accounts."[16] To Tout's cautions we might add that sums are easily misread or overlooked in accounts using Roman numerals and paragraph form, and that interpretation of

[14] James F. Willard, "The Memoranda Rolls and the Remembrancers, 1282-1350," *Essays in Medieval History Presented to Thomas Frederick Tout*. J. Conway Davies, "The Memoranda Rolls of the Exchequer to 1307," *Studies Presented to Sir Hilary Jenkinson.*

[15] The Patent and Close Rolls contain a diverse collection of grants, orders, etc., the latter rolls addressed mainly to individuals, the former generally concerned with numerous people or administrative areas. Royal indebtedness for specific loans was often acknowledged in a letter patent. The Fine Rolls record not only offers or payments for grants, writs, licences, etc., but also include a great variety of information relating to the king's financial interests.

[16] T. F. Tout, *Chapters in the Administrative History of Medieval England*, II, pp. 86-87.

the figures is even more difficult because of terse and often vague explanations attached to the sums. Particularly troublesome is the overlapping of periods of account. The accounting year at the exchequer ran from Michaelmas (29 September) to Michaelmas; the wardrobe accounts are based on the king's regnal year (1 Edward I runs from 20 November 1272 to 19 November 1273); customs accounts often open and close at Easter; the accounting period of paymasters, clerks of the king's works, etc., show the predictable diversity. No researcher can harbor the slightest illusion that the accounts were written for his convenience.

Research in the manuscript sources in the Public Record Office, London, was made possible by a Woodrow Wilson Dissertation Fellowship for 1965–66 and by a grant from the Penrose Fund of American Philosophical Society for the summer of 1968. Revision and preparation of the manuscript were underwritten by a University of Rochester summer grant for 1970. All of this support is gratefully acknowledged.

It is no mere convention to thank those who have helped me. This study was written in its first form as a dissertation under the direction of Professor Joseph R. Strayer, Princeton University. I owe much to his guidance and judgment. Without the perspective and encouragement he provided I could easily have been swamped by the frustrating obscurities of medieval finance. Another special acknowledgment is owed to Dr. Edmund B. Fryde, University College of Wales, Aberystwyth, for most generously sharing his broad knowledge of English government finance, Italian bankers, and the use of archival evidence. He introduced me to the records, and our conversations while I was engaged in research were essential. The Public Record Office staff were most helpful in the months which followed. Professor Gaines Post, Princeton University, read this study in dissertation form and gave useful criticism. My original interest in the role of Italian merchant-bankers as financiers to the English government stems from work done with Mr. William J. Darcy when I was an undergraduate. Mr. Paul Cucci translated my transcriptions of the difficult Riccardi letters in E101/601/5, and Dr. Gino Corti translated those in the "Ancient Correspondence" (S C 1, 58). The index was carefully prepared by Richard King. My sincere thanks to all these men does not diminish my own responsibility for the accuracy of this study. The dedication page records a final debt of thanks which is difficult to measure.

Abbreviations of Sources Frequently Cited

DOCUMENTS (PUBLIC RECORD OFFICE, LONDON)

E 122	Customs Accounts
E 101	Exchequer Accounts Various
E 159	King's Remembrancer Memoranda Rolls
E 368	Lord Treasurer's Remembrancer Memoranda Rolls
E 372	Pipe Rolls
S C 1	Ancient Correspondence

PRINTED SOURCES

C.C.R.	*Calendar of Close Rolls, 1272–1307.*
C.D.I.	*Calendar of Documents Relating to Ireland, 1252–1301.*
C.F.R.	*Calendar of Fine Rolls, 1272–1307.*
C.P.R.	*Calendar of Patent Rolls, 1232–1313.*
C.C.R.V.	*Calendar of Various Chancery Rolls (Supplementary Close Rolls, Welsh Rolls, Scutage Rolls), 1277–1326.*
Cole, *Documents*	*Documents Illustrative of English History in the 13th and 14th centuries selected from the Records of the Department of the Queen's Remembrancer of the Exchequer.*
Foedera	*Foedera, conventiones, litterae et cuiuscumque generis acta publica inter reges Angliae et alios quosvis imperatores, reges, pontifices vel*

communitates. Ed. T. Rymer, Record Commision.

R.G. *Roles Gascons, 1242–1307.*

JOURNALS

B.I.H.R. *Bulletin of the Institute of Historical Research*, University of London

E.H.R. *English Historical Review*

T.A.P.S. *Transactions of the American Philosophical Society*

T.R.H.S. *Transactions of the Royal Historical Society*

Table of Contents

Bankers to the Crown

Chapter I The *Societas Riccardorum*

Numerous studies by distinguished scholars have familiarized us with the nature and importance of Italian merchant-bankers in early European history, the evidence and the coverage being especially good from the fourteenth century. Drawing on superior business organization, commanding significant capital resources, often enjoying papal patronage, the Lombards and Tuscans gradually crossed the Alps and penetrated Northwestern Europe in an Italian *diaspora* of vast importance.[1]

The latter part of the twelfth century marked a critical stage in this movement as the merchants began to frequent the famous fairs of Champagne, which had previously been purely local or regional markets.[2] They were at first "caravan merchants," peregrinators who lacked any permanent bases north of the Alps and accompanied their goods across streams and mountain passes. Working under adverse conditions in fairs designed with northern merchants in mind, the Italians made the most of a tough chal-

[1] See R. S. Lopez, "The Trade of Medieval Europe: The South," *C.E.H.*, II, Chapter V, pp. 287ff.

[2] O. Verlinden, "Markets and Fairs," *C.E.H.*, III, Chapter III, p. 130. Robert-Henri Bautier has questioned whether the mature form of the fairs was actually established by the late twelfth century in his article "Les foires de Champagne: recherches sur une evolution historique," *Bulletin de la Societe Jean Bodin, V, La Foire* (1953). R. D. Face has challenged this view in "Techniques of Business in the Trade Between the Fairs of Champagne and the South of Europe in the Twelfth and Thirteenth Centuries," *Economic History Review*, ser. 2 10 (1957-1958).

lenge and developed the economic techniques needed to succeed: partnerships, procuration, and agency agreements; advanced communication and transportation; sophisticated credit instruments.[3]

But an even more significant stage in the Italian penetration of *Oltremonte* came in the second half of the thirteenth century when the old traveling trade was replaced by a new and more efficient type of organization. In broad terms the "caravan merchant" gave way to the "sedentary merchant" who conducted his business from some fixed center while relying on partners or agents throughout a network extending across Western Europe. The change is so striking that it has been labeled the "commercial revolution" of the late thirteenth century.[4] Yet the merchants who inaugurated the change were simply continuing to devise more efficient methods of doing business. They created the *compagnia* or *societas* partnership, which associated for many years a number of partners who supplied both capital and management. This terminal partnership grew in place of the old *commenda*, which was a single venture partnership bringing together for a short term a resident partner who supplied capital and a traveling partner who supplied only management.[5] The

[3] R. D. Face, *Economic History Review*, ser. 2 10 (1957-1958). Cf. Rosalind Kent Berlow, "The Development of Business Techniques Used at the Fairs of Champagne from the End of the Twelfth Century to the Middle of the Thirteenth Century," *Studies in Medieval and Renaissance History* VIII (1971).

[4] The term "caravan merchant" is that of R. L. Reynolds. See his three related articles: "The Market for Northern Textiles in Genoa, 1179-1200," *Revue Belge de Philologie et d'Histoire*, VIII (1929) no. 3; "Merchants of Arras and the Overland trade with Genoa in the Twelfth Century," *Revue Belge*, IX (1930), no. 2; and "Genoese Trade in the Late Twelfth Century, particularly in Cloth from the Fairs of Champagne," *Journal of Economic and Business History*, III (1931) no. 3. N.S.B. Gras coined the term "sedentary merchant" in *Business and Capitalism*, Chapter III. Lopez is opposed to the restriction of the label "commercial revolution" to the late thirteenth century, asserting that this had been in process for at least three centuries before. *C.E.H.*, II, p. 335.

[5] Raymond de Roover, *Money, Banking and Credit in Mediaeval Bruges*, p. 12. Cf. his "The Organization of Trade," *C.E.H.*, III, Chapter II, pp. 42-43. Armando Sapori, *Le Marchand Italien au Moyen Age*, p. XXXI. R. S. Lopez, *C. E. H.*, II, pp. 323-324.

Italians also began to develop the bill of exchange, which made possible a transfer of purchasing power without costly and troublesome shipment of vast quantities of coins.[6] Equally important was the increasing sophistication of bookkeeping in which great strides were made even before the invention of double-entry notation.[7] With these business advances it was possible for a company based in Florence or Siena or Lucca to conduct its operations through correspondence with branches in Paris or Bruges or London as well as the Champagne fairs which were at this time shifting from a commercial to a more strictly financial character.[8] The famous Italian companies begin to appear.[9]

The attractions which brought the Italians north and stimulated their advanced techniques were numerous. Crusade finance was a factor of some importance; more than one merchant found that he had to travel to the court of a king or baron to recover money loaned for an expedition to the Holy Land. The stimulus of papal finance was even greater. Large sums of money were owed the papal camera by princes ecclesiastical or lay, in all parts of Europe; taxes for future crusades also had to be collected and transferred to Rome. What better means could be used than the great Italian companies with their networks of branches in major cities, their facilities for transfers without the carting of specie? For the merchant-bankers a commission as *mercatores domini papae* meant the opportunity of utilizing large sums of money before the tithes, taxes, etc., would be transferred to Rome. Finally, one of the most significant attractions was the flourishing trade involving the fine wool produced by English flocks and the beauti-

[6]De Roover, *L'Evolution de la Lettre de Change, XIVe-XVIIIe Siecles*, introduction and Chapter I. Cf. his *Banking in Bruges*, p. 12, and his *The Medici Bank, Its Organization, Management, Operations and Decline*, pp. 32-33.

[7]De Roover, *Banking in Bruges*, pp. 12–13, writes: "In the late thirteenth century and the beginning of the fourteenth century, perhaps more than at any other period of history, accounting advanced with great strides in order to adapt itself to the change in business organization."

[8]See the sources listed in note 2.

[9]A useful list of these companies is given by Raymond de Roover in *C.E.H.*, III, pp. 75-6.

ful cloths woven from this wool on Flemish looms. Through the twelfth century the Italian involvement in this trade increased and the northern industry came to depend in large measure upon the distant Mediterranean markets, both for some raw materials such as dyestuffs and for outlets in which the finished product could be sold. By the close of the following century the Italians were second to none in wool commerce. They were beginning, moreover, to develop a woolen industry at home, finishing cloths shipped from Flanders and even weaving the cloths themselves from raw English wool.[10]

The Riccardi must be seen in the framework of this "commercial revolution" of the thirteenth century if we are to understand their role in English government finance. The expertise and the capital they could place at the service of Edward I stem from the vast business opportunities available to men active in the wool trade and papal finance across northwestern Europe. Yet with few exceptions the sources from which their story can be constructed are English government documents. Unfortunately the accounts drawn up by exchequer or wardrobe clerks and the writs penned in chancery only infrequently yield information on the private business and structure of the company. We can learn enough, though, to allow us to examine the Riccardi as an early example of the merchant-banking companies that were becoming prominent in the economic life of Northwestern Europe. Moreover, we can supplement the official records with a series of business letters written by the Riccardi in Lucca to their London partners between 1295 and 1303.[11]

1. STRUCTURE AND PERSONNEL

The early history of the firm in England is naturally obscure, since its link with the crown was still tenuous. As early as the

[10] See Eileen Power, *The Wool Trade in English History*, pp. 53–55, Eleanora Carus-Wilson, "The Woolen Industry," *C.E.H.*, II, Chapter VI, Part III.

[11] See the appendix at the end of this chapter.

1240's merchants from Lucca had begun business operations which brought their names into the royal records, and on many occasions Henry III bought fine cloths and expensive ecclesiastical vestments from them. We first see the merchants supplying these goods in June of 1245 when the king paid "Reyner of Lucca and Peregrine his partner" about £50 for a length of samite and six orphreys.[12] These two partners appear again in 1251,[13] and on three occcasions in 1253 Peregrine is associated with a "Henry of Lucca."[14] In the following year the three merchants are mentioned together.[15] The surnames of these Lucchesi and two additional partners are given in letters obligatory which Henry issued them in July of 1254. The king is held to "Peregrino Sesmundi, Bartholomeo Bendini, Reynero Senaci, Henrico Saraceni, Luco Natali et sociis suis, civibus et mercatoribus de Luca."[16] In 1256 and again in 1262 the king deals with "Luke de Luka and his fellows."[17] Luke and Reyner provide certain necessaries for the wardrobe in 1263,[18] and a few years later Luke appears in the service of Archbishop Giffard of York with a partner named Reyner Magiari.[19]

This thin thread of continuity over twenty-five years is of interest, for in Lucasio Natale ("Luke de Luka") and Reiner Magiari we have an association of two Lucchese merchants who can be unquestionably identified as members of the company that served

[12]*Calendar of Liberate Rolls, 1240-1245*, p. 309.

[13]*Ibid., 1245-1251*, p. 328.

[14]*Ibid., 1251-1260*, pp. 14, 99, 146.

[15]*R.G.*, I, no. 4241.

[16]*Ibid.*, no. 3877. In March of 1255 King Henry assigned sums from the tallage on London and York to the following: "Pelegrin Cismundi, King's merchant, Henry the Saracen [an obvious misrendering of Enrico Sarraceni], Reyner Sinok, Bartholomew Bendini, Luke Natalis and fellows, citizens and merchants of Lucca." They were to receive 2,246 marks. *C.P.R.* 1247-1258, p. 404.

[17]Thomas Madox, *History of the Exchequer* (2nd ed., 1769), p. 95, *C.P.R. 1258-1266*, p. 218.

[18]*C.P.R. 1258-1266*, pp. 257-258.

[19]*Register of Walter Giffard, Archbishop of York*, I, p. 153. The surname of the latter is given as Mayarii.

Edward I.[20] The roots of the Riccardi company thus extend back into the 1240's, and it is possible that the company itself was in existence at that time. Yet as the evidence reveals an increasing number of merchants in association, we cannot know if we are watching the gradual construction of a *societas* or simply have more information concerning a company already fully established. The first appearances of the name Riccardi in official records do not solve the problem. Papal documents use it in 1276,[21] but English government sources are very slow to describe the company by any formula other than naming a prominent member or two and adding "and their fellows, merchants of Lucca." This changes only in the late 1270's and early 1280's.[22] We have no evidence as to when the merchants themselves adopted the name, but since several members of the home branch are surnamed Riccardi, we can conclude that men of this name formed the original partnership and gave the company its title.[23]

It would probably be safe to assume that by the time Edward came to a basic agreement with Luke and his fellows at the beginning of his reign, these merchants were the English representatives of a flourishing "international" firm which, if not constituted three decades earlier, at least had antecedents with many years' experience in England.

Two difficulties complicate the identification of Riccardi personnel at any period. One is the nature of the contract in which the merchants agreed to act in partnership for a specified term;

[20] Several scholars have similarly suggested a long history of these Lucchesi in England before the reign of Edward I. See R. J. Whitwell, "English Monasteries and the Wool Trade in the 13th Century," *Vierteljahrschrift für Sozial- und Wirtschaftsgeschichte* II (1904). Emilio Re, "La compagnia dei Riccardi e il suo fallimento alla fine del secolo decimoterzo," *Archivio della Societa Romana di Storia Patria* XXXVII (1914).

[21] Lunt, *Financial Relations*, Appendix VI.

[22] In their early days as king's bankers, Luke and his fellows on occasion are even called Florentines, E 403/1235, C 62/50 mm. 5, 6.

[23] See Table I at the end of this chapter. The name of the Italian family was undoubtedly spelled Ricciardi, but I will follow the spelling found in English sources which is also that used by most scholars writing on this period of English history.

when this time had elapsed they were free to withdraw and join another firm or strike out on their own. The capital was divided into shares held by the partners, who would divide profits and losses in proportion to their share of the capital each time the partnership expired. A successful partnership would, of course, be continually renewed.[24] The company of the Peruzzi, for example, which existed from 1275 to its bankruptcy in 1345, actually represents successive partnerships formed by new articles of association in 1300, 1308, 1310, 1312, 1324, 1331, and 1335.[25] The problem in the case of the Riccardi is that although we know that the company was constituted as a sworn *societas,*[26] we do not know how often a new partnership agreement was drawn up, nor what the terms were. It is possible that the accountings with the English government were timed to coincide with the expiration of the successive partnership terms. If so this would set the dates of new articles of association in 1279, 1281, 1282, 1286, 1290, and 1294.[27] But there is no assurance that these accountings were held because of renewals of the Riccardi structure rather than as a matter of simple royal convenience.

[24]E. Jordan, *De Mercatoribus Camerae Apostolicae Saeculo XIII*, pp. 37, 43. See Raymond de Roover, "The Story of the Alberti Company of Florence, 1302-1348, as Revealed in Its Account Books," *Business History Review* XXXII (1958), for the several methods of dividing profits among the members of this company. For his comments on the Peruzzi see *C.E.H.*, III, p. 77, cf. Saproi, *Le Marchand Italien*, pp. XXXI–XXXIV, LXIV. At a time when the society of the Riccardi was sliding towards bankruptcy, the commune of Lucca appointed arbiters to assess what each partner owed to the company, so that this sum could be collected from his goods and used to meet a part of the obligations of the company. There are numerous requests for this information in the letters from Lucca to London, E 101/601/5, *passim*.

[25]De Roover, *Banking in Bruges*, pp. 31-32.

[26]E 101/601/5, pp. 24, 40: letters of 5 August 1296 and 3 November 1301.

[27]The documents containing these accounts are E 101/126/1, E 372/124 m. 1d., E 372/125 m. 1, E 372/133 m. 32d., E 372/134 m. 3, E 372/143 m. 35d. The Riccardi themselves only once refer to a partnership agreement. In an undated letter they comment on a lawsuit brought against them by the heirs of a deceased partner "because they do not approve of the settlement of the partnership we had from '89 to '92, and they want to see the

A second difficulty is the distinction which must be drawn between the full partners (the *socii* or "fellows" in government documents who invested their funds and received a proportionate share of profits or sustained a proportionate share of losses) and the "factors," who were salaried agents and who could be hired or dismissed at any time.[28] Again, our specific information on the Riccardi is deficient. Neither in government documents nor in the Riccardi business letters is this important distinction drawn for the personnel of the company in England or on the continent. The important leaders in England certainly could have numbered among the partners; cases of partners going abroad to the branches are known among the Peruzzi in the next century.[29]

The nature of the evidence thus makes positive identification of the names and status of all the Riccardi staff in England difficult. Yet outside the fluctuations which might easily be explained by death or transfer of partners and changes among factors, the basic continuity of the company was broken only once. Sometime after Easter of 1286 Baroncino Gualteri, who had evidently been the leading member of the firm in England, left the company with his two sons, Brunetto and Riccardo, to form an independent group. The loss was a serious one, for Baroncino was

accounts of all partners." S C 1, 58 no. 15. This comment neither confirms nor rules out the hypothesis that royal accountings coincided with Riccardi partnership renewals: a 1290 royal account could have followed a 1289 expiration of the partnership term; if a new partnership agreement was drawn up in 1292 perhaps no royal account was thought necessary at that time. This same letter indicates that a single partnership agreement covered both England and Ireland. The Lucca partners write, "You know that . . . who managed the England partnership took all of Ireland and put on the England partnership all the profit made in that of Ireland. . . ."

28Some of the agents originally employed by the Riccardi as customs collectors in the English ports were actually members of other companies. See Chapter III, Section 1. They were probably temporarily hired as factors of the Riccardi. For the firing of a Riccardi factor see the undated letter E 101/601/5 pp. 46, 46d. Another undated letter, *ibid.*, p. 14, records the complaint of a certain Panello that he did not receive salary and expenses while in Riccardi service.

29De Roover, *Banking in Bruges*, p. 33. The partner then collected a salary as well as his share in the profits.

described in a later letter as having been the *signore et maesstro* of the company.[30] With this exception there is a notable continuity in Riccardi personnel across more than two decades.

During the period when the Riccardi were in the service of the English government there could have been as many as a dozen members in England, either *socii* or factors, whose activities were important enough to place their names in government records, and perhaps another three or four in Ireland. (See Table I.) This indicates that the *Societas Riccardorum* was a company of considerable size and that its English operations required a significant investment of personnel. In 1336 the Peruzzi, the second largest company of the day, employed ninety factors scattered in fifteen branches.[31] At the beginning of the fourteenth century the Acciaiuoli, third largest in Florence, also had fifteen branches, but employed only forty-one factors outside the home office, two of them residing in London. In 1372 the Guinigi company, largest in Lucca, numbered only nineteen men, including four factors in Bruges, three in Naples, and three in Venice.[32]

A few important families, and especially the da Pogio and Guidiccioni, provided much of the leadership and many of the members of the Riccardi. The reference to Baroncino as "lord and master" may indicate that a definite position and title were provided for one man as head of the company, but it is equally likely that age, experience, and natural ability normally gave to a small inner group of two or three the final direction of affairs.[33]

[30]E 101/601/5, p. 8; letter of 17 November 1301. Compare the position of Alberto in the Alberti company. De Roover, *Business History Review* XXXII (1958), p. 43.

[31]De Roover, *The Rise and Decline of the Medici Bank*, p. 3. He notes that the Medici Bank never reached the size of the greatest fourteenth-century companies. In 1469 the total Medici staff numbered sixty with four men in London. See the table in *C.E.H.*, III, p. 86.

[32]De Roover, *Banking in Bruges*, p. 39.

[33]The business letters often refer to special friends and clients as *signore*, so that the term may be a rather loose one. De Roover notes that in theory all partners in a company held an equal voice, but that in fact one leader was accepted. *The Medici Bank*, p. 6. In *Banking in Bruges*, p. 38, he suggests that whatever the legal structure (i.e., centralized or decentralized),

This question of leadership should be considered in the light of the distinction Raymond de Roover has drawn between two main legal and structural types of banking companies in early European history. The decentralized form is best seen in the fifteenth-century Medici Bank, which had separate partnerships, capital, and books for each of the major enterprises: the home bank in Florence; the branches, managed by junior partners; the three industrial establishments in Florence. In contrast, the earlier centralized form characteristic of the great fourteenth-century companies consisted of a single partnership; one group of men owned and directed the home office and all branches, usually managed by factors. De Roover suggests that the failure of so many companies constructed on this centralized pattern—the Franzesi (failed in 1304), Macci (1312), Frescobaldi (1315), Cerchi Bianchi (1320), Bardi, Peruzzi, and Acciaiuoli (1345)—led to the abandonment of the centralized organization which had grown up in the thirteenth century.[34]

In this classification the *Societas Riccardorum* predictably belongs to the centralized category and provides an early example of that form. Its failure in 1301 could be placed at the head of de Roover's list. Yet the degree of control exercised by the home branch should not be overestimated, and we cannot be certain that the leaders in England were generally factors rather than partners.

The very fact of slow communications among branches would lead us to expect that the Riccardi establishments in various countries had to have much freedom of action; and the correspondence between Lucca and London confirms the feeling that a rough equality existed between the partners in these cities. "We have the same trust and faith in you," the Lucca partners wrote to London, "as we have in ourselves."[35] If the Riccardi in Lucca

---

branch managers had to have much independence within a general framework of instructions from the central branch. cf. *C.E.H.*, III, pp. 78, 87. Riccardi correspondence refers to one man managing the partnership in England and Ireland. S C 1, 58 no. 15.

[34] De Roover, *The Medici Bank*, pp. 5-7, *Banking in Bruges*, p. 31.

[35] E 101/601/5, p. 19d., undated letter.

had a pre-eminence as the home branch, it was nonetheless not an absolute authority. They usually suggested or rebuked, but did not order. In 1301 they wrote to London that they had been receiving the requests for a replacement from Ghirardo Chimbardi. "And since this grieves us because we do not have any person from Lucca to send there now. . .we therefore ask you, among other things, that you send Betto Antolmini who is from here, and that you should send him or anyone else you think is good and appropriate, in the name of God, to live there for our affairs, for to leave that country without any representative from us does not seem good or wise."[36]

Yet although some degree of regional autonomy was necessary, the complicated business of international finance could not function smoothly if the company were merely a loose confederation of branches. An individual or another company would have an account with the *Societas Riccardorum*, not with the London Riccardi or the Paris Riccardi. In 1295 the Lucca Riccardi sent to London a rough list of the major debts outstanding on loans advanced in England. In each case they stated that the individual owed "us" a certain sum.[37] It was of considerable importance, thus, constantly to exchange the information necessary to keep accounts up to date, and the letters often contain requests of this sort. "We cannot speak clearly concerning ourselves [i.e., our affairs] unless we have your accounts and especially your bills of exchange. . . ."[38]

Thus the Riccardi represent the centralized form, but one in which the leadership of the London branch probably included partners as well as factors and certainly enjoyed even more independence of action than often was the case in the companies of the fourteenth century. The unusual importance of English trade

[36]*Ibid.*, p. 16, letter of 5 September 1301. At this time the company was nearly ruined. In normal times they maintained a number of Irish representatives.

[37]*Ibid.*, pp. 26d., 27, letter of 10 October 1295.

[38]*Ibid.*, undated letter, p. 37. Copies of bills of exchange were kept in addition to the account books. When the latter were seized, the Lucca partners still asked for the former. *Ibid.*, p. 24, letter of 5 August 1296.

and English government finance to the Riccardi easily explains why the leaders of the London branch enjoyed this degree of autonomy.

Without doubt, the man who shaped the fortunes of the company in its earliest years of association with Edward I was Lucasio Natale, the "Luk' de Luk' " of the documents. The merchants were probably already applying the name Riccardi to their company, but the English clerks always identify them simply as associates of Luke. It was Luke and his fellows who sent money to the Lord Edward on crusade, who concluded the agreement which resulted in Riccardi control of the English and Irish customs, who collected the fifteenth of 1275 and helped finance Edward's first war in Wales. At this time Luke may have been an old man, feeling that there were few years left to him, for before going to Rome in the king's service in 1277 he gave power of attorney to Orlandino and Reyner "to dispose and ordain of his debts, goods and chattels, whether he die or not, as they shall deem fit for his advantage. . . ."[39] Luke returned to England before his death, which occurred between June and November of 1279,[40] and he and Orlandino rendered account of the society's receipts and expenses for the first seven years of the reign in the summer of 1279.[41]

After Luke's death the affairs of the society went on without interruption. With his name in the grant of the customs in 1275 had been associated that of Orlandino da Pogio (latinized as Orlandinus de Podio), and from that time until our evidence on the society fades in the early fourteenth century, he was to be one of the chief members of the Riccardi in England. The 1276 view of account names both Luke and Orlandino, as does the general account in 1279. Orlandino represented the company at the mint during the following two years, and was apparently in charge of the extensive Riccardi financing of Edward's residence in Gas-

[39] *C.C.R. 1272-1279*, p. 413.

[40] He is mentioned in the order for the general account issued on 10 June 1279. *C.C.R. 1272-1279*, p. 531. By 13 November he is described as deceased. *Ibid*., p. 546.

[41] E 101/126/1. Cf. Re, *Archivio*, p. 98.

cony in 1286-1289. Along with Federigo, he accounted for Riccardi receipts and expenses for the king in the years 1290-1294. During the trying years between the fall from royal favor and the bankruptcy, 1294-1301, the letters from Lucca always place his name first in the salutation. He lived through the collapse of the company, but after 1306 we lose trace of him altogether.[42]

Orlandino's importance in the firm always overshadowed that of his brother Enrico, but Enrico was nevertheless given positions of considerable responsibility. With Baroncino he accounted for the customs during 1279-1281, and was in charge of numerous large transfers of money in Gascony in 1286-1289.[43]

From the spring of 1278 Baroncino Gualteri appears as a leading member of the Riccardi. Although he had been in England for at least twenty-three years, it is only at this point that he can be associated with the company. His sudden assumption of a position of influence indicates his abilities. He was evidently held in high regard by the Italian merchant community. When several merchants banished by Henry III bought their return into the king's grace in 1262, they came armed with a commendation from Urban IV but still thought it wise to obtain the backing of Baroncino and of Diutatus Guillelmi.[44] In the same year, when a dispute broke out over contracts between Diutatus and several other Florentines, they chose "Baroncinus son of Sir Walterius de Vulturna, citizen and merchant of Lucca" as arbitrator.[45] During the years of the Barons' War he engaged in some business with Simon de Montfort the Younger "and other the king's enemies," either of his own will or, as he said, to satisfy Simon, "whom of necessity he had to propitiate for his own salvation in those

[42]*C.P.R. 1272-1281*, pp. 131-132, E 101/126/1, E 372/143 m. 35d. *C.C.R. 1296-1307*, p. 427. These Riccardi services are discussed in detail in Chapter II, Sections 1 and 2.

[43]For the customs account, see E 372/124 m. 1d. On Gascony, see Chapter II, Section 2.

[44]Whitwell, *T.R.H.S.* n.s. 17 (1903) pp. 210-211, citing Liber A, fo. 209, 209d. Diutatus was a banker to Queen Eleanor and later farmed Edward's "new aid" of 1266. See below, Chapter III note 13.

[45]*C.P.R. 1272-1281*, pp. 129-131.

days."[46] The results of an inquiry concerning this are unknown, but even if he had been dealing with "the enemy" of his free will, it did not curb his career.

In fact, very little seemed to curb Baroncino's career. Of all the men associated with the Riccardi in England, he emerges as the most successful, joining the company once its profitable link with the crown had been forged but leaving it before the link was transformed into the fetters of arrest and failure. We would probably not be wrong in assuming that initially there was a mutual attraction between the rising fortunes of the Riccardi and his own ambitions and abilities. What motives or disagreements prompted him to leave the firm in 1286, however, remain unknown. The company was then enjoying prosperity and full royal favor. Along with his two sons Riccardo and Brunetto and a grandson, Nicholao, he remained active in money-lending and the wool trade while the Riccardi buckled and collapsed.[47] By 1314 he and one son, Brunetto, had died[48] and we lose track of the others. While in the company Baroncino had been most closely associated with the financing of the second Welsh War. He also twice accounted

[46]*Select Cases on the Law Merchant*, Selden Society 46, pp. 9-10. Baroncino evidently continued his connections with the Montfort family, for Earl Simon's widow owed him money on her death. See Table II, at the end of the chapter.

[47]Information on their money-lending and wool purchases is scattered through the Memoranda Rolls for these years. Baroncino and his sons continued some work for Edward, but on a very limited scale. It was perhaps with his eyes on future royal favor that Baroncino made a loan to Prince Edward, the future Edward II, in 1305, at a time when a quarrel between father and son had led to some reduction of the prince's revenues. The original request for the loan is preserved among the Ancient Correspondence, S C 1/30 no. 42. For the original letter obligatory for £466 13s. 4d., see C 47/13/1 no. 29. Hilda Johnstone prints the various documents concerning this loan in *Letters of Edward Prince of Wales, 1304-5* (1931), pp. 81, 98, 101, and notes in her introduction, p. xix, that this large loan "paid off the neediest or greediest of the prince's creditors. . . ." Cf. *C.P.R. 1313-1317*, p. 101.

[48]*C.P.R. 1313-1317*, p. 101.

for the customs–with Enrico da Pogio for 1279-1281, and with Riccardo Guidiccioni for 1281-1282.[49]

Riccardo was the most important member of the Guidiccioni family among the Riccardi in England. He answered for the customs receipts over a period of eight years, 1282-1290.[50] Furthermore, when the Welsh rebellion of 1287 caught the government by surprise, and the king, the wardrobe, and several of the leading Riccardi *socii* were in Gascony, the major burden of directing the financing of an expedition fell upon him.[51] Tomassino Guidiccioni, although not so prominent as Riccardo, was entrusted with some important missions by the king, such as that to Rome in 1290, and may have been in charge of the Riccardi branch at York for some time.[52] Aldebrandino and Marcassino, also members of this family, were apparently men of lesser abilities, though Marcassino appears only as Riccardi fortunes in England were fading.

Labro Volpelli was a fellow of Luke working in England in the early 1270's and perhaps again at the end of the decade, but he seems to have been basically concerned with Riccardi business at the *curia*. It was through Labro that Edward acted on several occasions, paying the *census* and showering gifts on key cardinals; the archbishops of Canterbury and York similarly used his services in Rome, as we shall see. In the years after 1294 the company entrusted him with winning papal support, and it was while thus engaged that he died, on 22 November 1300.[53]

[49] The various writs and the accounts are in his name. See below, Chapter IV, Section 2. The customs accounts are found in E 372/124 m. 1d. E 372/125 m. 1.

[50] E 372/133 m. 32d. E 372/134 m. 3.

[51] See below, Chapter IV, Section 4.

[52] See note 68.

[53] See Chapter II, Section 2. The letter to the London Riccardi announcing Labro's death says that "on the 22nd of November God called to Himself Labro Volpelli," but this letter is dated only as 4 December, without year. Yet it must be dated 1300, for on 30 November 1300 Boniface VIII instructed the bishop of Lucca to seize the goods of Labro who had recently died (Lunt, *Papal Revenues*, I, pp. 323–4); moreover, a letter from the Lucca partners, obviously written after April of 1300, refers to Labro as still living. E 101/601/5 pp. 43, 11. Cf. Re, *Archivio* XXXVII, p. 135.

Another fellow of Luke in the 1270's, Federigo Venture, comes prominently into view only later. He appeared with Orlandino to account for payments and receipts in the king's service 1290-1294,[54] and is frequently mentioned in the letters of 1295-1301. His name is almost invariably included in the salutation, reserved for the most important agents in England.

Direction of affairs in Ireland was first given to a "Hug' de Luk' " who was probably Hugolino Rossciompeli. Within a few years, however, he was eclipsed by Percival Gerarduci and Bendino Panici, who held the reins until the mid 1280's.[55] At this time a new pair came to the fore—Ghirardo Chimbardi and Francesco Malisardi. To them fell the task of conducting company affairs in an atmosphere of increasing hostility from the Irish administration.[56] These difficulties discouraged Ghirardo, who frequently sent complaints to Lucca, pressing for a replacement. His father plagued the Riccardi in Lucca on his behalf, as they wrote to London in 1301, "blaming us harshly and crying sorrowfully because of the fact that his son went to Ireland at the service of the company more than thirteen years ago; and he has spent no more than five months together with his wife since that time, so that he can very reasonably, and with many reasons, grieve much because of his assignment, and blame us."[57]

The sources tell us little about men of lower rank, though we occasionally see them in action. Two "men of the Riccardi" were wounded and ill-treated in a 1294 robbery involving the king's goods worth £220. Although we do not know their status within the Riccardi organization, the interesting fact is that they were Englishmen, showing that those employed by the society were not solely Italians.[58] Another Englishman, John de Redmere, is mentioned in an earlier document as an agent of the Riccardi.[59] He is a figure of some interest in that his legal case with James le

[54]E 372/143 m. 35d.
[55]E 101/230/5 mm. 1, 4, 5, 6.
[56]See Section 4 of this chapter.
[57]E 101/601/5, p. 39d., letter of 3 November 1301.
[58]E 143/3/6 no. 103 and 103/2.
[59]*C.P.R. 1281-1292*, p. 17.

Roy is regarded as one of the antecedents for the famous statute of Acton Burnell and its successor, the statute of merchants.[60]

The headquarters of the Riccardi in England were naturally located in London, and it was here that they transacted most of their business in a building which they either owned or rented.[61] It seems that a "northern branch" was located in York,[62] and there definitely was a Riccardi house in Dublin.[63] In addition to these few centers, they could operate through their agents who were customs collectors in the ports of England and Ireland. The buildings they maintained were probably part business office, part warehouse, and no doubt contained strongrooms for money and valuables. In the counting-house proper we can envision desks with brass and copper inkwells, tables for displaying and measuring cloth, a strongbox for cash, and perhaps even a case with pigeon-holes for classifying mail.[64]

[60]See H. Hall, ed., *Select Cases on the Law Merchant* II, pp. XXXII-XXXIV, 18-27. Powicke, *Thirteenth Century*, pp. 623-626. Although it is at first glance tempting to see some connection between the king's merchants and these statutes favoring foreign merchants, the Riccardi agent would have to be not Redmere but Le Roy, in order for such speculation to be valid. It was Le Roy who was in the position of the foreign merchant trying to bring an action against a native landowner and friend of the sheriff.

[61]A reference to a "house of Luke of Luka and his fellows in the city of London" appears in E 159/49 m. 26. In 1279 cloth of gold is carried "from the house of Luke of Luka to the tower when the king was at the tower." E 101/3/15. Until 1281 the merchants held a "capital messuage" of the king in the parish of St. Faith. It included tenements and five shops. In October of that year they surrendered it to the crown. *C.P.R. 1272-1281*, p. 458.

[62]In the account of wardrobe necessary expenses for 15 Edward I, E 36/201 p. 77, there is a reference to fellows of Orlandino *Eboracum morantibus*. The *Register* of Archbishop Romeyne, I, pp. 27-29, likewise mentions Tomassino Guidiccioni and fellows "dwelling in York."

[63]E 101/231/23. The Riccardi owned several buildings in Dublin, and after the company collapsed they were held by a king's sergeant. *C.C.R. 1302-1307*, p. 303.

[64]Not only would money and such valuables as cloth of gold be kept in the Riccardi house, but even bulky staples such as grain were stored there. A household roll of necessary expenditure shows grain being carted from

Our slight evidence for the Riccardi on the continent indicates that—outside of Lucca—they had establishments at the papal court, in France, Flanders, and Gascony. The Riccardi house in Paris, located in the Parroise Saint Merri,[65] was not their sole branch in France. The financial importance of the fairs of Champagne necessitated placing Riccardi agents there,[66] and another branch can be located in Nîmes.[67] The men in Flanders[68] would look to the receipt of wool shipped from England in addition to their other affairs. In Gascony, the Riccardi operated from a house in Bordeaux.[69]

Regular communications had to be maintained among these far-flung centers. One means was the occasional travels of members, on either the king's affairs or those of the company, but it was above all through a stream of business letters that the Riccardi coordinated their affairs from Ireland to Tuscany. The various Italian companies apparently cooperated in carrying letters for their friends,[70] and Sapori refers to "le service postal, que les

the Riccardi house to Westminster. E 101/3/15. De Roover notes the contents of a typical fourteenth-century counting-house in *C.E.H.*, III, p. 90.

65C. Piton, *Les Lombards*, I, pp. 126, 130. This information is taken from the records of the taille.

66E 101/601/5 *passim*. Luchese merchants rented a hall at Troyes, near the church of Saint Jean; the Riccardi probably shared it, for when the rent was renewed for five years in 1266, two men later identifiable as members of the company were named. Leon Mirot, *Études Lucquoises*, p. 3. The Riccardi are "Richardo Guidechonis and Theobaldino Maniumac." As we have seen, the former was an important member of the Riccardi establishment in England at a later date. The latter was, no doubt, related to the Francisco Maneumach of the Paris Riccardi, mentioned in C 47/13/1 no. 15.

67E 36/201 pp. 22, 61. C 47/4/3. Leon Mirot, *Études Lucquoises*, p. 3 n. 1, citing Piton, *Les Lombards*, I, p. 221.

68E 101/601/5 *passim*.

69E 36/201 p. 16.

70See the letter of 5 December 1297. E 101/601/5, p. 3d. A letter from London was sent by a Master John of Siena who gave it to a Florentine named Ristolo, of the company of the Spini, who delivered it, "being on horseback and coming from France to go to Florence." The Lucca Riccardi seem a bit displeased over this indirect delivery. On a later occasion Netto di Baroncino (i.e., Brunetto, the son of Baroncino) delivered a letter, long compagnies memes se chargeaient d'éxecuter à tour de rôle."[71] But the more common practice no doubt was to use the messengers maintained by the company, and we find the London Riccardi dispatching Stefano, Rubino, and Bocco with correspondence;[72] they spent about five or six weeks on the road between London and Lucca.[73] Directives, advice, inquiries, information, and occasional recriminations were carried across Europe in their packets, which must frequently have been bulky pouches, for the extant letters mention rolls of account, letters of exchange, and copies of communications to important people.

All these types of documents have disappeared save a few of the Riccardi business letters, but these provide a rich source. As Sapori noted of this type of source in general,

> La lettre du marchand, la plupart du temps, représente autre chose qu'une simple manifestation de civilité; elle remplace la journal moderne. On y trouve alternativement des renseignements commerciaux, des formulaires, des informations politiques, des chiffres arides et des personnages historiques, des previsions d'évenéments de toutes sortes donnant la mesure de la culture de l'ecrivain; et aussi des narrations agréables sur les intrigues de cour des seigneurs laics ou ecclésiastiques, jusqu'à des potins des personnages qui nous semblent d'une importance secondaire.[74]

---

after the group led by Baroncino had split off from the Riccardi. Undated letter, p. 45.

[71] Sapori, *Le Marchand Italien*, p. XXV.

[72] E 101/601/5, pp. 25d., 1, 44, letters of 10 October 1295, 5 December 1297, and 21 April 1298.

[73] *Ibid.*, p. 25d., letter of 10 October 1295. A letter sent from London on 18 August arrived in Lucca on 22 September. Another sent 24 February 1300 arrived on 5 April. *Ibid.*, letter, p. 11. Unusual circumstances no doubt delayed the letter sent on 5 September 1297, which arrived only on 5 December of that year. The hostility of the French government to the bankers of the English king throughout the period in which these letters were written may well have delayed most of the Riccardi letters.

[74] Sapori, *Le Marchand Italien*, pp. LXV-LXVI.

Although the extant letters represent only a thin slice from the bulk of Riccardi correspondence, the characteristics of the company and of the merchants themselves emerge more clearly with the aid of this sample,[75] which strongly underscores the "international" nature of the Riccardi operations.

> We tell you that, as you know, our men in Champagne have loaned to the Bonsignori of Siena a great amount of money, and they have told them to pay it back to our men over there [in England] and in Ireland. Therefore, until now we have not known, nor have we been able to find out, if they have been paid back, either all or in part, nor how much you have gotten back. Therefore we ask you to let us know both how much you have received, and when, both you and the men in Ireland.
>
> And just as you should let us know, so you should also tell our men in France, because the companions of the Bonsignori, when our men in France ask them for that money, make excuses and say that they do not know if that money has been paid there or in Ireland, nor how much has been paid. Therefore do not fail to send word both to us and to them, so that if that money has not been paid we can recover it. . . . Speak of this with their companions over there and have them and their companions in Ireland write to their companions in France.[76]

Here, in one transaction, we can see the networks of two firms stretching from Lucca and Siena across France and England to Ireland.

Exchange operations, which Raymond de Roover has empha-

[75] Although all the letters were written in the troubled period after the break with the king, they can tell us much about the workings of the Riccardi in more typical times.

[76] E 101/601/5 p. 5, letter of 5 December 1297. This international character was not limited solely to such large scale transactions between major companies. When an English knight, Thomas of Sandwich, borrowed £10 11s. 8d. from the Riccardi, his letter obligatory promised repayment either in London or Paris. E 159/106 m. 145 d.

sized as the central business of medieval banking,[77] appear throughout the Riccardi letters. Since these letters were written in the period of impending failure after the fall from royal favor, the efforts are usually directed to collecting on old transactions rather than initiating new ones. "If we do not get the money over there, we will never get it over here" is an opinion expressed more than once.[78] But it is evident that in normal times credit and exchange operations were common. In an era when the bill of exchange was slowly evolving as an informal letter missive from the more formal notarial *instrumentum ex causa cambii*, it is interesting that the Riccardi usually refer simply to letters of exchange; they occasionally mention specifically the letter of payment (*lettera di pagamento*), an order to remit (*mandare a recevere*), or a first copy (*lettera di prima*) of a multiple copy letter of exchange.[79] The development that would reach completion only in the second half of the fourteenth century is well on its way in a company like the Riccardi at the close of the previous century. This evolving exchange contract would prove compellingly attractive not only because of its purely financial merits, but also because it was free of any taint of usury in the eyes of churchmen.[80]

[77]*L'Evolution de la Lettre de Change, XIVe-XVIIIe siecles*, introduction and Chapter I. *The Medici Bank*, pp. 31–40. *Banking in Bruges*, pp. 12, 49-57. *The Rise and Decline of the Medici Bank*, pp. 11–12 and Chapter VI.

[78]See for example E 101/601/5, p. 14, probably written after September of 1301.

[79]*Ibid.*, pp. 3 d., 4, 4d., 7, 45, 45d. De Roover notes that the *lettera di pagamento* (by which a partner or factor was informed of a contract and told to pay the bearer what is promised in the notarial act) was not yet a true letter of exchange since it was not yet sent to the creditor but was sent directly by the drawer to the drawee. Yet he states that it was the last link in the chain of development. *L'Evolution de la Lettre de Change*, pp. 38–41. In *Banking in Bruges*, pp. 69–70 n. 29 he corrects some previous errors in terminology associated with exchange.

[80]In addition to the sources cited in note 77, see T. P. McLaughlin, "The Teaching of the Canonists on Usury, (XII, XIII, and XIV centuries)," *Medieval Studies* 1 (1939), and De Roover, "Les doctrines économiques des scholastiques à propos du traité sur l'usure d'Alexandre Lombard," *Revue D'Histoire Ecclesiastique* 59 (1964).

Although exchange and other transactions with companies of their fellow Italians were undoubtedly both frequent and sizable in normal times, in the extant letters we cannot observe the usual Riccardi relationship with other firms. Several companies with which the Riccardi dealt after 1295 were also failing. As we have noted, the Bonsignori of Siena had received large loans from the Riccardi in Champagne and the letters worry over the fading prospects of recovering the money.[81] But it is the Bettori, fellow Lucchesi, who are most frequently mentioned. At this point the Riccardi were not concerned with carrying on regular business with them, but were desperately collecting what they could of the money owed. Thus in Lucca they took legal action to obtain the houses and lands of Jacopo Bettori while their partners in France apparently collected wool from the Bettori in Soumiers and in Flanders, along with certain finished cloths and "half of certain debts." The Riccardi men in France were instructed to add the value of these goods and debts, subtract their expenses, and send the result to the Riccardi in London, who could then "do things clearly and close the books," sending to Lucca with full particulars (*per partite*) the debts the Bettori had assigned them in England and Ireland "and also other things which they might have assigned to you." The London partners got a reprimand for not acting more swiftly. "You would have done well and acted rightly if you had sent it to us, and as quickly as you can, by particulars. Also send us what they have to give you, both to you and to our men in Champagne, both in principal and in interest and up to what day you have counted the interest."[82] These interest rates are seldom specified in surviving Riccardi letters, but from the extant sample it appears that when one Italian company borrowed from another the interest it could expect to pay on this money would be in the range of ten to fifteen percent.[83] If our few clues as to the interest rate charged to the king by the Riccardi–discussed below–are valid, these rates between companies indicate that the Riccardi may on occasion have

[81] E 101/601/5 p. 5, letter of 5 December 1297. See E. Jordan, "La Fallité des Bonsignori," *Mélanges Paul Fabre.*

[82] E 101/601/5 p. 29d.

[83] E. g., *ibid.*, pp. 4, 5, 11.

borrowed money from other companies at ten to fifteen percent and lent it to Edward at more than twice this rate.

Relations were more positive with Musciatto Guidi who, along with Albizzo Guidi, headed the Franzesi firm, the leading Italian company in the service of Philip IV of France. Musciatto, whose name the French corrupted to Mouche, had in the past used his influence at the French court to obtain royal letters ordering the *baillis* to aid in collecting Riccardi debts. In their difficulties after 1294 the merchants of Lucca were hopeful that similar letters could be had once again.[84]

Much of their business was conducted at the great fairs of Champagne, mentioned in this letter and in others. If by the last quarter of the thirteenth century the commercial character of the fairs was declining, their financial character was actually growing. Money-changing and the regulation of the capital market now took precedence over the trade which had previously made the fairs centers of western "international" commercial activity.[85] The scale of transactions when the Riccardi were at the height of their power is reflected in the boast that they could borrow "100,000 and 200,000 *livres tournois* and even more" at these fairs.[86] From other sources we learn that the Riccardi also transacted business at the fairs of Laon; in England they often attended the fair of St. Botolph at Boston on the business of the company or that of the king. In 1277, for example, a mandate for a certain payment was sent by the king "to the merchants of Lucca, of the society of Luke de Luka, about to meet at Boston fair. . . ."[87]

[84]E 101/601/5 p. 8d., letter of 17 November 1301. See J. R. Strayer, "Italian Bankers and Philip the Fair," *Explorations in Economic History* 7 (1969).

[85]O. Verlinden, *C.E.H.*, III, p. 133. Robert-Henri Bautier "Les foires de Champagne: recherches sur une évolution historique," *Bulletin de la Société Jean Bodin, V, La Foire* (1953).

[86]E 101/601/5 p. 25, letter of 10 October 1295. As frequenters of the Champagne fairs the Riccardi were familiar with the "lettera della fiera" which could be sent to the judicial authorities in a debtor's home city or country. The use of such a letter is mentioned in this letter.

[87]*C.P.R. 1272-1281*, pp. 131–132, 214. Cf. pp. 195, 196, 210, E 159/54 mm. 12, 14.

The merchants were never sparing of criticism of any member who they felt had acted unwisely or any outsider who had harmed them. The matter-of-fact tenor of the letters is thus occasionally changed to one of smoldering ire. After the London partners fired an agent who had proved unreliable, the home office devoted nearly a page of one letter to raking his character. The following is only a sample: "Now it seems to us that he is so wicked and dangerous because of his wicked and lying tongue that you should warn your friends at court that he is not to be believed in anything he may say, as he is a drunkard, a liar, and wicked, without any principles. For what he said concerning the £30,000 that we had brought to Brabant he should have been burned, such an evident and false lie it was!"[88] As their affairs went from bad to worse in the last years of the thirteenth century, they often made statements of pious resignation. "May God in his mercy not look at our sins, but rather may He look at the good that our ancestors have done, and grant grace to those who hurt us so that they may see the right way. . . ." But the old fire never died completely. "Let us hope in God and in the Virgin that shortly we will be in the position to give back to everyone in the same way as they have dealt with us. For the time being it is more suitable if we keep our mouths shut."[89]

In the business letters, then, we not only learn much about the company, but move a step closer to seeing the merchants as men of flesh and blood instead of as Latinized names in accounts. Here they show something of their large and small concerns, argue, and make judgments, though we still know little of their individual personalities. Rarely does some personal trait come to light, such as Matteo Rosciompeli's fondness for hunting. He was caught taking hares in the king's warren of Northampton and it was necessary for his partners to stand surety for his appearance to answer for the trespass.[90]

Still, the common qualities of the merchants are not hard to surmise. It would require men of no small spirit and enterprise to

[88] E 101/601/5. Undated letter, p. 46d.
[89] *Ibid.*, undated letter, p. 18.
[90] *C.C.R. 1279–88*, p. 445.

leave their home city and not only engage in trade but enter into the perilous if profitable business of government finance. They were evidently adept at personal diplomacy, for they formed friendly alliances with several men in the highest circle about the king, and until the falling-out in 1294 appear to have been on close terms with Edward himself. They were obviously progressive businessmen, as can be seen in such small ways as their use of paper for letters and accounts, rather than the costly parchment.[91] We can guess that they dressed conservatively and were not eager to be publicly prominent.[92]

Yet their outstanding characteristic was the desire and ability to drive a hard bargain. There was no room for sentiment or personal feelings. On one occasion the partners in Lucca defended themselves from the charge of just these "faults." "About the special consideration (*sofferenza*) which you say we have given to Ranuccio Ronsini . . . for which you blame us greatly, we tell you that what we have done we have not done out of love for him or because he is related to any one of us, or because of any request he might have made to us. Whatever we have allowed we have done for our benefit and not for his. . . ."[93]

The point is most clearly made in an incident concerning John Pecham, Archbishop of Canterbury. Faced with the costs of consecration and the trip to England from Rome, Pecham "whose vows of poverty were not the most convenient preparation for the costliness of the archepiscopal state," borrowed 4,000 marks from the Riccardi in Rome.[94] Repayment was promised within a

[91]On 18 September 1295, a clerk of the Treasurer, William March, delivered into the exchequer "i librum papiri ligatum et i quaternum papiri in i pucha sigillata que sunt mercatorum de societate Ricardorum de Luca, videlicet de lanis eorum." E 159/68 m. 43d. The letters of the society were also written on paper.

[92]This is the advice of a member of the Frescobaldi who wrote a sonnet of advice for "him who is passing into England." "Clothe yourself in dingy colours, be humble, stupid in appearance, subtle in act. . . ." The sonnet and a free translation are printed by Walter Rhodes in *Historical Essays*, edited by T. F. Tout and James Tait, pp. 151–152 and note.

[93]E 101/601/5, p. 5d., letter of 5 December 1297.

[94]This discussion is based on Dorothy Sutcliffe, "The Financial Condition of the See of Canterbury 1279–92," *Speculum* 10 (1935). She cites

month after Michaelmas 1279. When he had previously borrowed money from the Riccardi—probably in much smaller amounts—he had been given the delays he needed, up to a year or two. But when this loan was not repaid, the Riccardi, in July of 1279, obtained a papal bull threatening him with excommunication unless he repaid the loan within a month from the coming Michaelmas. This was not an unusual tactic,[95] but the archbishop's correspondence at this time complains of the Saracenic cruelty of men aided by the devil and puts the chief blame on the Riccardi who were, he thought, aided by Nicholas of Terracenses, a papal chaplain. In moving terms he described the miseries his high position had brought and threatened to leave England and give up his pastoral office, preferring death to the disgrace of excommunication. Eventually the Riccardi gave Pecham an extension, and a settlement was reached in May of 1285. The threat of excommunication may have been formal, and if so was probably recognized as such by the archbishop, whose fear of the bull "dreadful to see and terrible to hear" may have been somewhat feigned to evoke sympathy at Rome. But it cannot be doubted that the Riccardi were applying pressure of the most effective sort, and that it probably gave them most favorable terms in the final settlement.

To ask whether these merchants were capitalists brings us all too close to the quicksands of definition. In Marxist theory the answer would clearly be negative, since men like the Riccardi did not own the means of production and live from the labor of a propertyless proletarian class. As Maurice Dobb insists, the acquisitive use of money, large-scale trading, and the existence of a professional merchant class are not be be equated with capitalism.[96] Other historians, against Marxist objections, speak of a long era of specifically commercial capitalism preceding industrial capitalism, and see the great medieval merchants as its early stan-

---

the *Register Epistolarum* of Pecham. The quitclaim issued by the Riccardi to the archbishop in 1285 is Lambeth MS 1212 fol. 185.

[95] See Adolf Gottlob, "Kuriale Prälatenanleihen im 13. Jahrhundert," *Vierteljahrschrift für Sozial- und Wirtschaftsgeschichte* I (1903).

[96] Maurice Dobb, *Studies in the Development of Capitalism*, revised ed., pp. 8, 17.

dard bearers.[97] Moreover, if we choose to adopt the idealist conception of Werner Sombart or Max Weber and speak of a "capitalistic spirit," then what we know of the Riccardi, of both their methods and their motives, demands that we recognize this spirit as that which informed the activities of the merchants of Lucca long before the appearance of the Calvinist ethic which so stimulated Weber's imagination. A fusion of an adventurous and enterprising spirit with a typically "bourgeois" calculation and rationality (Sombart), or an "attitude which seeks profit rationally and systematically" (Weber) fits the case of the Riccardi perfectly: not only were they adventurous in seizing the dangerous opportunities of trade and finance from Ireland to Italy, but they were also thoroughly rational and calculating in their manipulation of that trade and finance for their considerable profit.[98] If the label of capitalist is to be applied to any group of men in early European history, the Riccardi must be included.

2. MONEY-LENDING AND THE WOOL TRADE

The household and administration of a great lord approximated, on a smaller scale, that of the king and shared with the royal finances the problems of slowly collected revenues and a

[97]See, for example, the introduction to David S. Landes, *The Rise of Capitalism*. De Roover, *The Rise and Decline of the Medici Bank*, p. 7, states that the Medici give the lie to the Weber thesis, although commercial and not industrial capitalism is involved. R. S. Lopez argues that "The golden age of medieval trade certainly knew many of the characteristics which we regard as typical of capitalism." *C.E.H.*, II, p. 320. Henri Pirenne's classic article, "The Stages in the Social History of Capitalism," *A.H.R.*, XIX (1914), makes a case for recognizing that "capitalism is much older than we have ordinarily thought." (p. 497). Eileen Power writes of the great exporters, industrialists, and financiers as "representatives of capitalism in a pre-capitalistic age." *The Wool Trade*, pp. 105–106.

[98]See Dobb, *Studies*, p. 5. De Roover challenges Sombart's view that there was no economic rationalism in the Middle Ages in *Banking in Bruges*, p. 29. Cf. N.S.B. Gras, "Economic Rationalism in the Late Middle Ages," *Speculum* VIII (1933). Sapori is likewise critical of Sombart. See *Le Marchand Italien*, pp. XLV-XLVI.

perennial shortage of cash. The firms of Italian merchant-bankers offered them, no less than the king, a way out of these difficulties. We know that in the early fourteenth century Walter Langton, the treasurer, used the Ballardi of Lucca as his bankers, that slightly later Hugh Despenser the Younger employed the Bardi and Peruzzi of Florence, and that Henry de Lacy, Earl of Lincoln, kept deposits with the Frescobaldi.[99] These merchants held money on deposit, invested it, and conducted business in England and abroad for their clients, in much the same way that they served the king. It can hardly be doubted that a few decades earlier the Riccardi were providing similar services, but our evidence is disappointingly meager. Government documents only rarely give some indication of this sort of private financial management.[100] In June of 1275, for example, the sum of £900 owed to Antony Bek by the abbot and convent of Fountains was received by Luke Natale "to the use of the said Antony."[101] We have very little further information on the relations between Bek and the merchants and cannot determine whether this is one glimpse of their handling of his affairs or merely an isolated transaction. But we do know that they referred to him as one who had been a "special lord" to the company and a friend who helped and advised them in their great affairs.[102] At the time of the fall from royal favor Bek owed the company £1200.[103]

In a similar fashion we catch occasional glimpses of a long-term relationship between the Riccardi and the prior and convent of Lewes. Prior John used the services of the merchants for about a

[99] Alice Beardwood, "The Trial of Walter Langton, Bishop of Lichfield, 1307–12," *Transactions of the American Philosophical Society*, n.s., 54, Part 3. E. B. Fryde, "The Deposits of Hugh Despenser the Younger with Italian Bankers," *Economic History Review* ser. 2, 3 (1950–1951).

[100] For some of the few extant examples of deposits with the Riccardi see *C.C.R. 1288–1296*, p. 205; *C.P.R. 1290–1292*, pp. 417–418; E 159/63 m. 16.

[101] *C.P.R. 1272–1281*, pp. 97–98.

[102] E 101/601/5, p. 25d., letter of 10 October 1295.

[103] E 101/126/7.

decade. His debt to them stood at £300 in 1283,[104] but it increased considerably over the next two years, for in September of 1285 a final concord made at London stated that a former obligation of 1,000 marks was now reduced to 800.[105] Within a year not only had the debt risen to 900 marks but the religious had also pledged twenty-three sacks of the wool of their estates, valued at 13 marks a sack.[106] This large monetary debt was repaid by 1290, but the house was by that time again in need and the merchants were given a recognizance for £50.[107] Hard-pressed for 2,000 marks owed the king in 1292, the monks turned to the Riccardi in a final arrangement. Through the influence of Labro Volpelli, a leading member of the company, they got a three-year extension of terms from the king. But it seems that for services rendered the Riccardi expected 200 marks a year.[108]

It is more certain that the merchants were bankers over an extended period to Otto de Grandson, Edward's Savoyard friend and trusted diplomat. It is, in fact, likely that they came into contact with Otto while providing funds for his journeys on be-

[104]E 159/57 m. 13d. N. Denholm-Young, *Seignorial Administration*, pp. 55–56, cites an earlier debt of 700 marks owed to the Riccardi in 6 Edward I, but the merchants involved were not members of the company. See E 368/52 m. 15.

[105]E 101/126/4. This is one portion of the original chirograph.

[106]E 159/59 mm. 10d., 12d. The wool obligation is separate from the monetary debt, which was to be repaid at a rate of 200 marks a year in equal installments at Michaelmas and Easter. This house continued to sell its wool to merchants from Lucca, but it dealt with the group which Baroncino led away from the Riccardi. See E 159/61 m. 14 for a sizable contract with them involving 400 sacks of wool worth 2,500 marks.

[107]E 159/59 m. 10d. E 159/64 m. 25d.

[108]The "Liber A" contains a copy of the letter of Labro, dated August 19, 1292, by which he agreed that the 2,000 marks would be deducted from the king's debt to the Riccardi if it were not paid at the end of the term of three years. E 36/274 mm. 212–213. Cf. E 159/66 m. 3; E 368/64 m. 1. The Riccardi letters occasionally mention this business with "la prioria de lliesa" and indicate the profit expected. E 101/601/5 pp. 34d., 39. For the final settlement of this debt between king and prior see E 159/68 m. 38.

half of Edward's foreign affairs. Grandson proved a loyal friend of the company and continued his connections with them even after their fall from royal favor. He is familiarly referred to as "Messer Otto" in their letters, which more than once mention his account with the firm.[109] In 1288-1289, when the bishop of Emly was in debt to Grandson for lands held at farm in Ireland, the sheriffs of Limerick and Tipperary were instructed to levy the money from the bishop's possessions and pay it to Bendino of the Riccardi on behalf of Otto.[110] Similarly, a few years later, when Grandson was fighting as a crusader in the Holy Land, his bailiffs in the Channel Islands (granted to him by the king in 1275) were ordered to levy all arrears of farms and debts, turning over the money to a representative of the Riccardi.[111] Not only did Otto himself deal with the Riccardi but he apparently introduced them to others of his family as well. In the 1290's at least, his brother, the bishop of Verdun, and his nephews received loans from the merchants.[112]

Probably the most useful case in which we can follow their banking activity over a number of years concerns Isabella de Fortibus, Countess of Aumale.[113] As early as 1260 they had a long-term contract for the wool of her estates centered on Holderness in Yorkshire; until 1280 they bought the best grade wool at a fixed price of 8-1/2 marks a sack. Sometimes the price of the wool was simply entered as a credit to her account in the merchants' books. That they were also transacting some of her wider financial affairs is shown by a bond they gave to Walter Giffard, Archbishop of York, in March of 1276 or 1277. If he would pay to the countess within the quinzaine of Easter the 1,000 marks he

[109] E.g., E 101/601/5 p. 44d., letter of 21 April 1298, and p. 4, letter of 17 November 1301.

[110] Henry Cole, ed., *Documents Illustrative of English History in the Thirteenth and Fourteenth Centuries*, pp. 102–103, 104, 106, 100–101, 63. *C.D.I. 1285–1292*, pp. 259, 283–289.

[111] *R. G.*, III, no. 1924.

[112] E 101/126/7. E 101/601/5, p. 26d., letter of 10 October 1295.

[113] This has been discussed by N. Denholm-Young, *Seignorial Administration*, pp. 17, 60–66, 80.

owed them, they promised to return his letters obligatory.[114] A debt of £206 11s. 11d. owed to Isabella in Trinity term of 1275 was to be paid "in the house of Luke of Lucca and his fellows in the city of London."[115] When the countess brought Adam de Stratton into her administration in 1278, his financial reorganization gave the Riccardi increased prominence. Proceeds from Holderness were often taken to the merchants at York in order to save transporting them to the countess at Carisbrooke Castle on the Isle of Wight, or elsewhere. In return they would make the payments requested of them by Stratton. In 1276-1277 a messenger delivered letters to the countess "concerning money paid by them [i.e., the merchants] in Boston Fair and to be received by them in Southampton." In 1277-1278 the countess' receiver was paid £600 from Holderness "by the hands of Mathei Rugepeil, merchant of Lucca, and by the hands of Adam of Stratton and letters of the said Mathei by two tallies." We have examples of letters given to Isabella in 1281-1282, 1287, and 1290 "for money paid by the merchants." These could be used as drafts on the company whenever she needed money.[116]

Although our sources are inadequate to show other instances of this type of regular relationship between the Riccardi and great lords, there is abundant evidence that they were at least money-lenders to great and lesser men alike on a considerable scale. The recognizances given them in the exchequer or chancery do not by any means represent an exhaustive list of their loans,[117] but they

[114]Giffard's *Register*, I, p. 153. This could not be simply a means of purchasing wool, for the average number of sacks bought in 1260-1285 was about 30, at 8-1/2 marks a sack. Denholm-Young, *Seignorial Administration*, p. 60.

[115]E 159/49 m. 26.

[116]Denholm-Young, *Seignorial Administration*, p. 65 and note.

[117]No recognizances appear for the Countess of Aumale or for Otto de Grandson, though we know they were important clients of the firm. Perhaps the Riccardi did not expect formal recognizances from those who had standing accounts with the society. Loans to the royal treasurers similarly did not result in recognizances. A note on the K.R. Memoranda roll for 14-15 Edward I states that John Kirkby, the treasurer, has satisfied them for a loan of 1,204 marks 6*s*. 8*d*. which he owed them "in a cer-

do show the numbers of magnates who negotiated loans with the Riccardi and give some idea of the scale on which they carried out lending to men of varying ranks. The amount of these loans secured through recognizances increased to a peak in the early 1280's before tapering off in the last decade the firm served as king's bankers. In especially active years the total of these recognizances came to approximately £2,500, as in 1280–1282, 1283-1284, and 1286-1287.[118]

The Riccardi were creditors to a broad section of the upper ranks of society, ranging from earls and archbishops to simple knights and townsmen. The amounts loaned show a roughly corresponding scale. Thus the obligation of Roger Bigod, earl of Norfolk, in Michaelmas term of 1281 came to 1,700 marks, while one William de Cotton owed them £5 in Easter term of that year.[119] Many great lords, lay and religious, evidently managed their affairs through occasional but sizable loans from the merchants. The more important of these are summarized in Table II, at the end of this chapter.

For high-ranking ecclesiastics, a firm with representation at Rome had an additional attraction. They could use the merchants to pay sums due to the *camera* and through them could distribute the gifts appropriate to the successful conclusion of business at the papal court. Archbishop Pecham not only borrowed money from them at the time of his elevation to the see of Canterbury, but he also transferred 500 marks to the *curia* through the company in 1282.[120] Two archbishops of York, William Wickwane

tain writing obligatory." No recognizance in chancery or exchequer was made. This writing was cancelled before the barons and turned over to Nicholas de Ocham, Kirkby's clerk. E 159/60 m. 20. In 1295 the merchants note that it should be easy to recover the 2,000 marks owed by the bishop of Bath "now that he has left the treasury." E 101/601/5, letter of 10 October 1295. He was dismissed in August of 1295.

118 Based on the exchequer recognizances in the K.R. Memoranda Rolls, with additions from the L.T.R. Memoranda Rolls, and also the chancery recognizances, in the *Calendar of Close Rolls*. It is likely that these recognizances include interest charged on the loans.

119 E 159/55 mm. 10d., 12.

120 Sutcliffe, *Speculum* 10 (1935), p. 59.

and John le Romeyn, also effected payments in Rome by means of the Riccardi. The latter seems to have had a special understanding with Labro Volpelli concerning the prosecution of his interests and rights. In a letter sent in 1286 to Labro in Rome he wrote that if this business could be advanced he would provide 300 marks, "if you are not able to achieve the aforesaid for a lesser sum."[121]

The extent of Riccardi money-lending at the end of their two decades of royal service can be discovered from a file of documents written in the fall of 1294.[122] After Edward broke with his bankers in the summer of that year he seized their books, causing the company no end of trouble. Although these books unfortunately have not survived, we do have several abstracts of the debts owed them at this time, drawn up by government clerks. Two membranes entitled "Debts owed the merchants of Lucca for which there are not yet writs" list about 140 debtors and the sums they owed, along with a notation of the county in which the debtors lived. Most of the names are those of unknown men who had borrowed relatively small sums. Some were clerks or servants of the illustrious–such as the Hugh Pessim, *clericus Domini W. de Valencia*, who owed £12 14s.–while others were in the royal service, such as Ricardus Gentilcors, *valletus regis*, who owed 20s. Yet among these men of small status and correspondingly slight credit we also find a number of important figures. The bishop of Bath and Wells (William March, the treasurer) owed £1,200; the archbishop of Dublin (John de Sanford) an unspecified sum; John de Sulleye, knight, £600 6s. 1d. Certain foreign debts also appear: the bishop of Verdun (brother of Otto de Grandson) owed £314 0s. 17d.; the count of Bar £650, the count of Holland 200 marks. The total of the debts listed comes to about £6,928. But this gives neither an accurate idea of the volume of the debts owed the Riccardi nor the extent of their im-

[121]Wickwane's *Register*, pp. 245–246, 259–260. Romeyn's *Register*, pp. 138–39. His letter to Labro reads "Et, si hec premissa omnia efficaciter impetraveritis, satisfaciemus vobis de CCC^{tis} marcis, si predicta pro minori summa non poteritis impetrare."

[122]E 101/126/7.

portant clients at this time. Sewn to the membranes is a long narrow strip of parchment listing names without sums. The two exceptions are the counts of Bar and Holland who appear with the debts as on the first list. Although we would like to know the indebtedness of the others, it is still a highly informative document, for it shows that the following had debts outstanding to the Riccardi: the earls of Lancaster, Gloucester, Warwick, Surrey, and Lincoln, the bishops of Durham, Ely, and Carlisle, two of the king's daughters, and ten important men in the king's service.[123] If any confirmation were needed that this is indeed a list of debtors, it could be found in a letter written by the Riccardi in Lucca to their London partners in October of 1295. Since the books of the latter were not available to them, the home branch sent a rough list of important debts owed in England. Most of the names on the Riccardi abstract also appear in the government list, and from the letter we learn the amounts of their obligations, in round figures. Although the names appear strange in Italianized form, we see that "messer aimondo di mortomieri (Edmund Mortimer)" owed 300 marks, "lo chomto di guarvichi (the earl of Warwick)" 400 marks, "lo veschovo de bai (the bishop of Bath)" 2,000 marks, and so on.[124] A complete list of the recipients of Riccardi loans approximates a *Who's Who* for late thirteenth-century England.

These lords who were rich in lands but short of cash sometimes found it necessary to pledge one or more of their manors as security, or to assign manorial revenues for repayment of loans. Thus Thomas de Clare, brother to the earl of Gloucester, borrowed £409 17s. 0d. and placed in Riccardi hands his manor of Agni in County Limerick, Ireland, until the proceeds should repay the debt.[125] In a similar way the earl of Warwick turned over

[123]John de Havering, John de Berwick, Hugh de Cressingham, Walter Beauchamp, Philip Willoughby, John Kirkby, Walter Langton, Richard Louth, John Droxford, William Pershare.

[124]E 101/601/5, p. 26d., letter of 10 October 1295. See Table II at the end of this chapter.

[125]E 159/58 m. 13d. *C.D.I. 1252-1285*, no. 2312.

his manor of Borsete to the merchants in repayment of some unspecified debt,[126] and John Sudley demised his manor of Dersete for a term of nine years.[127] Earlier, William de Breouse acknowledged a debt of £300 "for which he commits to the merchants his manor of Wicham in the county of Kent." They were to recover the loan in two installments, at Easter of 1282 and 1283.[128] Several wardships, even, came to the merchants. Maurice de Craon sold them his rights of wardship over four manors and parts of two others for £730 13s. 4d. in 1278. The Riccardi obtained the king's special permission in a letter patent.[129]

Committing landed revenues to the merchants was a practice not limited to secular borrowers. In 1293 the archdeacon of Lincoln, William de Estamato, owed the Riccardi £826 2s. 6d., and for repayment assigned them all of the fruits and proceeds of his archdeaconry, as well as a number of prebends and churches which as a pluralist he held.[130]

The wool trade was one of the attractions which originally drew Italian merchants to England, and it may well have retained a primary place in their own estimation, even after they had developed extensive credit transactions with lay and religious lords and with the king. Government documents cannot be expected to show the degree to which this trade occupied the energies of

[126] E 159/71 m. 44d. This is the order for seizure of the manor into the king's hands in 1298, when Edward was collecting the debts owed the Riccardi.

[127] Since this was done late in 1293, the merchants' fall cut short their profit. *C.P.R. 1292-1301*, p. 41. Edward later allowed Sudley (who was to become one of his chamberlains) to take possession once more, but demanded £97 8*s*. 5-1/2*d*. for goods and chattels of the Riccardi on the manor. See C 47/87/4 no. 51, E 368/74 m. 17. The loan from the merchants may have been 900 marks. E 101/601/5, p. 1d., letter of 5 December 1297.

[128] E 159/55 m. 9.

[129] C 47/13/1. Cf. *C.C.R. 1272-1279*, p. 502. *C.P.R. 1272-1281*, p. 256.

[130] E 159/67 m. 66d.

Italian companies,[131] but they can illustrate the nature of the arrangements and give some idea of the scale of the transactions.

We have seen that over a long period the Riccardi bought some of the wool produced on the great Fortibus estates centered on Holderness. Many laymen of smaller means in both England and Ireland also sold their wool to the merchants of Lucca.[132] The total of these purchases could be of some consequence; in 1287-1288, for example, men of this rank recognized before the exchequer that they owed thirty-nine sacks of wool to the Riccardi.[133] A few of them can be classed as regular customers, such as Robert Boson, the Bailiff of the Peak, who sold his wool to the merchants in 1288, 1289, and 1290.[134]

But most important by far were the estates of the great monasteries, of which the Cistercians stood in the front rank.[135] Not only were abbots and priors eager to sell the wool of their flocks but they were often in need of the loans which could be obtained from the Italians. The late thirteenth century brought financial distress to many monasteries. Faced with papal and royal taxation, hurt by the ravages of murrain in their flocks, attempting extensive building operations, more than one house contracted a series of loans on the security of its wool, sometimes pledging at an undervalue the entire produce of the estates of the house for years in advance.

The lively Riccardi share in this business can be seen in the

[131] See the comment by Georges Bigwood, "Un marché de matières premières: laines d'angleterre et marchands italiens vers la fin du xiiie siècle," *Annales d'Histoire Economique et Sociale*, 2 (1930), p. 205.

[132] E 159/53 m. 12d.; -54, mm. 15, 18, 20; -55, m. 9; -58, m. 14d.; -59, m. 8d.; -61, mm. 17, 19, 12d.; -62, mm. 14, 16d.; -63, *passim*; -64, m. 25d.; -65, m. 33.

[133] E 159/61 mm. 17, 19, 12*d*. A sack was a quantity of wool weighing 364 English pounds.

[134] *Ibid*., m. 17; -62, m. 14; -64, m. 25d. Eileen Power mentions Boson as an example of the middleman collecting wool from small producers for sale to the Italians. *The Wool Trade*, p. 45.

[135] See the article by Bigwood, cited in note 131, and that by R. J. Whitwell in *Vierteljahrschrift für Sozial- und Wirtschaftsgeschichte* 2 (1904).

example of the great Cistercian house of Meaux in Holderness.[136] By 1274, if not earlier, the Riccardi were contracting to buy the abbey's wool. In that year the Riccardi contracted to buy 120 sacks of the wool of the abbey at Boston fair, paying the price of 1,200 marks in advance. When the abbot would not deliver the wool, the merchants obtained a royal order directing the sheriff of Yorkshire to levy the debt from the abbot's goods. Anticipating his next move, the Riccardi then wrote to John Kirkby, the treasurer, and to Otto de Grandson, one of the king's closest associates, asking them to advise Antony Bek, later Bishop of Durham, and Robert Burnell, the chancellor, to ignore the pleas the abbot would present at court. When he argued his version of the case, he could have found few to listen. But the abbot must have taken this defeat in stride, for he continued to sell wool to the merchants of Lucca, as did his successor. Several years after the dispute fifty-three sacks of *collecta* (wool collected from scattered estates) were sold to the Riccardi at a price of 12-1/2 marks a sack. They were to receive twenty-five sacks at Hull on the quinzaine of the Nativity of St. John the Baptist, 1281, and the remaining twenty-eight sacks on this feast in the following year.[137] At the same time Abbot Robert negotiated a loan of £130 from the merchants, payable at Boston fair.

He must have obtained many such loans from one source or another, for he left the sizable debt of £3,678 to his successor, and had allowed the flocks to deteriorate. In 1282 Abbot Richard could contract to sell only nine sacks of wool to the Riccardi, though still at 12-1/2 marks a sack.[138] Five years later Abbot Richard agreed to deliver eleven sacks to the Riccardi at Hull on 9 July 1289, in return for 15 marks a sack, paid in advance.[139] Things were going better still in 1287, for an advance of £220 was

[136]This is discussed by Whitwell, pp. 25–28. For the original letters see S C 1 X, no. 114; XXX no. 101; and VIII no. 81.

[137]For the specific conditions laid down for the wool, see the document printed by Whitwell, p. 29 note. The discussion of Riccardi trade with this house which follows is based on this article, pp. 28–33.

[138]E 368/57 m. 11d., cited by Whitwell, p. 31.

[139]E 159/60 m. 18, cited by Whitwell, p. 33 note.

obtained when sixty sacks were sold to the merchants; delivery was scheduled in equal portions between 1290 and 1294. A special clause in the contract guaranteed the full quantity to the Riccardi. They were to be allowed £44 on the delivery of each twelve sacks, while agreeing to pay at the rate of £10 a sack in every year that the twelve sacks were delivered. If there were any shortage, the £44 allotted to that year would be full payment for the wool delivered. That this severe clause was later modified is shown by the fact that in 1294 all the wool produced on the estates of the house was pledged to the Riccardi at 12 marks a sack.[140]

The merchants' dealings with the ancient Benedictine house of St. Swithun in Winchester are particularly instructive, since they show the interconnection between Riccardi involvement in the wool trade and their functions as private financiers and as king's bankers. Although the merchants may have been in contact with this priory at an earlier date, the first recorded transaction took place at the fair of St. Giles, Winchester, in 1278. This involved a loan of 310 marks given the keeper of the house during vacancy, on the king's order.[141] Once the vacancy had ended, the new prior, Brother Adam, negotiated loans on his own, receiving £168 in Easter term of 1281, and a further £81 10s. 0d. in Trinity term of the same year.[142] Two years later a new prior, Brother William, and his monks again met with Riccardi *socii.* On the Sunday after St. Clement the Pope (8 November) in the chapter house of the priory, they sealed a letter obligatory for £310 "for themselves and the great and arduous business and serious necessities of their church." Repayment was due on half the loan within the quinzaine after Easter, and on the remainder within a similar period after Michaelmas. The prior pledged his goods and his church, similarly obligating his successors.[143]

140Whitwell, citing E 101/126/7 (2) m. 2, E 159/61 m. 14.

141In January of 1279 Edward ordered the keeper, William De Brayboef, to send the money to Thomas Bek for the wardrobe. *C.C.R. 1272-1279*, p. 519. Only £190 were forwarded, leaving 25 marks arrears unpaid for nearly a year. *C.P.R. 1272-1281*, p. 304. *C.C.R. 1279-1288*, p. 3.

142E 159/54 mm. 19, 23.

143E 159/57 m. 9. E 368/57 m. 8d.

Up to this time there is no indication that the merchants were buying the wool of the house, but in the spring of 1285, "on the Tuesday after Sunday when the Jubilate is sung," a long-term contract was arranged by Brother William. The Riccardi were to have the entire supply of wool "*bene levata et siccata*" for six years, beginning in 1287, at a price of 6 marks a sack. According to the agreement a minimum of forty sacks must be provided every year, and more if it were available. The monks received £300 at once. They were to repay this advance by deductions from the price of the wool: 190 marks in the first year, 80 marks in the second, 40 marks in each of the final four years. Since these deductions come to only £286 13s. 4d., we may reasonably assume that the Riccardi were buying the wool at a price below normal market value.[144] Apparently the monks were later unable to meet these conditions, for in 1291 Brother William acknowledged at the exchequer that he owed the Riccardi thirty sacks of wool, promising to repay at the rate of five sacks a year on each feast of the Nativity of St. John the Baptist between 1291 and 1296. At the same time he also acknowledged a debt of £60 for himself and his house.[145]

But before the terms of this sale began to be implemented the need for more cash drove the prior and his monks to negotiate still another loan and to extend the advance sale of their wool through 1295. By an agreement embodied in a cyrograph executed early in 1286, the monks were committed to sell 200 sacks of good-quality wool "*de eorum proprio stauro*," in portions of fifty sacks each, delivered at Winchester on the Nativity of St. John the Baptist (24 June) in 1286, 1293, and 1294, and on "the other feast of St. John" (29 August) in 1295. The price was again set at 6 marks, but since a loan of 804 marks was received, the conditions for buying the wool and repaying the loan were

[144]E 159/58 m. 16. The priory possessed vast flocks on its estates; they numbered 20,000 sheep in the early fourteenth century. Eileen Power *The Wool Trade*, p. 34.

[145]E 159/64 m. 22d. In 1293 a sum of £15 was still outstanding and terms were given by which it could be paid in three installments of £5 each. E 159/66 m. 49d.

combined. The first delivery of fifty sacks of wool would go free to the Riccardi, who were to deduct 300 marks from the sum owed them. They would also receive much of the wool contracted to them earlier in the year at no cost. Allowances of 50, 160, and 24 marks were to be deducted from the price of the wool to be sold to them in 1287, 1288, and 1289. The remainder of the debt was to be paid to them in six cash installments of 45 marks each: at London on 1 August and at Winchester on St. Giles (1 September), during 1286, 1287, and 1288. Apparently the Riccardi would pay cash for the remaining 150 sacks delivered in three installments in 1293, 1294, and 1295. As was true in the earlier agreement, the priory was held to sell all of their wool, even if it exceeded the fifty sacks specified for any year.[146]

Even these arrangements and the large loan did not set the house on firm financial ground. In 1288 it was necessary to borrow a further £298 8s. from the Riccardi, as well as 50 marks from the group of former members of the company led by Baroncino.[147] Since the wool of the house was pledged until 1295, it could not conveniently be used as security. The same was true of another loan, of £126 13s. 4d., negotiated four years later.[148]

The account was becoming complex, and a final concord was arranged in 1293 when Brother William met with Orlandino and Riccardo Bonefaci in London to set in order their records "concerning each and every matter concerning wool, and the particulars, and also the sums of money between the said parties from the beginning of the world to the said day. . . ." The monetary debt stood at £217 11s. 4d., for which payment was promised on the Nativity of St. John the Baptist. But the prior further pledged 200 sacks of wool over the next four years, "as is more fully

[146]E 159/59 mm. 4, 5.

[147]E 159/61 m. 15. The prior in that same year was attached to answer to various members of the company of the Mozzi for £163 6s. 8d., but the sum was paid only in 1291 "in the presence of Riccardo Gwydicionis, merchant of Lucca." E 13/13 m. 14.

[148]E 159/65 m. 27d. A few months before this the Riccardi were given a further claim on the priory through a third party. William of Estdene named them, along with several Englishmen, annually to seek and receive 100 marks which the house owed him. *Ibid.*, m. 34.

contained in a certain cyrograph made between them concerning this," plus a further twenty sacks of wool which were owed over the next four years by an earlier recognition.[149]

The seizures of the wool of Italian merchants in 1294 and the fall of the Riccardi from royal favor cut short the collection of the priory's debts to the society, substituting the king as creditor. When Riccardi wool was sold abroad by the king, seventy-two sacks and twenty-four nails of wool which they had bought from the prior of St. Swithun was included.[150] An accounting among the king, the prior, and the merchants was held in December of 1295. The prior had owed £89 15s. 8d. to the merchants, but his delivery of the wool, worth £289 17s. 0d., meant the Riccardi obligation to him stood at £200 1s. 4d. Since Edward had actually seized this wool, he allowed the £89 15s. 8d. to the Riccardi on their debt to him and acknowledged his responsibility to the prior for the £200 1s. 4d. plus the £10 4s. 11d. spent in transferring the wool from Winchester to London. However, the prior owed £86 11s. 5-1/2d. for the tax of one half from the clergy and also £116 3s. 10d. from the time he was collector of the clerical twentieth in the archdeaconry of Winchester. The £7 10s. 11-1/2d. remaining of Edward's obligation was simply deducted from a debt of £20 owed for two transgressions. In February of 1296 four tallies were issued, three to the prior and one to the Riccardi. A writ of *liberate* in favor of the prior and the merchants was ordered. No money had actually changed hands.[151]

Although there is less information available on the organization

[149]E 159/66 m. 49d. The twenty sacks represent the residue of the five sacks yearly pledged in 1291. Of the 200 sacks, 150 had been promised for 1293, 1294, and 1295, and the additional 50 probably represent a defaulted payment from 1286.

[150]E 372/146 m. 54.

[151]E 159/69 m. 62. Some further transactions may have taken place between the company and this priory, for as late as March of 1305 Orlandino and Federigo came before the exchequer and certified that "Brother Henry, recently Prior of St. Swithun, Winchester, and now Bishop-elect of Winchester, and his predecessors, have satisfied them fully of all debts, both wool and money and all other things from the beginning of the world to the day when this present recognition was made." E 368/75 m. 65.

of the Riccardi wool trade than on its sources, some further details concerning both aspects can be found in the customs accounts from particular ports. We learn that the Riccardi hired ships owned by Englishmen to transport their wool to the continental market. The various Italian firms, which were no doubt keen rivals when seeking the best wool suppliers, seem frequently to have cooperated when it came to hiring ships for exporting the wool. The customs particulars give many examples of hulks shared by several different societies.[152]

This series of customs particulars for the late thirteenth century is fragmentary, and a certain suspicion lingers that the Riccardi, as customs collectors, did not report every sack of their own wool going into the hold of a ship. Yet we can get an occasional glimpse of their agents sending the wool they have purchased to foreign markets. Tomassino Guidiccioni supervised customing of the following cargoes of wool from Hull in 1275:[153]

7 July	37 sacks
21 July	76 sacks 10 stone
25 July	27 sacks
3 August	74 sacks 1-1/2 stone
10 September	20 sacks 21 stone
	45 sacks 1-1/2 stone
30 September	20 sacks
	299 sacks 34 stone

A similar series of exports from Newcastle, overseen by Hugelino Gerarduci, can be observed in 1293–1294:[154]

152E 122/36/2. E 122/5/2.

153E 122/55/1.

154E 122/148/4. The total wool export was 572 sacks and 2 stone. The Riccardi also exported a quantity of hides. Hugolino may be the Hugonis Gerarding who was a customs collector in Sandwich in 15–16 Edward I, E 122/124/1. His Italian surname may have actually been Gerarduche, since this name appears in government documents, E 101/231/23 m. 1.

26 June	1293	25 sacks
8 August	1293	14 sacks 3 stone
24 August	1293	18 sacks
30 September	1293	12 sacks
14 February	1294	10 sacks
2 April	1294	10 sacks
6 April	1294	11 sacks
		100 sacks 3 stone

Since wools commanding high prices were produced in Lincolnshire and Yorkshire, we would expect Hull and Newcastle to figure prominently as ports for wool export.[155] But Riccardi wools were also laden in southern ports, though the export is of lesser volume. In 1277-1278 Riccardo Guidiccioni exported forty-three sacks eleven nails of wool for the Riccardi from Southampton; in 1286-1287 another agent shipped sixteen sacks thirty-six nails; in 1290-1291 Riccardo was again in charge and thirty sacks nineteen nails were exported. The company sent seventeen sacks ten nails from Shoreham in 1286-1287.[156]

These figures are illustrative, but they give us no idea of total Riccardi exports in any year nor of the relative standing of the firm among wool exporters. There are two occasions on which we might expect to gain an idea of their total export and its relation to that of other firms: the issue of wool licenses during the Flemish embargo at the beginning of our period, and the wool seizures at its close. However, in both cases we must be satisfied with only an indication. The German scholar Adolf Schaube has carefully examined the licensed wool export in 1273, and from his conclusions we learn that 24.4 percent of this export was in the hands of Italian merchants, proportioned as follows:[157]

155Eileen Power, *Medieval English Wool Trade*, p. 22. In 1291-1292 a Lucchese merchant whose name appears as Wan Tadelin, and also a John Lambert, shipped considerable quantities of wool from Hull, but it seems that they were not members of the Riccardi. E 122/55/2.

156E 122/36/1, 2, 3. The heading of this third prosaic roll of customs duties begins "In nomine patris et filii et spiriti sancti amen." E 122/135/3.

157Adolf Schaube, "Die Wollausführ Englands vom Jahre 1273," *Vierteljahrschrift für Social- und Wirtschaftsgeschichte* 6 (1908), pp. 68, 183.

Cerchi of Florence	400 sacks
Macci of Florence	640 sacks
Falconieri of Florence	620 sacks
Nicholas Testa of Lucca	700 sacks
Bardi of Florence	700 sacks
Frescobaldi of Florence	880 sacks
Riccardi of Lucca	1,080 sacks
Scotti of Piacenza	2,140 sacks

Although this might represent the rough scale of operations for each of these firms, the unsettling fact is that the Riccardi, as king's bankers, collected more than £13,000 in fines for unlicensed export between 1272 and 1279, much of it probably in the early years of this period.[158] At 10s. a sack this represents an enormous volume of illegal wool traffic. The Riccardi were themselves pardoned for offenses against the regulations; a fine of £1,495 5s. was assessed against them but was never collected.[159] Thus Schaube's figures cannot possibly be pressed into serving as conclusive statistics.

The second case is much the same. In 1294, at a time of crises on all fronts, the king decided to seize the wool of foreign merchants and sell it abroad himself. From the records of these seizures[160] we find that the Riccardi total is larger than that given for any other firm.

Cerchi Neri of Florence	350 sacks
Cerchi Bianchi of Florence	301 sacks
Bardi of Florence	99 sacks
Frescobaldi of Florence	360 sacks
Frescobaldi Neri of Florence	154 sacks 10-1/2 stone
Pulci of Florence	257-1/2 sacks
Mozzi of Florence	261 sacks 11 stone
Spini of Florence	153-1/2 sacks
Bettori of Lucca	35 sacks
Riccardi of Lucca	412 sacks 17-1/2 stone

These are evidently not total figures for the entire year, for even

158E 101/126/1.

159*C.P.R. 1272-1281*, p. 125. *C.C.R. 1277-1279*, p. 532.

160E 101/126/7.

the licensed export in 1273 was several times higher. The merchants must have shipped out some of their wool before the king's seizures in 1294. Yet again these figures are valuable in indicating that the Riccardi ranked as one of the greatest companies of wool merchants operating in England. Their dominant position is established beyond doubt by the specifics of Riccardi purchases drawn up by the king's clerks. These specifics show that in addition to the more than 412 sacks of wool noted, the Riccardi had purchased the entire supply of wool for the year from eleven religious houses, listed without figures' being given.[161] The actual quantity of wool the company was preparing to export at the time of the seizures is thus considerably larger than 412 sacks.

Although the evidence is spotty it indicates that if the company was only one of a group of several important wool-exporting Italian firms at the time it entered the king's service, it had probably achieved the largest share in this trade by the time it fell from royal favor.

The purchase and export of wool were by far the most important trading activities of the Riccardi; however, they took advantage of other opportunities as well. A letter close of 1290 refers to the merchants as "trading in the king's realm and the parts subject to him in diverse merchandise, cloth, wool, horses, and other things."[162] The silks and precious stones they supplied the king probably found a market among the great lords as well. In the 1280's we find evidence of Riccardi purchases of grain, consistently managed by Eliseo of the company.[163] All of these incidental references to Riccardi trading activity, along with the more substantial traffic in wool, emphasize the fact that the

[161] See Bigwood, *Annales d'Histoire Economique et Sociale* 2 (1930), p. 202 and note, citing E 101/126/7. He incorrectly states that twenty religious houses sold their entire supply of wool for 1294 to the Riccardi. The following eleven houses had made such a pledge: St. Swithun's, Woburn, Bindon, Dingham, Newminster, Fountains, Snitewite, Cokersand, Hailes, Clyne, and Birsope. The process of seizure and sale abroad will be discussed in the following chapter.

[162] *C.P.R. 1292–1301*, p. 360.

[163] E 159/58 m. 19d.; -59, mm. 1, 6, 7, 10d.; -60, m. 11; -61, m. 20. Cf. E 101/352/16.

Riccardi were indeed merchants at the same time they were financiers.

3. THE RICCARDI AS PAPAL BANKERS

A full discussion of the Riccardi as papal bankers lies outside the scope of this study and would of necessity be based on different sources. Here we can only note that for about half of the period when they were closely linked to the English government, the Riccardi were also papal bankers. Early in the pontificate of Martin IV, in May 1283, they are first described as cameral merchants, along with several Florentine firms: the Pulchi and Rimbertini, the company of Thomas Spilati, and that of Bonaventura Bernardini. From this time until the bankruptcy the Riccardi were among the companies retained by succeeding popes to transact cameral business.[164]

Thus the Riccardi were not officially *mercatores domini papae* when chosen by Edward I to function as *mercatores domini regis*. But as early as 1273 they stood in a very close relation to the papacy, for in August of that year the papal collector in England sent an order to the Irish Dominicans instructing them to deposit with two fellows of Luke Natale all the proceeds of the tax of a tenth for Edward's crusade which had thus far been collected.[165]

The relationship between pope and banker was probably something like that between king and banker, with the exception that the pope did not rely so heavily on a single firm. Riccardi agents held deposits of papal taxes, arranged for transfer or shipment of money, and provided loans for papal needs. They took at least some role in the financial administration of the Holy See as well, for a member of the firm held the office of *thesauraria* in the March of Ancona, and others helped in the audit of accounts.[166]

It is not surprising that students of cameral merchants in this

[164] Jordan, *De Mercatoribus*, pp. 24–25.

[165] August Theiner, *Vetera Monumenta Hibernorum et Scotorum Historiam Illustrantia*, pp. 107–109, cited by Re, *Archivio della Societa Romana* 37 (1914) p. 91, note.

[166] Jordan, *De Mercatoribus*, pp. 110, 119–121.

period have been unable to find satisfying evidence on the matter of interest paid for loans, but the bankers must have received premiums in the form of "damages and expenses," and must have been assured of profits from the immense sums placed with them in deposit over long periods. In addition they enjoyed the backing of the pope, whether they were dealing with kings or trying to collect from a recalcitrant abbot. In any transfers of money or delivery of gifts between king and pope, the Riccardi were logical agents and no doubt thus strengthened their position with both rulers.[167]

Although we have little information on the Riccardi as papal bankers, it is fortunate that much of what we do have touches the tax of a tenth for the aid of the Holy Land; it is in this connection that their ties to the *camera* most concern their English affairs. The proceeds of this sexennial tenth imposed by the council of Lyons in 1274 added considerably to Riccardi resources. The amounts deposited with the Riccardi at various times up to 1283 are given below:

	£	s.	d.	
20 October 1276	£ 6,596	5s.	8d.	collected
	1,596	5	8	paid to papal collectors at New Temple
	5,000	0	0	held in deposit
16 March 1278	14,163	9	3	collected
	4,163	9	3	paid to papal collectors at New Temple
	10,000	0	0	held in deposit
17 February 1281	13,229	0	11	held in deposit
20 December 1281	10,309	5	7	held in deposit
8 February 1283	11,003	11	5	held in deposit

[167] *Ibid.*, pp. 126–127. "Fateor tamen nihil in materia, quam agressus sum, obsecurius esse, quam quae ad salarium mercatorum pertineant." In general, see Lunt, *Financial Relations*, pp. 599–603.

This final figure represents nearly 16 percent of the tenth deposited with the Italians in England. The remainder was divided among fifteen other firms, with the Scotti holding £9,220, the Bonsignori £8,550, and the Bettori £7,114.[168]

Comprehensive figures are not available after 1283, but some further sums from the tenth passed through Riccardi hands: A deposit of £6,000 with the merchants in December of 1285 was probably a thinly disguised loan to Edward from the papal tax; the king acted as surety for his merchants, in case of their failure to pay within one month of a request.[169] In May of the following year a similar deposit of £8,000 is recorded, but this probably represents only an additional £2,000 beyond the previous £6,000.[170] At about this time the Riccardi carried £2,000 from the tenth to Paris as a part of their financing of Edward's sojourn on the continent.[171] We will encounter further use of the Riccardi position as depositaries of the tenth when considering the finance of Edward's Welsh campaigns.[172]

4. RESENTMENT AGAINST THE RICCARDI: THE CASE OF IRELAND

We have seen that the Riccardi, or men like them, were often necessary and always useful to those in the upper echelons of English society, and that they established relationships with a number of important individuals which were as close to friendship as any connection based primarily on financial considerations can be. But we would also suspect that as rich merchant-bankers and as foreigners in high position the Riccardi would evoke feelings of envy and resentment. There is no evidence of this is England; an occasional robbery of a Riccardi strongbox is to be expected and argues no particular feeling against foreign

168 All of this information is taken from the work of Lunt. See *Financial Relations*, Appendix VI, and *E.H.R.* 32 (1917) p. 89.

169 C 202/H/3 no. 20.

170 *C.P.R. 1281–1292*, p. 244.

171 C 47/4/3 m. 16.

172 See Chapter IV, Section 5.

money-lenders.[173] The royal protection was no doubt an ample shield against persecution or exploitation in the realm.

Ireland, however, was more remote, and a more primitive society; the king's authority was less sure and swift here, and there was greater opportunity for resentments to find expression. This was particularly the case among the class of government officials struggling to carry on an administration while men and revenues were drained for non-Irish endeavors, such as the Welsh campaigns and castle-building.[174] It was especially galling for them to see Irish revenues delivered into the coffers of Italian merchants whose services to the crown were not apparent to them. Special conditions in Ireland thus set the stage, and provided a stimulus, for incidents, of hostility.

If the Riccardi had not previously maintained agents in Ireland they placed them there for the first time in order to collect the new custom of 1275. As we shall see,[175] they met with difficulties from an early date, for Bonasius Bonante, who shared the collection with them, was murdered by unknown "malefactors and disturbers of the king's peace" in 1277. In the following year it was necessary to send an order to the justiciar and the officials of the Dublin exchequer warning them "not to intermeddle further with the collection or receipt of the said custom, but to permit the merchants to receive the said custom freely and entirely as the merchants ought to answer to the king for all the money from that custom in Ireland. . . ."[176]

A more serious situation developed in that same year when the leading member of the society and several other Italians were

[173]See, for example, E 143/3/6 no. 103 and 103/2.

[174]See, for example, Powicke, *Thirteenth Century*, pp. 564–565, 568–571.

[175]Chapter III, Section 3.

[176]*C.C.R. 1272-1281*, p. 441. Some further orders may have been necessary. A document preserved in the Chancery Files and calendared in *C.D.I. 1252-1284* no. 1615 (dated only 6–7 Edward I), orders the justiciar and treasurer to pay over to Percival and his fellows, by hands of those through whom they had received it, all money from the custom on hides. To hasten action it was added that "the king marvels that he has had to send so many mandates on this subject." The reference to hides may be shorthand

indicted for usury and clipping coins "to the damage of the king and the people."[177] Pleading not guilty, they put themselves under inquisition by a jury of twelve men before the bishops of Waterford, Clonfert, and Meath, Jeoffrey de Geneville, and John de Saunford. Although surprisingly cleared of usury, they were with one exception found guilty of paring down coins collected as customs duties "for the purposes of trade as regards the smaller pieces and concerning the larger in order to make silver vessels." At this point the judges' sense of politics must have tempered their sense of justice, for they released the men with their goods and chattels until the morrow of Trinity (29 May). On this day they were given a further delay by order of the king's council and were allowed to stand pledges for each other "in order that they may in the meanwhile seek grace from the king." It seems that in the case of Percival, the chief Riccardi representative in Ireland, a second inquisition had meanwhile been conducted by Robert Bigod, Eustace de Poer, and Thomas de Chaddeworth, with the result that Percival was thrown in prison. The leading members of the Riccardi in England quickly pledged themselves as his bail and sureties and the king ordered his release. Two days later Edward ordered the justiciar to send a transcript of the inquisition, repeating at the same time his earlier mandate to release Percival.

The king was undoubtedly angry with the Irish administration for not handling a delicate situation with more tact. In fact, unless the coin-clipping was on a much greater scale than is apparent, Edward was probably more displeased with his officials than with his bankers. It may not be coincidental that less than two weeks after ordering Percival's release, the king also ordered the justiciar to come to England "to confer with the king regarding Irish affairs. . . ." A letter sent by the bishop of Waterford, the treasurer, gives further indirect evidence of Edward's feelings. The bishop prays that the king will not find fault with him if he

for the new custom in its entirety (wool, woolfells, and hides), or may indicate that the Irish officials had previously returned only the duties on wool and were trying to keep those on leather.

177For what follows see *C.D.I. 1252–1284*, nos. 1509 (citing Inquisitions Post Mortem 6 Edward I, no. 90), 1562, 1563, 1565, 1881.

has not been able to perform the royal commands, as it was his duty to do, in appeasing the merchants lately placed in Ireland.

The Riccardi themselves gave a concise summary of the next incident–the abduction of the head of their Irish branch in 1283. They added it, wisely enough, as a postscript to a letter announcing to the king the delivery of a sum of money desperately needed for the second Welsh war. This is their account of what happened:

> Furthermore, we have learned from Bendino Panichi, your merchant and our fellow in Ireland, that he was forcefully seized by Eustace de Poer [de Podere] and his brother Robert with the posse in the city of Waterford, led to a certain wood, and held there for two days and two nights against God and your peace; his seal was taken from him, and they forced him to redeem his head for £100 and all the cloth bought from certain religious to a value of twelve marks before they would release him, because if he would not do so they would cut off his head. Whence, concerning this may it please your lordship to provide for your merchants and your company what is appropriate to your majesty and what shall be to your honor.[178]

Apparently Bendino wrongly identified one of his captors, who were not Eustace and Robert le Poer, but Robert and his brother Peter.[179] But his basic testimony was accepted. Edward decided that what was appropriate to his majesty was royal wrath. The sheriff of Dublin conducted Robert to the king in Wales, where

[178]The original letter is preserved among the Ancient Correspondence, S C 1, XIX, no. 73. It is printed by Rymer in *Foedera,* I, ii, p. 644, with some errors in proper names. He dates the letter in 1284, but the reference to an *excertitus* places it during one of the Welsh wars, and the fact that Baroncino is writing for the society indicates the 1282–1283 war.

[179]At the time of Robert's offence, Eustace gathered his kinsmen before the sheriff "and the whole country" and swore to take him "living or dead and kill him" to clear the family name. *C.D.I. 1285-1292*, pp. 307-308. Eustace had been one of the justices before whom the Riccardi were brought when accused of coin-clipping.

he was imprisoned first at Caernarvon and later, with Peter, at Conway.[180] His relatives in Ireland dutifully trooped into the exchequer at Dublin on several occasions, adding their contributions to his fine "for having the king's peace." But it was only after the intercession of Eustace and the earl of Ulster in 1290 that the brothers were pardoned and released—on condition that they answer any charges against them in the king's court, and in general conduct themselves well.[181]

Though less clear-cut, their next difficulties are equally revealing.[182] When Edward was in Gascony for three years he leaned heavily on Riccardi support and in return committed the total proceeds of Ireland to the company.[183] But he was also draining Irish revenues for the castles and fortified towns rising in North Wales. In September of 1289 he ordered the treasurer of Ireland, Nicholas de Clere, to send 2,000 marks for this purpose to Caernarvon, disregarding other payments in order to meet this one. Since Clere had paid over the proceeds of the previous year to the

[180] *C.D.I. 1285-1292*, p. 74. *C.C.R.V.* (Welsh) pp. 294, 327-328. The constable of Caernarvon castle was paid a penny a day for his maintenance over a period of fifty-one days.

[181] *C.D.I. 1285-1292*, pp. 26, 97, 100, 123, 307-308, 341-342.

[182] The basic information on this case can be found in the report of the inquest taken by royal order. A Latin version cites the various writs in full. E 101/231/23. For the Riccardi complaint written in the original French, see E 101/231/22. Both are printed in Cole, *Documents*, pp. 112-121. There is little mention of the two Clere brothers in secondary literature. For some facts on their careers see Richardson and Sayles, *The Administration of Medieval Ireland, 1172-1377*. Elsewhere they comment on the complex nature of this dispute: "Irish Revenue, 1278-1384," *Proceedings of the Royal Irish Academy* 62 (1962), Section C, p. 89, note 5. The king's order for an inquisition reads as follows: "Nos qui mercatores predictos in personis et omnimodis rebus eorum suis exigentibus meritis affectione prosequimur speciali et ab oppressionibus violenciis et injuriis quibuscumque tenemur eosdem specialiter confovere de transgressione predicta si patrata fuerit et qualiter et qua causa plenius certiorari volentes, Vobis mandamus quod inquisita super hoc veritate facti seriem et modum et causam vel occacionem ejusdem ac omnes circumstancias contingentes nobis dictincte et aperte ad proximum parliamentum nostrum a die Paschae in unum mensem constare faciatis."

[183] See Chapter II, Section 2.

Riccardi, and since he thought that the merchants had received 2,000 marks of customs duties for which they had not yet accounted, he asked them to provide the money. They refused, saying that the money had been sent to their London partners. At this point Nicholas was summoned to England to explain his failure to provide the sum. His defense naturally involved the Irish issues held by the Riccardi, but the members in London repeated what their Irish partners had said.

Edward then sent a second order to the Irish exchequer officials, now led by William de Clere, *locum tenens* for his brother. After Nicholas had left for England, William received 1,021 marks of the issues of Ireland which he, in company with Peter Ballymore, chamberlain of the exchequer, deposited with the Riccardi "for reasons which the said William explained to the Lord King *viva voce*." What these reasons were we do not know, but William soon changed his mind and asked that the money be sent to Wales. The Riccardi, however, defiantly replied that even if he sent them to the castle he would not get a penny from them.

Clere's reaction shows a compound of the apprehension resulting from his difficulties in meeting the king's demands, his anger at the resistance of the merchants, and probably resentment toward their wealth and position as well. Despite the resistance of some officials, he effected the arrest of all Riccardi goods and chattels in Ross, Waterford, Cork, and Youghal, placing seals on their treasure chests. He then prohibited debtors from paying the merchants in Limerick, Cork, and Waterford. Guglielmo Gerarduchi, collector of the custom at Ross was held to answer for the custom at the exchequer. A few days later, after noon on 18 January, William came to the house of the society in Dublin, bringing with him the mayor and provost of the city, the clerk of the bailiwick, the porter of the castle, some sergeants, and a host of others unknown to the Riccardi (*et quampluribus ignotis*). Hugolino Rosciompeli, Raimondo Rapundi, and Ghirardo Chimbardi met their demands for the 1,021 marks with refusal, stating that they would pay this only on warrant from the king. On William's order they were arrested and guarded by sergeants who followed them about "as if they were thieves (*cum si il fussent larrons*)."

Moreover, their boxes and chests were sealed so that they could not carry on business. But they could complain indignantly: to the chief justice at Cloyne on that same day and again on the following day at Dublin. A compromise was reached before the justice of Common Pleas and the exchequer officials on Monday. The merchants were to restore £200 at once, 200 marks before Easter, and the residue on the morrow of the close of Easter, unless they could get other conditions from the king. Upon the "gratuitous" payment of £200 their goods were restored. As the officials had obviously expected, however, they sent a full complaint to England, and on the basis of this Edward ordered an inquisition be held before the archbishop of Dublin. The king's attitude was clear. Since he held the merchants in his special favor and wished to protect them from all oppression and injury, the inquest was to determine if an offense had occurred and to report full details at the next parliament.

How Edward balanced his concern over the treatment of his merchants with his anger over the delays on the important Welsh castles does not appear. Yet William de Clere could hardly have escaped the king's anger. Aside from Edward's touchiness whenever the Riccardi were concerned, William was confronted during the inquest with questions about tampering with the rolls of the Dublin exchequer. He admitted to coming to the exchequer early in the morning before the other officials had arrived, opening the bags of records, and "inspecting" some rolls of debts owed the king. We may doubt that the investigators believed his assertion that this was merely out of zeal to check possible sources of funds with which the king's orders might be fulfilled. Both William and Nicholas de Clere were soon in disgrace, the specific charge against William being meddling with exchequer records. But we have no way of knowing what part of his disgrace can be linked to his excessive zeal in recovering money from the Riccardi.[184]

[184] On Nicholas, see for example *C.D.I. 1285-1292* pp. 425 ff, E 159/69 m. 7. On William, see *C.D.I. 1293-1301*, p. 208, E 368/64 m. 61. He was imprisoned in the Tower, and his goods sold to pay for arrears of his account as treasurer.

Despite its murky close, the incident illustrates clearly the pressure on Irish officials, the constant drain of funds away from the island, the problems of dealing with a company of rich, foreign merchant-bankers who were virtually a branch of government. The temptation to vent feelings on these merchants is understandable. Yet the reaction of the Riccardi can also be understood. Although the revenues of Ireland were pledged to them for their very heavy outlay of cash in the king's service, a substantial sum was nonetheless demanded from them by an official who seems to have been surrounded with an atmosphere of corruption. Well might they refuse to hand over money without special royal orders.

Ill-feelings toward the society continued into the 1290's and possibly even increased. In 1292 the king learned that "twelve sworn men, in divers counties of Ireland, appointed to denounce delinquents to the king's bailiffs and ministers, denounce them [the Riccardi], though they have committed no delinquencies, in order that money may be extorted from them." Furthermore, they were being charged tolls, murages, and customs which they were not accustomed to pay. The king, therefore, announced that they were under his protection and ordered his officials not to harass or aggrieve the Riccardi because of these charges, but to protect them and acquit them of the unwonted exactions.[185]

In a letter written to the king by the Riccardi in England, the merchants once described the efforts they were currently making on his behalf. For we realize, they said, "nous ne avoms nul issi especial ami en Engeltere apres le Rey. . . ."[186] This statement could with more truth be taken as a concise summary of their position in Ireland.

185 *C.P.R. 1281–1292*, pp. 500–501. *C.D.I. 1285–1292*, p. 495.
186 S.C.1, XLVIII, no. 74.

Table I Riccardi Personnel[1]

ENGLAND

Name	*From*		*To*	
Lucasio Natale	1256	*Cal. Lib. Rolls*, p. 337	1277	*C.C.R.*, p. 546
Orlandino da Pogio	1275	E 403/28	1309	*C.P.R.*, p. 120
Enrico da Pogio[2]	(1250)	(*Cal. Lib. Rolls*, p. 273)		
	1276	Lunt, *Fin. Rel.*, Appendix VI,	1293	E 159/66 mm. 43, 44
Dono da Pogio[3]	1287	E 159/61 m. 1d.	1316	E 159/63 m. 31d.
Baroncino Gualteri	(1255)	(*Cal. Lib. Rolls*, p. 16)		
	1278	E 159/51 m. 20	1286	
			(c. 1314)	*C.P.R.*, p. 101
Riccardo Guidiccioni	1279	*C.P.R.*, p. 354	1301	E 101/601/5.
Tommasino Guidiccioni	1273	*C.C.R.*, p. 33	1301	E 101/601/5.
Reiner Guidiccioni	1285	E 159/58 mm. 13, 18	1290	*R.G.*, II, no. 1765
Aldebrandino Guidiccioni	c. 1278	*C.C.R.*, p. 492		
Marcassino Guidiccioni	1293	E 159/67 m. 66d.	1297	E 101/601/5
Labro Volpelli[4]	1274	*C.P.R.*, p. 44	22 Nov., 1300	E 101/601/5
Federigo Venture	1277	C 47/13/1 no. 12	1309	*C.P.R.*, p. 120
Reiner Magiari[5]	(1244)	(*Cal. Lib. Rolls*, p. 248)		
	1266–67	Giffard's *Register*, I, p. 153	1286	Arias, *Studi*, p. 158
Riccardo Bonefaci	1286	C 47/4/3 m. 18d.	1293–94	E 13/19 m. 83d.
Matteo Rosciompelli	1276	Lunt, *Fin. Rel.*, Appendix VI	1292	Giffard's *Register*, II, 421
Adiuto Rosciompelli	1278	*C.C.R.*, p. 492		
Giovanni Simonetti	1281	E 159/54 m. 11	1286	Arias, *Studi*, pp. 157–166
Gualteri Simonetti[6]	1289	E 159/62 m. 5	1290	E 159/63 m. 23d.

Name	*From*		*To*	
Abbate Talgardi	1277	E 368/50 m. 9d.	1286	Arias, *Studi*, pp. 157–166
Peregrino Sesmundi[7]	(1244)	(*Cal. Lib. Rolls*, p. 248)		
(Peregrine de la Pointe)	(1271–72)	(E 372/117 m. 6d.		
Opiso Malisardi[8]	(1269–70)	E 372/125 m. 3	(1292–93)	E 159/66 m. 51d.
Francesco Malisardi	1286	*C.P.R.*, p. 229	1293	E 159/66 m. 26
Eliseo Barreli[9]	1281	E 159/54 m. 11	(1305)	C.P.R., p. 396.
Fregiotto da Montechiaro[10]	1290	E 159/64 m. 26d.	(1297)	E 101/601/5
Fornario da Fornaria	1285	E 122/135/2	1291	E 159/64 m. 25d.
Guido	1275	C.F.R., p. 61	1292	E 122/148/3
Bernardo Leal	1288–89	E 122/32/2		
Mametto Russelino	1287	E 122/93/1		
Riccardo Honesti	1290–91	E 122/135/4 B		
"Rokejohan Canel'"	1286	E 122/135/3	1291	E 122/32/3
Hugolino Gerarduci	1287–88	E 122/124/1		
Guillelmo Gerarduche	1290	E 101/231/23 m. 1		
Conte	1297–98	E 101/601/5		
Amadeo Fiadoni	c. 1300	E 101/601/5		
Bacciomeo Toringhelli	1297	E 101/601/5	c. 1300	E 101/601/5
Grasuccio Callianelli	c. 1295–1301	E 101/601/5		
Paganuccio	1295	E 101/601/5		
Leonis Sesmundi	1292–3	E 122/213/1		
IRELAND				
Percival Gerarduci	(1258)	(*Cal. Lib. Rolls*, p. 436)		
	1276	*C.D.I.*, p. 233	c. 1285	E 101/230/12 m. 9

Table 1 Cont, Ireland

Name	*From*		*To*	
Bendino Panici	1278	*C.P.R.*, p. 260	1286	*C.P.R.*, p. 229.
Ghirardo Chimbardi[11]	c. 1287	E 101/601/5	1301	E 101/601/5
Francesco Malisardi[12]	1286	*C.P.R.*, p. 218	1293	C 62/69 m. 2
Reiner Nicholai	c. 1282	*C.P.R.*, p. 44.		
Reiner Broccholi	1280	*C.P.R.*, p. 369	1285	*C.P.R.*, p. 193
Hugolino Rosciompelli[13]	1275	E 101/230/5	1290	E 101/231/23 m. 1
Vanni Rosciompelli[14]	c. 1297	E 101/601/5		
Giustoro Damasci	1282	*C.P.R.*, p. 33	1286	*C.D.I.*, no. 248
Raimondo Rapundi	1290	E 101/231/23		
LUCCA				
Andrea Parenti Riccardi Filippo Riccardi Reiner Bandini Guidiccione Paganini Filippo Talgardi Sarraceni Macchi [15]	1286	Arias, *Studi*, pp. 157–166		
Bonino Riccardi	1295	E 101/601/5		
Nicholao Chiavari	1295	E 101/601/5		
Stefano Buzolini	1295	E 101/601/5		
Chino Christofanni	?	E 101/601/5		
GASCONY				
Riccardo Rosciompelli	1279	*R.G.*, II, no. 351		
Bonaventura Lombardo	1289	E 101/352/14		

Name	*From*		*To*	
Nicholao Mingosi[16]	1289–90	*R.G.*, II, nos. 1463, 1772	(1301?)	E 101/601/5
Nigello	1286	C 47/4/13 m. 18		
Galfrido Riccardi	1287	*R.G.*, II, no. 1463		
Graziano Perdriz	1290	*R.G.*, II, no. 1772		
FRANCE				
Francesco Maneumach[17]	1279	C 47/13/1 no. 15		
Lotto Aldebrandini[18]	1279	C 47/13/1 no. 15		
Giovannino Bandini[19]	1299–1300	Piton, *Les Lombards*, I, pp. 142, 149		
Benetuccio del Barcanchera	1301	E 101/601/5		
Betto Cremondelli [20]	1297	E 101/601/5		
(Labruccio Simonetti) [20]	(1297)	E 101/601/5		
LOW COUNTRIES				
Giovanni Paganel	1296	E 372/146 m. 54		
Giovanni "de St. Andonio"	1296	E 372/146 m. 54		
Giovanni "de Kaioby"	1296	E 372/146 m. 54		
Guido Guidiccioni	1287	E 36/274 mm. 371d–372	1297	E 101/601/5

Table II Important Debts Owed the Riccardi

EARLS			
William Beauchamp, Earl of Warwick	200 marks	1278	E 159/52 m. 12
	500 marks	1282	E 159/55 m. 15
	£100	1287	E 159/60 m. 19d.
	£240	1287	E 159/60 m. 19d.
	£400	1295	E 101/601/5
(James, his brother)	(£22 2s. 6d.)	(1288)	(E 159/61 m. 22)
	(£36 15s. 0d.)	(1290)	(E 159/63 m. 29d.)
Roger Bigod, Earl of Norfolk	£330	1277	E 368/50 m. 9d.
	£762 11s. 7-1/2 d.[21]	1278	E 159/51 m. 19
	£1,000 10s. 1d.	1278	E 159/52 m. 12
	£950 6s. 6-1/2 d.[22]	1279	E 368/52 m. 14
	1,700 marks[23]	1281	E 159/55 m. 10d.
	£182 5s. 0d.	1284	E 159/57 m. 17
John de Warenne, Earl of Surrey	£933 7s. 0d.	1285	E 159/58 m. 18
	£100	1287	E 159/60 m. 19d.
	100 marks	1287	E 159/61 m. 13
(William, his son)	(200 marks)	(1286)	(E 159/59 m. 6)
Gilbert de Clare, Earl of Gloucester and Hertford	500 marks	1295	E 101/601/5
(Thomas, his brother)	(£409 17s. 0d.)	(1284)	(E 159/58 m. 13d.)
Henry de Lacy, Earl of Lincoln	£300	1286	*C.C.R.*, 427
	1,000 marks	1295	E 101/601/5
Eleanor de Montfort, Countess of Leicester	£600[24]	1282	*C.C.R.*, p. 183
Margaret de Clare, Countess of Gloucester	£178 17s. 8d.[25]	by 1294	E 401/140, 141, 148, 149

ARCHBISHOPS			
Robert Kilwardby, Canterbury	not stated[26]		
John Pecham, Canterbury	4,000 marks	1279	*Register*, I, pp. 17, 21–23
	500 marks	1282	*Register*, I, pp. 296–297
Walter Giffard, York	1,000 marks	1266–67	*Register*, p. 153
	200 marks	1270	*Register*, p. 115
	£648[27]	1275	*Register*, p. 274
William Wickwane, York	316 marks[28]	1279	*Register*, pp. 257–258
	30 marks	undated	*Register*, pp. 259–260
John le Romeyn, York	£21	1286	*Register*, p. 155
	200 marks	1287	*Register*, p. 161
John Sanford, Dublin	not stated	1294	E 101/126/7
BISHOPS			
John of Pontoise, Bishop of Winchester	500 marks[29]	1284	E 159/57 m. 16d.
William Middleton, Bishop of Norwich	517 marks	1280	*C.C.R.*, p. 59
Antony Bek, Bishop of Durham	800 marks[30]	1294	E 101/601/5
Thomas Bek, Bishop of St. David's	£100[31]	1286	
William of Louth, Bishop of Ely	not stated	1294	E 101/126/7
John of Halton, Bishop of Carlisle	not stated	1294	E 101/126/7
ABBOTS, PRIORS, ARCHDEACONS			
Prior of Wenlock	£200	1275	E 159/49 m. 26d.
	200 marks	1281	E 159/54 m. 22
	100 marks	1290	E 159/63 m. 31d.
Abbot of Kirkstall	£119 6s. 8d.	1276	E 13/4 m. 11

ABBOTS, PRIORS, ARCHDEACONS (cont.)

Prior of Lewes	£300	1283	E 159/57 m. 13d.
	800 marks	1285	E 101/126/4
	900 marks	1286	E 159/59 m. 12d.
Abbot of Glastonbury	£801 0s. 8d.[32]	1279	E 159/52 m. 15
	£175	1291	E 159/65 m. 30
Abbot of Hyde	£100	1286	*C.C.R.*, p. 465
Abbot of Faversham	200 marks	1286	E 159/60 m. 12
Abbot of Ramsay	800 marks	1287	E 159/61 m. 14
Prior of Cokefield	210 marks	1287	E 159/60 m. 17d.
Abbot of Vaudey	305 marks	1280	E 159/54 m. 11
Abbot of Meaux	£130	1280	E 159/53 m. 13d.
	165 marks	1287	E 159/60 m. 18
	£220	1287	E 159/61 m. 14
Prior of St. Swithun's, Winchester	310 marks	1278	*C.C.R.*, p. 519
	£168	1281	E 159/54 m. 19
	£81 10s. 0d.	1281	E 159/54 m. 23
	£310	1283	E 159/57 m. 9
	£300	1285	E 159/58 m. 16
	804 marks	1285	E 159/59 mm. 4, 5
Abbot of Deulacres	£42 6s. 0d.	1294	E 401/141, 144, 145
Abbot of Glastonbury	£20 0s. 0d.	1294	E 401/138
Abbot of Cokefield	£20 0s. 0d.	1294	E 401/138
Abbot of Cumbermere	£84 10s. 0d.	1294	E 401/139, 140, 144
Abbot of St. Augustine's, Bristol	£47 13s. 4d.	1294	E 401/139, 140, 141

ABBOTS, PRIORS, ARCHDEACONS (cont.)			
Prior of Holy Trinity, Ipswich	£88 13s. 4d.	1294	E 401/139, 140, 141, 143, 144
Abbot of Tilletye	£36 6s. 8d.	1294	E 401/141, 144, 148, 153
Abbot of New Monastery	£41 13s. 4d.	1294	E 401/155, 159
William de Estimato, Archdeacon of Lincoln	£826 2s. 6d.	1293	E 159/67 m. 66d.
Master James de Hispania, Canon of St. Paul's, London	£203 6s. 8d.	1292	*C.C.R.*, p. 260
Gerald de Wyspayns, Archdeacon of Richmond	£388 10s. 10d.	1294	E 401/140, 141, 144, 147
William de Stevie, Archdeacon of Lincoln	£60 0s. 0d.	1294	E 401/140
GOVERNMENT OFFICIALS			
William March, Treasurer, Bishop of Bath and Wells	2,000 marks	1295	E 101/601/5
John Kirkby, Treasurer	1,204-1/2 marks	1290	E 159/60 m. 20
	not stated	1294	E 101/126/7
			E 368/62 m. 9
Walter Langton, Treasurer	1,000 marks	1295	E 101/601/5
John Droxford, Keeper of the Wardrobe	not stated	1294	E 101/126/7
John Berwick, king's clerk	not stated	1294	E 101/126/7
John Havering, Seneschal of Gascony, 1288–94	not stated	1294	E 101/126/7
Hugh Cressingham, justice and Treasurer of Scotland (1296)	not stated	1294	E 101/126/7
Walter Beauchamp, Steward of Household	not stated	1294	E 101/126/7
Elias de Hauville, constable of Rockingham Castle, etc.	not stated	1294	E 101/126/7

GOVERNMENT OFFICIALS (cont.)			
Philip de Willoughby, Chancellor of Exchequer, repeatedly acting treasurer	£68 7s. 6d.	1294	E 101/126/7
Adam de Creting, marshal in Gascony	300 marks	1295	E 101/601/5
William Latimer, household knight	sum obliterated	1280	E 159/53 m. 16d.
a magnate	not stated	1294	E 101/126/7
John de St. John, lieutenant in Gascony, 1293,	sum obliterated	1280	E 159/53 m. 16d.
and household familiar	£40 12s. 4d.	1281	E 159/54 m. 23d.
	84 marks	1283	E 159/57 m. 11d.
	£229 9s. 6d.	1286	E 159/59 m. 3d.
	£320 9s. 5d.	1292	E 159/65 m. 27d.
OTHERS			
Henry le Waleys, mayor of London	300 marks	1274	E 159/48 m. 12
London citizens, led by Henry le Waleys	1,200 marks	1274	*C.C.R.*, pp. 122–123
Nicholas Segrave	1,000 marks[34]	1276	*C.C.R.*, p. 427
Roger Mortimer	230 marks	1276	*C.C.R.*, p. 342
	not stated	1294	E 101/126/7
Edmund Mortimer	£255 9s. 2d.[35]	1287	E 159/60 m. 16d.
Pain de Chaworth	100 marks	1279	E 159/53 m. 9
	£100	1280	E 159/54 m. 14
	£200	1281	E 159/54 m. 21d.
	105 marks[36]	1281	E 368/54 m. 20
Thomas de Berkeley	700 marks[37]	1284	*C.C.R.*, pp. 300–301

OTHERS (cont.)			
John le Gros	£584 14s. 0d.	1279	E 13/8 m. 9
John de Eyvill	£135 10s. 0d.	1287	*C.C.R.*, p. 477
William de Bosco	£102 6s. 8d.	1294	E 401/138, 140, 141, 145, 149
Jacob d'Ispannia	£56 0s. 4d.	1294	E 401/138, 141, 144
John de Vescy	1,600 marks	1276	*C.C.R.*, p. 326
John de Sulleye, knight	£600 6s. 1d.	1294	E 101/126/7
Richard Louth, clerk	not stated	1294	E 101/126/7
Geoffrey Welles	not stated	1294	E 101/126/7
Joan of Gloucester and Margaret, the king's daughters	not stated	1294	E 101/126/7
John l'Estrange (de Estrattengges)	£200	1292	*C.C.R.*, p. 309
FOREIGN DEBTS			
Count of Bar[38]	£650	1294	E 101/126/7
Count of Holland[38]	200 marks	1294	E 101/126/7
Bishop of Verdun, brother of Otto Grandson	£314 1s. 5d.	1294	E 101/126/7
Jacopo Bettori	£2600	1294	E 101/126/7
John, Duke of Brittany	not stated	1294	E 101/126/7

NOTES TO TABLE I

[1] These men would have been partners and important factors, but any attempt to determine the status of each man would be largely guesswork. The dates in parentheses refer to an uncertain identification of the agent at that time, or an uncertain or terminated association with the society. They are explained in the footnotes if the meaning is not clear from the discussion in the body of the chapter. The dates given show the time during which the agent was active in England, but do not imply continuous residence there.

[2] A Henry of Lucca appears in 1250, but the surname da Pogio only in 1276. The earlier Henry may be Henry Saracini, mentioned in *R. G.*, I, no. 3877. Enrico da Pogio was a brother of Orlandino. *C.P.R. 1281-1292*, p. 318.

[3] His full name was Dono Bernardini da Pogio, *C. C. R. 1288-1296*, p. 31. Since he had been knighted by 1300 and went abroad in that year, he must have left the company prior to the 1294 fall from royal favor. *C. P. R. 1292-1301*, p. 492.

[4] Labro was abroad for many years of this period. Our earliest evidence, cited in the table, shows him going to Rome. He returned by 1279, *C. P. R.*

1272-1281, p. 354. By 1290 he was once again in Rome, C 47/4/5 m. 15. As we have seen, he died in Italy.

[5] A Reiner of Lucca appears in 1244, the surname in 1266-1267. In 1294 there is a reference to "Reiner of Lucca who was a king's merchant in the year 10 [1282]," implying that he had died or left the firm by 1294. E 159/67 m. 25d. This is probably Reiner Magiari.

[6] He may be the Gualteri who was a customs collector in 1287. E 122/50/2.

[7] Peregrino and Peregrine de la Pointe may be the same man. There was also a Peregrino da Chiatri or Peregrine de Chartres who was known by the Riccardi and in contact with them, but he cannot be clearly linked with the society. He owed money to the Riccardi in 1290-1291. E. 159/64 m. 16.

[8] Episonis, fellow of Luke appears in an account running from 1269-1270 to 1281. Opiso was a son-in-law of Baroncino, and went with his group after it split off from the Riccardi. E 159/61 mm. 15, 19d. Yet in 1293 he assigned to the Riccardi 1,100 marks which Baroncino owed him. He named all the Riccardi members as his attornies against Baroncino to seek the money in partial payment of his debts to the company. E 159/66 m. 51d.

[9] He owed money to Enrico da Pogio in 1288-1289, and may have been out of the company by then. E 159/62 m. 3.

[10] By 1297 he may have left the Riccardi. E 101/601/5, p. 5, letter of 5 December 1297.

[11] The letter of 3 November 1301 states that he had been in Ireland for more than thirteen years. He was given permission to leave at this time. E 101/601/5, p. 39d.

[12] He was in Wales in 1287. *C.C.R.V.* (*Welsh*), p. 310.

[13] A Hug' of Lucca accounted for Irish customs in 1275-1277. It seems reasonable to identify this man as Hugolino Rosciompelli.

[14] He was a member of the Riccardi by 1286. Arias, *Studi*, pp. 157-166.

[15] The document which gives these names is a formal contract of deposit for a papal tax and lists numerous important Riccardi members. The others on this list can be placed in England or Ireland at this time. Since these names appear at the top of the list and include men of the Riccardi family itself, we may conclude that they were from the Lucca branch.

[16] His area of operation in 1301 is uncertain.

[17] In Paris.

[18] In Paris. He was mentioned in 1297, but the location is uncertain. E 101/601/5, letter of 5 December 1297.

[19] In Paris.

[20] These men may have worked in France or the Low Countries or both.

NOTES TO TABLE II

[21] Invalidated because included in the recognizance given for £1,000 10s. 1d. in E 159/52 m. 12.

[22] A note on the L. T. R. Memoranda Roll specifies that this debt is entirely separate from the £1,000 10s. 1d.

[23] This represents his total debt and not an entirely new obligation.

[24] Edward eventually discharged this debt, along with the "damages" of £400, because of money owed her as a dowry by Henry III. The countess assigned £1,000 to Baroncino at the exchequer. The executor of her will renounced the assignment as contrary to the form of the will. E 159/60 mm. 13, 2d. (1286–1287). But the payment was ordered anyway. E 159/65 m. 25d. Cf. Denholm-Young, *Seignorial Administration*, p. 64. Turner, *Manners and Household Expenses in England in the XIIIth and XIVth Centuries* (Roxburghe Club), pp. 90–92. For some reason the money was to go to Baroncino personally and not to the company. There was considerable confusion over this sum as late as 1301, since Baroncino claimed the Riccardi had not turned the money over to him. E 101/601/5, letter of 17 November 1301.

[25] This loan, and all loans citing the E 401 series, are taken from the records of debts owed to the Riccardi and collected by the exchequer after

their fall. The receipt rolls record what the king actually collected, and not necessarily the total debt owed; the figures are nonetheless useful as minimal sums.

[26] A part of his debt was outstanding when Pecham succeeded him. See Pecham's *Register*, I, pp. 156-158.

[27] This is a summary obligation for more than one loan. But when he died four years later, in April of 1279, he still owed the Riccardi an unspecified sum. See the *Register* of his executor, Bishop Godfrey Giffard of Worcester, II, p. 123.

[28] This sum and the following one represent payments made at the papal *curia*.

[29] At the time they made this loan the Riccardi agents, Baroncino and Giovanni Simonetti, mainperned that several merchants of the Cardellini company would not seek damages, expenses, or interest on a loan of 4,000 marks which the Cardellini had made to the bishop, provided that he repay this loan by the next feast of St. Martin. If he failed to do so, interest for the entire term of the loan could be collected. However, it is clear that the bishop had already paid a sizable interest charge; no less than 1,000 marks had been delivered to his creditors "in recompensacionem expensarum dampnorum et interesse," although it is immediately added "et dicte mille marcas fuerint de mero dono suo et eas alia de causa non dedit."

[30] The debt had previously been 1,000 marks.

[31] The Riccardi were to collect this from a third party for the bishop's debts to them.

[32] The Riccardi had paid the abbey's share of the tenth for the Holy Land.

[33] This is a comprehensive statement and may include parts of previous debts.

[34] On the importance of the Segrave family see Powicke, *Thirteenth Century*, pp. 331-332.

[35] This contains £100 paid to him by order of the queen consort. Edmund has to repay if she did not.

[36] A sum of perhaps £132 remained to be paid in 1284 after his death. *C.C.R. 1279-1288*, pp. 250-251.

[37] In December of 1284 the Riccardi remitted the sum to Thomas and "looked to the king for it." Edward paid his merchants. The obligation had been sealed under the statute of merchants.

[38] These two counts were among Edward's most important allies in the continental coalition he was constructing against Philip the Fair. Although we have no further evidence on these loans, it is possible that they were made on Edward's orders.

APPENDIX THE RICCARDI LETTERS

Most of the surviving Riccardi business letters are preserved as a bundle of loose leaves among the Exchequer Accounts Various (E 101/601/5). One additional letter and one fragment (four sheets) are in the Ancient Correspondence (SC 1, 58 nos. 15, 20A, B, C, D). All are written in an abbreviated Italian on heavy paper, possibly the oldest paper documents in the Public Record Office. At least three distinct hands can be detected. Although the E 101 pages have been numbered, the order of the letters is not now chronological, nor is there any certainty that pages from one letter have not been misplaced among those of another letter. Those letters that can be dated give a time-span of 1295-1303. Many are damaged and incomplete so that it is impossible to determine the exact number of letters or the precise dates of all of them. But we can be sure that there are at least fifteen letters, or parts of letters, since there are this many pages beginning with a salutation. From internal evidence it is quite possible that more than twenty letters or fragments are represented.

Emilio Re drew on these letters for his useful article on the Riccardi in the *Archivio della Societa Romana di Storia Patria* XXXVII (1914), and printed parts of some of them, modernizing the originals somewhat in word-division, punctuation, capitalization, etc. To a much lesser extent he utilized the letters in a later article, "Archivi inglesi e Storia italiana," in *Archivio Storico Italiano*, serie vi, I (1913), printing a few more passages from them. But he apparently did not study the letters at great length, nor did he attempt to correlate their contents with the bulk of unpublished documents relating to the company in the Record Office. His stated intention was to carry out a larger study, based on the letters. In the *Archivio Storico Italiano* he writes (p. 261 n. 5) "Esse formerano il soggetto principale di un volume di prossima pubblicazione: *Mercanti italiani in Inghilterra*." If this work was ever completed, it was apparently not published. Moreover, several of the letters have been classified only recently, and so were unavailable to Re. He could not have known of pp. 36–46 of E 101/601/5, nor of the pages in SC 1, 58. Only eight of the minimal number of fifteen letters are cited in his article.

Without inferring more confidence than is warranted by the condition of the letters, I would divide and date them as follows:

E101/601/5

Pages	*Date*	
25–30	10 October, 1296	Letter begins on P. 25*d*., continuing on pp. 25, 26, 26*d*., etc. Page 29 may well represent a part of a new letter.
24	5 August, 1296	
45–46	probably 1296–1297	No salutation page. May be more than one letter.
31–35	probably 1296–1297	May be more than one letter.
36	15 November, 1297	
1–6	5 December, 1297	Possibly two letters, but not more. Re misread this date as 1298.
17–23	between 1297–1300 Re dates this "1298 (?)"	Of what is legible there could be two letters, but not more. Many pages are completely illegible.
44	21 April, 1298	
42–43	4 December, 1300	The year is omitted in the letter date, but it can be established by references to the death of Labro Volpelli. This letter states he died 22 November. A papal letter of 30 November 1300 refers to him as recently deceased. The letter of pp. 11–12 was obviously written after April of 1300 and speaks of Labro as alive. The year of his death, and this letter, is thus 1300.
11–12	after April, 1300	Could be more than one letter.
15–16	5 September, 1301	Could be more than one letter.

Pages	*Date*	
13–14	probably after September, 1301	
38–41	3 November, 1301	Could be more than one letter.
7–10	17 November, 1301	Could be more than one letter.
37	1 November, year uncertain	Only four paragraphs long.
S C 1, 58		
no. 15	possibly 1297 or 1298	Only two paragraphs long. No salutation. Subject of first paragraph is similar to letter of 5 December, 1297.
nos. 20A, B, C, D	12 April, 1303	

Chapter II The Relationship Between King and Banker

1. A SOLUTION TO THE PROBLEM OF ROYAL FINANCE

A serious and persistent shortage of funds plagued Western European monarchs throughout the thirteenth century. As governments developed more elaborate and active administrations and more magnificent courts, as the costs of warfare rose and expensive alliances became more common, the gap between traditional revenues and the new costs widened. Ordinary revenues barely covered the king's day-to-day needs and in the face of war or sudden emergency they failed utterly. To meet the problem, monarchs and their advisers were beginning to levy extraordinary revenues, but their subjects were not yet reconciled to the "painful necessity" of recurrent taxation. Since men saw the collection of taxes as closely akin to robbery, only a crisis was sufficient warrant for a king's asking all his subjects for financial support. Even then the process of collection would probably still be going on when the next crisis arose. The task was thus not only to establish adequate sources of revenue, but also to insure a supply of cash. To this twofold problem was added the condition that the solution must not alienate the politically powerful groups within the realm which were committed to the idea that a ruler ought to be able to "live of his own." The countries of Western Europe were not impoverished or unable to support larger and more active government establishments; the wealth was there, in the fields, on the backs of sheep, in the merchants' shops, and in the vineyards, but it would have to be tapped carefully.[1]

Although occasional borrowing had been a feature of earlier periods, it was only about the middle of the thirteenth century that capable and ambitious rulers were able to institute a more regular use of loans as a way out of their difficulties. To do this they turned to the companies of Italian merchant-bankers which were penetrating Northwestern Europe as collectors of the various payments owed the papacy and as merchants anxious to put their superior financial resources and business techniques to good use in the thriving wool trade.

These two factors were particularly operative in the England of Henry III (1216-1272), with its strong papal ties and the finest wool in Europe. The Italians were not newcomers in England at this time, for they had lent money on occasion to Richard (1189-1199) and John (1199-1216) and had been competing in the wool trade as early as the reign of Henry II (1154-1189). But it was during the reign of Henry III that they began to flourish.

Numerous dealings with foreign merchants have left their mark in royal records from this reign. A Florentine whose name usually appears as Diutatus Guillelmi is especially prominent, being described as "one of the king's household," "the king's merchant," "the queen's merchant," and the like.[2] Over a period of more than a decade he can be seen advancing moderate loans and making purchases for the royal family.[3] Lucchesi were also involved and were sometimes men who were later to serve Edward I as members of the Riccardi.[4] In July of 1254, for example, King

[1] See the discussions by J. R. Strayer in the introduction to *The English Government At Work, 1327-1336*, II, pp. 3-4; by E. B. and M. M. Fryde, *Cambridge Economic History*, III, pp. 431-433; by T. F. Tout, *Chapters in the Administrative History of Medieval England*, II, p. 99; by Edouard Perroy, *The Hundred Years' War* (Capricorn edition), pp. 44-47, 55-57; and by Eileen Power, *The Wool Trade*, pp. 63-64.

[2] *C.P.R. 1258-1266*, p. 570. *Ibid., 1266-1272*, p. 335.

[3] He loaned money in Gascony on the order of Henry III in 1255, and in 1271 he is still described as being engaged on the king's business. *C.P.R. 1258-1266*, p. 570. *Ibid., 1266-1272*, pp. 530-531.

[4] See Chapter I, Section 1.

Henry owed these merchants 2,000 marks: 1,000 marks for an old debt and 1,000 marks for goods delivered for the knighting of the Lord Edward.[5] Less than a year later the king owed them 2,246 marks 11s. 11d. for goods supplied to Henry and Edward, with repayment promised partly from the exchequer and the wardrobe, but mainly from the tallage levied on London and York.[6] Edward was beginning to learn important lessons in the usefulness of foreign merchant-bankers, even making contact with the men who were to become his financiers once he ascended the throne. "Luke of Lucca" (Lucasio Natale), who occasionally served Edward's father during the trying years of baronial strife, would figure as a leading Riccardi partner when the relationship with Edward I was established.[7] In the case of both the Florentines and the Lucchesi the Lord Edward must have observed his father repaying Italian loans from the proceeds of taxes,[8] and utilizing branches of Italian companies in Rome for loans to royal diplomats.[9]

Yet though these lessons were not lost on Edward, it must not be thought that Henry III had created anything like the financial system his son would devise. Neither in the resources committed to the Italians nor in the scale of their loans to the crown can Henry's realization of the potential in their liquid wealth and financial expertise be compared to Edward's. King Henry used the Italians intermittently, when pressing need forced him to turn to them; his transactions were generally of no great size. King Edward made them a cornerstone of his total financial structure.

[5]*C.P.R. 1247-1258*, p. 315. The merchants are "Peregrine Sesmundi, Bartholomew Beudini [probably Bendini], Reyner Senac', Henry Saracen', and Luke Natal' and fellows, merchants of Lucca."

[6]*Ibid.*, p. 404.

[7]See Thomas Madox, *History of the Exchequer* (2nd ed., 1769), p. 95, *C.P.R. 1258-1266*, pp. 218, 258. Edward's uncle, Richard Earl of Cornwall, also dealt with Luke. *C.P.R. 1266-1272*, p. 487.

[8]*C.P.R. 1266-1272*, pp. 27, 92-93, 207, 224.

[9]See Glenn Olsen, "Italian Merchants and the Performance of Papal Banking Functions in the Early Thirteenth Century," *Economy, Society and Government in Medieval Italy*, pp. 53-55, for several examples early in the reign of Henry III.

Moreover there are elements of a love-hate relationship in Henry's dealings with the alien merchants. He professed to hate their usury, yet he needed their loans. In 1240, 1245, 1251, and 1253 he withdrew the royal protection from foreign merchants, set a date for their expulsion, and then collected loans—the price of continued business in England. For much of Henry's reign the greatest royal creditor was not some Italian merchant-banker, but rather the king's brother Richard, Earl of Cornwall, who could draw upon his extensive holdings, which included the lucrative tin mines of Cornwall.

A new dimension was opened after Henry accepted the papal offer of the kingdom of Sicily for Edmund, his second son. The price was no less than the mounting of an expedition to Sicily and the satisfaction of papal debts to Italian merchants standing at 135,541 marks. Alexander IV obligingly placed his bankers at the disposal of the English king, and Henry was able to borrow at least £54,000 from them in Italy before the barons took over the reins of government in 1258, ending "the Sicilian business."[10]

The security arranged for these loans is enlightening. It seems that the property of English monastic houses was pledged, sometimes without their knowledge, in return for the Italian loans to the king. Although the money was to be repaid ultimately from the papal tenth collected for the crusade, the monastery had to meet its particular share in the meantime, notwithstanding any privilege, protection, or legal action.[11]

This was the central difficulty blocking a more productive use of the great resources obviously available through Italian loans. Without adequate security even small loans brought occasionally onerous stipulations. Thus when Florentine merchants gave Henry a loan of 780 marks in 1260, he not only promised prompt

[10]Much of the preceding discussion is based on E. B. Fryde, *C.E.H.*, III, pp. 451–454. Cf. F. M. Powicke, *King Henry III and the Lord Edward*, I, pp. 313–315; R. J. Whitwell "Italian Bankers and the English Crown," *T.R.H.S.*, n.s., XVII (1903). W. E. Lunt, *Financial Relations of the Papacy with England to 1327*, pp. 598–600. Tout, *Chapters*, II, pp. 99, 122 ff.

[11]Powicke, *Henry III and Lord Edward*, I, pp. 372–373. W. E. Lunt, *Financial Relations*, pp. 255–290.

repayment under penalty of 200 marks, but added "besides which the king promises to pay all loss, interest, and expenses incurred by them, on their simple word, renouncing any privileges of jurisdiction, of crusades, indulgences, letters obtained from the Pope, or other privileges."[12] In one of the loans from the period of "the Sicilian business" he even found it necessary to place himself and his heirs under the coercion of the bishop of Florence and the papal nuncio for enforcing payment.[13]

The Lord Edward realized the potential represented by the Italian companies and realized also that the key to a successful means of tapping their resources was a steady source of income which could be used as collateral for their loans. His efforts to create a customs system show this awareness,[14] as does his crusade finance. On the security of the customs of Bordeaux he negotiated a loan of 70,000 *livres tournois* from Saint Louis, with repayment from these customs to begin in March of 1274. In the interval, moreover, these same customs were farmed to merchant-bankers in order to raise further sums for the expedition to the Holy Land.[15]

Once Edward came to the throne he bolstered his income with new revenue sources: the 1275 wool custom and much more frequent direct taxes on lay and clerical property. Thus, as E. B. Fryde has observed, "Edward's increased use of credit facilities represented simply a more effective deployment of resources in themselves considerable."[16] These two sources—the wool custom and taxes—went a long way toward solving the primary problem of an adequate supply of royal funds.

But although his resources were augmented, their collection was still slow and often irregular; it was still difficult if not impossible to set aside any significant reserve. As Tout noted of Edward,

[12] *C.P.R. 1258-1266*, p. 71.

[13] *C.C.R. 1247-1258*, p. 631. May 29, 1258.

[14] Below, Chapter III, Section 1.

[15] Powicke, *Thirteenth Century*, p. 281. Jean-Paul Trabut-Cussac, "Le financement de la croisade anglaise de 1270," *Bibliothèque de l'École des chartres*, CXIX (1961).

[16] E. B. Fryde, *C.E.H.*, III p. 455.

"His was the eternal problem that still besets both individuals and nations that their creditors call upon them to pay their accounts before they have been able to collect the accounts owing to them."[17] There was a crucial necessity to smooth the curve of incidence of royal revenues and insure sufficient cash for great or sudden need. It was with this in mind that Edward established his special relationship with the Riccardi of Lucca. He committed his new revenues largely to the Italian *societas* and in return received a steady supply of cash when and where he had need of it. The merchants were expected to anticipate the revenues in their charge with frequent and sizable loans to the king and by payments on his behalf. A system of finance was thus created which met the royal needs handsomely. By borrowing from the Riccardi, Edward could act vigorously in any situation and repay the Italians in a more leisurly fashion and perhaps in a less politically charged atmosphere.

In short, for the first twenty-two years of his reign the Riccardi of Lucca would act as the king's bankers in a sophisticated system of government finance which assured Edward of liquidity. By using the credit facilities of the Riccardi, Edward was able to order payment of almost any reasonable amount of money and be sure that it would be rapidly accomplished, regardless of the state of the royal revenues or the rate at which they were being received.

Although the Riccardi would not always have to anticipate royal revenues to meet these orders, the wording of many writs confirms that they were expected to do so. These mandates direct the Riccardi to make payments "out of the king's money or their own." Thus when rebellion broke out in South Wales in 1287, the merchants were told to pay what would be required for the army, either out of the king's money in their keeping, or from loans, or from any other source whatsoever.[18] And after the first of Edward's campaigns in Wales they were required to pay 1,000 marks

[17] *Chapters*, II, p. 99. Cf. Eileen Power, *Wool Trade*, pp. 63–64.

[18] The original is preserved among the Ancient Correspondence, S.C. 1, XIII, no. 63. It is quoted in the Riccardi account for this war, E 372/132 m. 1. Cf. *C.C.R.V.*, p. 309.

to Roger Bigod, Earl of Norfolk, out of royal funds or their own.[19] It was not only the largest payments which are thus described. Orders for two gifts of 100s. each in 1279 are followed by the same phrase.[20] From the majority of the writs, which make no mention of the source of revenue, we may draw the same conclusion.

In most instances it is not possible to determine whether the royal revenues held by the Riccardi actually could meet a particular assignment at that time, but Edward was constantly in debt to his bankers and these revenues were committed to their control as sources of repayment. Thus, unless for brief periods the proceeds of royal revenues in Riccardi hands exceeded the king's debt to them at that time, their payments on royal orders were indirect loans, even if the money was actually drawn from these royal revenues. There can be no doubt that the Riccardi were in fact making sizable advances. In 1272-1279 their excess of payments over receipts is listed as £23,000;[21] in 1290-1294, £18,924.[22]

We do not know exactly when Edward came to a definite agreement with the Riccardi partners, outlining the special relationship between the king and the company; but it is most likely that some such understanding was reached during the period of his crusade. For although Edward had been in touch with Riccardi agents for some time before this venture, it was while he was wearing the cross that their services first became regular and sizable.

When Edward was still in Acre the merchants shipped 2,000 marks to him under the supervision of one of their agents, Peregrine de la Pointe, and an English wardrobe clerk, William de Blyburgh.[23] But it was above all on his return journey that their resources were tapped. Between Edward's landing at Trapani in Sicily in November of 1272, and his landing at Dover in August

[19]*C.P.R. 1272-1281*, p. 195. This is also the phrase used in connection with their purchases of wine for the king. *Ibid.*, p. 361.

[20]*Ibid.*, pp. 319-320.

[21]E 101/126/1

[22]E 372/143 m. 35d.

[23]E 101/350/5/1.

of 1274, they advanced £23,364 4s. 5d. Moreover, the company had provided an additional credit of £7,687 13s. 8d. to Robert Burnell "carrying on the king's affairs in England during his absence."[24] This included discharging the king's debts to merchants of Acre at the fairs of Laon and Provins, and meeting other obligations at the Paris Temple. Early wardrobe accounts and orders sent to leading members of the Riccardi show them busy in the king's service, lending money to his household, receiving money on its behalf, transferring to Edward in Paris the sums exacted from Jews in England, frequenting the great fairs.[25]

By the time Edward had once again set foot in England there must have been substantial agreement on the role the Riccardi would play in English government finance. He had learned at first hand what their employment could mean to an ambitious king and had undoubtedly pledged the proper inducements.

The "Ricardi system" which had thus emerged by Edward's accession was an entirely new and a crucially important instrument of English government finance. In the first place it was a feature of Edward's system that this single firm of merchant-bankers was chosen to act as *mercatores regis* and was placed in a special relationship to the king. This was in marked contrast to the multiplicity of lenders used by his father. Although Edward transacted business with other firms between 1272 and 1294, the revenues placed in Riccardi hands, the scale of payments and loans provided by them, and the privileges they enjoyed placed the merchants from Lucca in an entirely separate class. As we shall see, when he wanted to deal with the Italian community at large, Edward often negotiated through this chosen firm.

Second, it must be stressed that this single Italian company

[24]See their 1276 account, *C.P.R. 1272-1281*, pp. 131-132. Cf. Tout, *Chapters*, II, pp. 4-5, and 6 n.1. The wardrobe account covering a slightly longer period shows a total receipt of £31,457, but only £9,763 from the Riccardi. E 372/121 m. 21. Tout suggests that short advances, soon repaid, may not have been included in the accounts. Perhaps many of their advances were made on the king's personal order, without entering the domain of the wardrobe, and only at the time of the account were lumped with those paid to the keeper or paid out by his directive.

[25]E 372/121, E 101/350/5/1, *C.P.R. 1272-1281*, pp. 4, 51, 52.

became, in effect, a branch of the English government, a special treasury supplementary to the financial administration based on the exchequer and wardrobe. The Riccardi did not stand on the sidelines, occasionally lending money only when formal negotiations for specific sums had been conducted and elaborate promissory instruments had been given them; they required only a royal order. The king's writs went with great regularity to the *mercatores regis* not only ordering them to provide the cash needed by royal officials, but also directing them to make payments personally. The sums might range from the inconsequential to figures of several thousand pounds.[26]

Third, although the Riccardi received large sums *de thesauro*, i.e., from the exchequer, the new system based on their loans was tied more closely to the wardrobe, the flexible financial department of the king's household, than to the exchequer. It was almost invariably to wardrobe officials that the Riccardi delivered cash when the king's requests came to them. Sums "de mercatores de Luka" form a significant part of the receipt of most wardrobe accounts, but the receipt rolls of the exchequer show no such loans.[27] This close link with the wardrobe appears in other ways as well. Orlandino da Pogio of the Riccardi was the only layman accorded the privilege of sleeping in the wardrobe. At the opening of the reign the Riccardi even fulfilled the characteristic wardrobe function of making provision for the coronation, handling nearly a quarter of the sum spent "on wardrobe purchases for the coronation."[28]

At times meeting the king's demands must have strained the merchants' resources almost to the breaking-point. A letter to John Kirkby, the treasurer, probably in the autumn of 1284,

[26]For example, the Patent Roll alone shows 27 orders for payment between mid-July of 1276 and mid-November of that year. The total sum for this four-month period comes to nearly £5,000. *C.P.R. 1272-1281*, pp. 152, 155, 157, 159, 164, 167-168, 169.

[27]Whitwell found no Italian loans on the receipt rolls before Michelmas 1294-1295. *T.R.H.S.*, n.s., XVII, p. 219. My own search of a sampling of these rolls confirmed this.

[28]Tout, *Chapters*, II, pp. 29, 45. The sum of 1,000 marks was given to Luke of Lucca for this purpose. E 372/118 m. 18.

makes this abundantly clear. Kirkby had written to them asking that £1,000 be sent to Northampton by a certain time "pur les bosoignes le Rey." To this they replied that they had no money at hand, nor could they collect any so quickly. But, they explained, as soon as they had talked with Kirkby's clerk Nicholas, who brought the request, "nous enveiames a nos compaignons de la outre q'il nous enveissent argent par de ca pur meime cele b[osoigne] issi q' si deu plest nous averoms ces deniers de dents ces xv iors." Having thus promised the sum required by drawing on their cross-Channel credit network, the Riccardi pointedly list the payments they have recently made for the king. After Kirby had left London the following orders for payments had been fulfilled: £1,400 to Gascons, presumably mercenaries still in England following the 1282-1283 Welsh war; £900 to Hamo de la Legh, keeper of the great wardrobe; more than £1,000 "de autres mandements q' le Rey nous a mande"; £450 "pur lenterrement mon sire Amphus"—that is, for the funeral expenses of Edward's eldest son Alfonso. The letter concludes, "et chescun ior nous venent mandements du Rey de paier deners q' nous ne savoms quel part tourner. Por quei il nous peise mult q' nous ne avoms nul issi especial ami en Engleterre apres le Rey pur ky nous feisoms issi volunters cum nous feisoms pur vous."[29]

Detailed records of all the transactions were kept, and general accountings were held periodically. The first of these was a "view of account" at Winchester in 1276, conducted before unspecified auditors. When the records had been reviewed a summarized statement was placed on the patent roll.[30] The next came in the summer of 1279, with Robert Burnell (chancellor, and bishop of Bath and Wells), Brother Joseph de Chauncy (the treasurer of the exchequer), John de Vescy, Otto de Grandson, Antony Bek, and Master Thomas Bek ("treasurer of the king," i.e., keeper of the wardrobe) examining the accounts. This was clearly an audit be-

[29]S. C. 1/48 no. 74. Alfonso died August 19 1284 and though the burial costs might have been paid at some later time, the mention of payments to Gascons makes a date in the autumn of this year likely. J. E. Morris states that some Gascon contingents hired for the war stayed on into 1284. *The Welsh Wars of Edward I*, p. 189.

[30]*C.P.R. 1272-1281*, pp. 131-132.

fore the king's council.[31] Between 1279 and 1290 we have no comprehensive accounts, but only those dealing with the customs or the proceeds of a tax, or other revenue. These show only those payments which were charged on these revenues.[32] Finally, the Riccardi answered for all their receipts and expenditures for 1290-1294 in a general account at the exchequer. No auditors are named, but the exchequer officials were no doubt in charge, for the account was entered on the pipe roll.[33]

It is worth noting that this kind of system was not reproduced on the other side of the Channel, that Philip the Fair did not depend upon the credit facilities of any group of Italians to the degree that Edward I did. Although he taxed Italians and used the Franzesi firm as his bankers for a time, there was nonetheless a "failure to take full advantage of the presence of the large and wealthy community of Italian bankers who lived in France during his reign."[34] Various arguments have been advanced to explain this. It has been suggested that England, standing at the end of the trade routes stretching from the Mediterranean, presented a single face to the continent and sold above all a staple which was easily taxed to give a basis for credit operations. France, by contrast, was essentially a country of transit between the Low Countries and Italy and was not dominated by a single commodity in its trade. This situation contributed to a general instability in government finance which hindered the use of Italians.[35] But the reasons cannot be confined to the sphere of economics for, as J. R. Strayer has recently pointed out, political motives must be

[31] An order for the account was issued in June, *C.C.R. 1272-1279*, p. 531, and an acquittance given them in August, *C.C.R. 1279-1288*, p. 32. For the account itself see E 101/126/1. A later document states this account was held before the council—"reddiderunt magnum compotum suum in fine anni vii coram consilio Regis." E 101/351/16.

[32] Sources for the customs accounts are listed in Table I of Chapter III.

[33] E 372/143 m. 35d.

[34] J. R. Strayer, "Italian Bankers and Philip the Fair," *Explorations in Economic History*, 7 (1969), pp. 113-121. This article also appears in David Herlihy, R. S. Lopez, Vsevolod Slessarev, eds., *Economy, Society and Government in Medieval Italy*, pp. 113-121.

[35] Edward Miller, "The Economic Policies of Governments," *Cambridge Economic History*, III, Chapter IV, p. 291. J. R. Strayer, *loc. cit.*

considered as well. Philip's "search for sovereignty" left "no place for independent or quasi-independent groups in his political system." Since the Italian banking houses were international, having centers of power and income outside France, they would not be given the same important place within the royal finances as was true in the England of Edward I.[36]

2. TYPES OF RICCARDI PAYMENTS AND SERVICES

The Riccardi might be expected to meet any royal obligation, and the accounts which record their activity are at best terse summaries of involved transactions; nevertheless we can establish some of the general categories of expense for which Edward regularly relied on his bankers. Their credit facilities were especially important in four areas: warfare, diplomacy and foreign affairs, household expenses, and the king's works–i.e., royal building.[37] The last three types of expenditure can be examined briefly as illustrations of the basic services the Riccardi provided. The costs of warfare, which predictably made the greatest demand on the king's bankers, will be considered in detail in Chapter IV.

Diplomatic expenses were a logical charge on a company with a credit network spread across Northwestern Europe. Although Edward's foreign relations in the first twenty years of his reign were not as costly as they became in the last decade, still there were many payments to be made abroad, emissaries and messengers to be sent in some state, and costly gifts to be given. The Riccardi could arrange for these expenses through a letter to their partners in Rome or Paris, eliminating the cost and danger of transporting silver pennies by the barrelful over long distances.[38]

[36] J. R. Strayer, *loc cit.*

[37] E. B. Fryde has shown that in the early years of the reign of Edward III, before the war with France, loans were needed most for household expenses and next for diplomacy and other foreign business. "Loans to the English Crown, 1328–1331" *E.H.R.* LXX (1955), pp. 201–202.

[38] The Riccardi often made payments for this purpose in England. Occasionally they provided the money needed by a clerk setting off on a diplomatic mission–such as the £50 paid to two men being sent to Brabant in 1279–or discharged the debts incurred on a return journey to England

The most important case in point was the series of loans made to Edmund, Earl of Lancaster, when he was in France in 1293-1294 trying to negotiate the differences which soon led to war between Philip IV and Edward I. The Riccardi in France lent him 25,031 marks 5s. 6d. "en temps qil estoit en France por les besoignes nostre seignur le Roy."[39] But there are numerous other instances. In 1278, 1285, and 1289, when delegations were sent to the papel court, the Riccardi were told to pay whatever costs the envoys should incur.[40] This instance is particularly instructive. It was the "stately mission" led by Otto de Grandson and William of Hotham, "with forty-seven horses, sometimes with fifty, sometimes with sixty." The instructions for financing this large group, sent to Labro Volpelli of the Riccardi, are worth quoting.[41] "The king to his dear Labro Volpelli and his partners, citizens and merchants of the Company of the Riccardi of Lucca dwelling at the Roman curia, greetings and sincere affection. Since we have sent our dear secretary and faithful man the noble Otto de Grandson, knight, to the said court, in order to expedite certain of our affairs there, we ask you that the loan which the said Otto has sought be freely and securely advanced to him. And we will be held to repay fully the sum which Otto receives from you as witnessed by his letters." The convenience of having the services of the various Riccardi branches is further seen in an order sent them in August of 1277. Several *clerici regis* were going to the French court on the king's business and the Riccardi were ordered to lend them 200 marks; they were also to instruct their fellow-merchants in Paris to advance any further amount

---

–such as the expenses of £5 for two envoys coming from Rome in the same year. *C.P.R. 1272-1281*, p. 303. The money could be delivered in London as the recipient going abroad would have little difficulty carrying sums of this size.

39 S C 8 File 260, no. 12970.

40 *C.P.R. 1272-1281*, p. 256, *Ibid., 1281-1292* p. 213. *R.G.*, II, no. 1448.

41 Powicke, *Thirteenth Century*, p. 265, quoting a contemporary wardrobe account. The order to the Riccardi is found in *R.G.*, II, no. 1448. The objectives of the mission were to procure a dispensation for the marriage between Prince Edward and Princess Margaret of Scotland, to settle arrears of the annual tribute to the pope, and to discuss King Edward's crusade.

needed during the envoy's stay.[42] Hugelin de Vikio and a clerk, setting off for the papal court in 1287, were given £100 in the form of a letter of credit addressed to members of the company in Nîmes.[43]

The Riccardi branch in Rome was particularly useful to Edward. As one of the firms of merchants attached to the papal camera, the Riccardi were in a position to transact much of Edward's business there. One part of this business concerned the fees of the various advocates and notaries retained in the king's service.[44] The most interesting of these went to "the Lord Honorius, Supreme Pontiff, who was formerly called Jacobus de Sabelli, of his fee for the years 13, 14, 15 [1285-1287] . . . £200."[45] But occasionally Edward used Riccardi agents themselves on his affairs at Rome, as when Lucasio Natale was sent there in 1277 "by the king's orders for his affairs."[46] In 1290 English ambassadors were negotiating the highly important business of a tenth to be imposed on the clergy for the king, and a dispensation for the marriage of Edward, prince of Wales, to the heiress to the Scottish throne. The king strengthened his bargaining position by dispatching Tommasino Guidiccioni of the Riccardi, with four men and a page in escort, as a bearer of "various gold vessels and certain noble jewels" to Nicholas IV. Edward paid Tommasino's expenses, and those of

[42]*C.P.R. 1272-1281*, p. 226. Cf. E. B. Fryde, ed., *Book of Prests, 1294-1295*, pp. 136, 205-206.

[43]E 36/201, p. 22. When Edward was on the continent the Riccardi network could work in the opposite direction. In 1287, wanting to pay some back wages owed in England, the king, who was then in Gascony, told Orlandino to write to the Riccardi in York to effect payment. E 36/201 p. 77.

[44]See E 403/50, E 403/1248, C 62/56 m. 3, C 62/57 m. 31, E 403/1245, E 372/136 m. 31d., E 372/138 m. 26, E 101/351/16, E 36/274 fo. 181, *C.P.R. 1272-1281*, p. 274.

[45]E 372/136 m. 31d. This was Jacopo Savelli who became Honorius IV.

[46]*C.C.R. 1272-1279*, p. 413. Three years earlier Labro Volpelli of the Riccardi was given a safe-conduct for his journey to the court of Rome, but it is not stated if he had any royal business to transact. *C.P.R. 1272-1281*, p. 44.

his companions, over a period of 137 days. At this time Labro Volpelli of the company was already in Rome and it was by his hands that the gifts necessary for the smooth progress of the king's affairs were distributed to various cardinals. The king was evidently pleased with his success at the curia; Labro was given a riding-horse "de dono regis" and a Lombard knight who accompanied him on the return from Rome was also given his travelling expenses.[47] The exact extent of the Riccardi advances in Rome at this period cannot be determined, but in November of 1290, various members of the society were named in a grant of 5,000 marks, "for their service at the court of Rome."[48]

The most costly of Edward's obligations to the camera was the payment of the annual 1,000-mark *census* which had originated when King John accepted the lordship of Innocent III. Although Edward resented this tribute and often delayed its payment, he found it a useful lever in bargaining with successive popes. Thus when he wanted a favorable response on business before the curia, he paid the *census* and usually did so through his bankers.[49] After ignoring one request from Gregory X in late 1274, the king decided to comply when a second was sent two years later; by this time the *census* was eight years in arrears. Before the death of John XXI on 20 May 1277 the Riccardi had satisfied the papal camera for 3,000 marks, and on 23 February 1278 his successor, Nicholas III, issued an acquittance for this amount, plus an additional 5,000 marks, all received from Labro Volpelli of the Riccardi.[50] As W. E. Lunt has shown, Gregory X's letter states that the tribute for eight years fell due in March of 1275, but John's sets Michelmas of 1277 as the date due. Since there is no evidence that the gap was ever closed by another payment, the conclusion is that 2,000 marks were overlooked by accident or design.[51]

[47] C 47/4/5 mm. 14, 15. E 101/624/51. E 101/352/21.

[48] *C.P.R. 1281-1292*, p. 394.

[49] Lunt, *Financial Relations*, pp. 157, *et seq.*

[50] *Foedera,* I, ii. p. 553. E36/274 m. 88d. The sum is also listed in the first general Riccardi account, E 101/126/1.

[51] Lunt, *Financial Relations*, pp. 159-160.

However, the Holy See was soon repeating its requests for payment, and in late 1281 Edward again discharged the obligation through the Riccardi. They delivered 4,000 marks to Geoffrey de Vezanno, papal collector in England, and were given a writ of *allocate* for this amount out of the customs revenue.[52] When the king next complied with a papal request the Riccardi probably received a part of the money instead of supplying it. In July of 1284 Edward ordered payment by the exchequer of 2,000 marks for the years 1282-1284. Again Vezanno was to receive the tribute, and his instructions were to transfer the money to the papal merchants in England–the Florentine firm of the Pulci and Rimbertini, the firm of Bonaventuro Bernadini of Siena, and the Riccardi of Lucca.[53]

The last payment was delayed until after Edward's return from Gascony. Since the particularly important delegation headed by Otto de Grandson and William Hotham was at the curia, it was decided to pay the *census* due for five years through them. To strengthen the papal resolve to aid Edward, an additional 1,000 marks was included when the Riccardi transferred the money to the papal camera. The acquittance for 6,000 marks was issued in November of 1289.[54] For the remainder of his reign Edward turned a deaf ear to papal requests for payment.[55]

Paris was another center of Riccardi activity in the king's service. In 1278, for example, working through the Riccardi, Edward loaned 100 marks to Bernard de Bordelia on the security of a castle and sent the Riccardi a transcript of the form of letters obligatory he wanted from Bernard.[56] In the following year when Edward loaned £500 to Henry de Lacy, Earl of Lincoln, the Riccardi paid a part of the sum to the earl's clerk in London, while the larger part was advanced by their fellows in Paris.[57]

[52] *C.C.R. 1279-1288*, pp. 189-190. E 36/274 fo. 205, m. 244d. C 62/57.

[53] *Foedera,* I ii, p. 644. Lunt, *Financial Relations*, p. 162. O. Jensen, *T.R.H.S.*, n.s., XIX, p. 261.

[54] *Foedera,* I, ii. p. 719. Cf. E 101/352/22.

[55] Lunt, *Financial Relations*, p. 165.

[56] *C.P.R. 1272-1281*, p. 265.

[57] For the order, see *C.P.R. 1272-1281*, p. 303. The earl's receipt was entered in the Liber A, E 36/275 fo. 25-26.

During the second Welsh war, payments to a buyer of provisions in Gascony were similarly divided between London and Paris.[58] In February of 1284 the Riccardi were ordered to pay 5,000 marks to the bishop of Cadiz, envoy of Alfonso of Castile, the delivery to be made in Paris during the first week in August.[59]

Since marriage was a prime tool of medieval diplomacy, it is not surprising that the Riccardi provided sums needed in the marriage negotiations of several of Edward's children. Early in 1279 the merchants were directed to pay to John, Duke of Lorraine and Brabant, two sums for the marriage to be contracted between his son John and Edward's daughter Margaret. The order, dated 24 January, specifies the payment of 20,000 *livres tournois* at Leyngny within the quinzaine of the Purification (2 February), and by Midsummer (24 June) a further 10,000 *livres tournois* on behalf of Eleanor, the queen consort.[60] The duke did receive his money, but it is hard to determine when payment was made and whether the Riccardi actually provided the sums. The receipt is undated and no details are given concerning the source of the money.[61] The marriage did not actually take place until 1290, and a wardrobe document for the previous year shows that the merchants gave 10,000 *livres tournois* (£2,285 14s. 4d. sterling) to Edmund, Earl of Cornwall, for the purposes of the marriage.[62]

When Edward's daughter Elizabeth was married to John, son of Florence, count of Holland, the Riccardi role is clearer. A writ of

58 C 47/3/17. *R.G.*, II, p. 774.

59 *C.P.R. 1281-1292*, pp. 113-122. A letter on this subject written by Eleanor of Castille was entered in the *Liber Epistolarius of Richard de Bury*, no. 59., p. 31 (ed. N. Denholm-Young). Things did not go as first planned, for the site of the transaction was evidently shifted to La Rochelle and then the king died before the money could be sent to him. Upon hearing of Alfonso's death, the mayor and community of the town arrested the money and held it until a clerk arrived with orders to return it to the Riccardi.

60 *C.P.R. 1272-1281*, p. 299. At the same time the Riccardi were directed to pay £333 6s. 2d. to the count of Gueldres and 20 marks for the traveling expenses of Master Robert de Belvero going as envoy to the duke of Brabant.

61 E 36/275 fo. 25-26.

62 E 101/352/15.

liberate directed the exchequer to repay them the £1,496 13s. 4d. which they had advanced for her dowry.[63]

Finally, a loan of 2,000 marks made in 1286 to the king of Norway may well be related to the proposed match between Edward of Caernarvon and the Maid of Norway, Margaret, heiress to the Scottish throne. A daughter of the king of Norway, she was still living in that country when her grandfather died, leaving her next in succession. Perhaps the 2,000 marks loaned by the Riccardi to King Eric's procurator, Oliver, Count of Maresburg, was intended to pave the way for the marriage.[64]

The transactions considered up to this point indicate the diversity and scope of Riccardi payments abroad. But their major contribution to the king's affairs overseas naturally came when Edward himself was on the continent.[65] We have already seen to what extent he relied on their loans while traveling through Italy and France in the opening years of his reign. This was repeated on a much grander scale during the three-year stay in Gascony 1286-1289. When Edward turned to pressing continental affairs and crossed the channel in May of 1286, the wardrobe went with him as his traveling treasury. But the *Societas Riccardorum* also accompanied the king in the person of Orlandino da Pogio, one of the chief representatives of the firm in England. Other members of the company later joined the king, adding their services to those of Riccardi agents normally operating in France. During

[63] E 403/68, 72, 73.

[64] The documents recording the authority given to the count by Eric, and the receipts for the loan, were entered on the K.R. Memoranda Roll, E 159/62 m. 2d. One receipt is dated 21 September at Yarmouth, the other, 20 July at London. Edward was in Paris when he decided to loan the money to Eric and effected the transaction by a letter to the Riccardi in London. A copy is preserved in the Liber A, E 36/274 fo. 178, m. 217d. The marriage never took place, for Margaret died en route to England.

[65] It was evidently during his short journey to France in 1279, for discussions with Philip III over his rights under the Treaty of Paris, that Edward ordered the Riccardi to pay 1,000 *livres tournois* to the constable of Bordeaux "ad negocia nostra." *R.G.*, II, no. 351. The order is dated 13 June 1279, at Valloires.

these years the king had heavy financial requirements to meet[66] and he relied on the Riccardi to a greater degree than in any comparable period of their relationship. Unfortunately the evidence does not allow detailed analysis of the Riccardi transactions, but we can sketch the broad outlines.[67]

The Riccardi were at once busy arranging transfers of money in order to supply the wardrobe with cash. We can follow some of their activities from the wardrobe records of necessary expenditure, which not only note the small payments made to Riccardi members for these transfers but also conveniently give the sums themselves and the points between which they were conveyed. Edward went first to Paris at the end of May for the ceremony of homage to the new French king, Philip IV, and within a month of his arrival Enrico da Pogio brought over £2,000 from London.[68] In August, Riccardo Bonefaci of the society conveyed 3,000 marks from London to Paris and then on several occasions during that month and the next he and Nigello carried sums in

66 See Powicke, *Thirteenth Century*, pp. 282–283, 304–305. Especially expensive was the lavish entertainment of Alfonso of Aragon at Oleron in 1287. The heavy expenditure during these years is reflected in a series of orders sent to sheriffs, urging them to hasten the levy of debts owed the king, etc. See E 368/59 m. 26d., E 368/60 m. 21, E 368/61 m. 40d. In the second of these orders it is specifically stated that the king owes a great sum of money "to certain merchants."

67 Marcel Gouron noted their importance in these years in an article dealing with Queen Eleanor. "Aliénor de Castile en Guienne (1286–1289), *Le Moyen Age* 37 (1927), pp. 23–24. Few relevant documents were found in the Public Record Office. One which might have been very helpful, a list of acquittances issued by Louth, E 101/152/5, is almost totally illegible. From the number of times the clerk's bold "L" in "Lucca" appears, these acquittances may all refer to the Riccardi. Another potentially useful document, described in an index as a draft account of wardrobe receipts, 1286–1289, E 101/352/5, is also useless because much of the left half of the manuscript is gone. Furthermore, the Gascon Rolls for 1286–1288 are missing. To circumvent these gaps, the rolls of necessary expenses of the wardrobe were used.

68 C 47/4/3 m. 16. The money was received by the Riccardi from Geoffrey de Vezzano, which indicates that it was a loan from the papal crusade tenth. See the painstaking itinerary compiled by J. P. Trabut-Cussac, "Itinéraire d'Edouard Ier en France, 1286–1289," *B.I.H.R.* XXV (1952).

various currencies from Paris to the several southern destinations designated by the king: 1,000 *livres tournois* to Melun, £290 sterling, 431 *livres tournois*, and 2,000 *livres tournois noirs* to Orleans, 2,930 *livres tournois noirs* to Bordeaux, etc. Between 2 September and 15 October Enrico da Pogio was once again in charge, carrying 8,000 marks received in England from London to Paris via St. Omer.[69] In December he supervised the shipment of 200 "libra chipotensis"[70] from Sens to the port of St. Mary; in January he was paid for carrying unspecified sums. Sometime before March of 1287, 4,292 *livres tournois noirs* were sent from Nîmes to Toulouse. In March the Riccardi transferred 4,400 *livres tournois noirs* from Nîmes to Bordeaux. In April and May money was carried to the King from their house in Bordeaux. Similar shipments can be found in July and October.[71] There is no evidence for most of 1288, but the Riccardi are again found carrying specie across France for the king's affairs in late November of 1288 and on through the summer of the following year. At the end of this period the flow turned northward as Edward began his return. Finally, when Edward returned to England Orlandino crossed the channel also, landing at Whitsand with the jewels of the wardrobe in his charge.[72]

The Riccardi clearly were active in the king's service, and their small caravans of packhorses burdened with loads of silver pennies must have been frequent sights on French roads. They had also continued to pay the expenses of emissaries sent to Paris, Rome, the Empire, and Sicily; they provided money for fees and salaries; and they made prests—frequently of several hundred

[69] For all these payments see C 47/4/3 mm. 18, 24d., 25, E 101/352/2. Appropriately enough, at this time Enrico paid the wages of certain men "helping to count money for the king." An unspecified member of the Riccardi was paid his expenses "remaining in Bordeaux on the King's business," and Enrico was himself given an allowance for expenses "seeking money for the king."

[70] This was the currency of Bigorre; see Tout, *Chapters*, II, pp. 6–7, n. 2.

[71] E 36/201 pp. 5, 8, 9, 11, 13, 16, 22, 32.

[72] E 101/352/14 mm. 2, 4, 5, 6. Once again members of the Riccardi were given allowances for expenses on the king's service, either with the court or on the road, during this period.

pounds–to the keeper of the great wardrobe. When Otto de Grandson was sent to "extend" the lands ceded to Edward in Périgord, the Riccardi paid his expenses. They were entrusted with the delivery to Charles of Solerno of all the golden cups and plates Edward gave his kinsman upon his release from captivity by Alfonso of Castile.[73] They even helped establish the proper salary for the assayer of the king's money in the duchy.[74]

The rate at which Edward's enormous obligation to his bankers grew can be followed by five successive statements. The dates and amounts in these statements are given below:

Date	*livres tournois noirs*	*Sterling (in addition)*	*Source*
20 November 1286	49,418		E 372/136 m. 31
1 July 1288	212,572	9,010	E 36/274 m. 218
20 June 1289	353,424	11,898	*R.G.* II, no. 1094
31 July 1289	378,424	12,098	*R.G.* II, no. 1249
12 August 1289	380,609	12,632	*C.P.R. 1281-1292*, p. 318

The first of these is taken from the wardrobe account for 14 Edward I, where the sum is entered both in *livres tournois noirs* and in sterling. The second is actually a statement by the Riccardi upon receipt of royal letters obligatory. They pledge an accounting for all the king's money they received during this period, at

[73] For the messengers and household goods see E 36/201 *passim*. The gifts to Charles are mentioned in p. 33 of this wardrobe book. For a fee of £500 paid to Queen Eleanor see E 101/352/15. Examples of prests can be found in E 36/274 mm. 371d., 372, C 47/4/3 m. 23, E 36/201, *passim*. Edward arranged to repay a loan of 1,000 *livres bordelaises*, obtained from the Bishop of Agenais, via the Riccardi. *R.G.*, II, no. 1610.

[74] C 47/24/2. Orlandino acted with William Turnemeyer who had been in charge of the actual process of coining the new money in England in 1279. The Riccardi continued dealings with him as long as the company existed; he owed them money at the time of the collapse. See their letter, E 101/601/5 p. 12d.

which time the receipts would be deducted from the total of their loans. The remaining three letters were issued by the king and give his promise to repay by a certain date; the following Christmas is specified in the June and July letters, Easter in the August letter. For the merchants' security, all the Gascon revenues were pledged for repayment in case of the king's death,[75] and in the letter of 31 July no less than all the movable and immovable goods of Edward and his heirs back the promise of repayment. The final statement indicates that the Riccardi had delivered to the wardrobe, or paid out in its name, the equivalent of approximately £103,733 sterling.[76] although this figure undoubtedly contains interest charges.

The vast sums required to finance Edward's Gascon stay were not duplicated in the ordinary costs of running the royal household; yet the need for Riccardi loans appears with equal clarity in this basic matter of daily operating expenses for the king's immediate entourage. In September of 1281, for example, the chief representative of the Riccardi in England received a request for a loan to the wardrobe of £500 for household expenses, "the king not having money in hand at present."[77] Only two months earlier it has been necessary to send a similar request for £300 "as the king needs money for the expenses of his household."[78] The lack of funds for the household can be read more eloquently in a wardrobe journal of receipt and expenses for 1277-1278.[79] On

[75] Orders for payments by the merchants in 1289 refer to them as "collectors of our great custom of Bordeaux." *R.G.*, II, nos. 1176, 1617.

[76] Tout gave a figure of £107,784, based on the 1279 exchange rate of four black *livres tournois* to one sterling. *Chapters,* II, p. 123, n. 2. Powicke states that the sum was £107,725, but gives no source. *Thirteenth Century*, p. 305. But by this time the exchange rate had dropped. In 1290 it was £1,000 sterling to £4,162 10s. in the black money of Tours. E 101/352/21. This rate has been used to obtain the total figure given here. Powicke mistakenly refers to the Riccardi as the merchant family of the Pozzi, obviously converting the Latin surname of Orlandino and Enrico da Pogio into Pozzi.

[77] *C.P.R. 1272-1281*, p. 456.

[78] *C.C.R. 1279-1288*, p. 97.

[79] C 47/4/1.

fourteen occasions between late February 1276 and mid-November 1277, an *exitus* (i.e., a supply of money) is listed, its sources given, and its subsequent expenditure detailed. Out of the total legible receipt of approximately £12,220 the known Riccardi contribution was £8,097 7s. 8d.; but they also provided two sums beyond this amount which are obliterated in the document. For some weeks at a time in this period the household operated solely on Riccardi advances. Despite the uncertainties of an incomplete and badly damaged document, this information can be tabulated (see following page).

We have seen that a similar underwriting of household expenses must have occurred while Edward was in Gascony, 1286-1289, although comparable specifics are lacking. Moreover, a few years later, in 1293, the Riccardi loaned £10,000 for the same purpose in the two and one-half months between 1 August and 18 November.[80]

At times it was necessary or at least convenient to use Riccardi funds in a similar way for the miniature household which surrounded the king's children. While Edward and the wardrobe were abroad between 1286 and 1289 the cost of maintaining this establishment came to £12,814; the Riccardi furnished £11,183.[81] Furthermore, during the first seven years of Edward's reign, they loaned £1,346 "for the expenses of the king's children."[82]

Generally the payments which make up these large sums for the household are lost to us and we are not told the specific purposes for which the money went, but a few cases can be noted. The quantity of wine consumed by any medieval household was con-

80E 372/139 m. 6. C 81/7 no. 597. *C.P.R. 1292-1301*, p. 59.

81E 372/138 m. 26d. E 101/352/15. The general account for the household of the king's children for 14-18 Edward I, E 101/352/8, also refers to the money provided by the wardrobe "as well by the hands of the treasurer and chamberlains of the exchequer as by the hands of the merchants of Lucca" during 15, 16, and 17 Edward I, but the account was left in an unfinished state.

82E 101/126/1. In 2 Edward I the Riccardi loaned 150 *livres tournois* (£37 10s. 0d. sterling) to the keeper of the household of Edward's son Alfonso. E 372/121 m. 22.

Table I Riccardi Loans for the Household, 1276-1277 (c47/4/1)

Page	*Date*	*Total Exitus*	*From Riccardi*	
7	late February	£647 9s. 7d.	£600 0s. 0d.	paid at least partly in London
12d.	before 15 March	£1,998 7s. 4d.	(obliterated)	Glastonbury
16d.		£243 5s. 0d.		
17d.	circa Easter	£1,040 0s. 0d.	£473 6s. 8d. (with one sum obliterated)	Winchester and Westminster
21	late April, early May	about £160		
22	5 May	£1,000 0s. 0d.	£1,000 0s. 0d.	Westminster
25d.	13 May	£1,133 6s. 8d.	£500 0s. 0d.	
27	late June	£1,024 0s. 12d.	£1,024 0s. 12d.	Westminster
31	12 July	£508 0s. 10d.	£500 0s. 0d.	
34	15 August	£1,029 12s. 0d.	£1,000 0s. 0d.	Gloucester
37d.	14 September	£1,412 10s. 19d.	£1,000 0s. 0d.	Basingwerk
43d.	29 October	£1,000 0s. 0d.	£1,000 0s. 0d.	Westminster
48	12 November }	£1,024 0s. 0d.	£700 0s. 0d.	
	18 November }		£300 0s. 0d.	
		approximately £12,220	£8,097 7s. 8d. two sums missing	

siderable, and for the royal household an expenditure of hundreds of pounds a year was necessary. In the opening years of the reign the merchants of Lucca occasionally bought a part of these wines for the king. In 1277 their role in financing these purchases began to be more important, and in 1278 Edward arranged for the Riccardi to pay for all of the wines taken by his butler, Matthew de Columbar, by the right of prise, under the direction of the keeper of the Tower of London. While in control of the *cambium*, 1279-1281, they were often ordered to pay for wines out of the profits of the recoinage. Throughout the years of their service as king's bankers they continued to act with Columbar, new directives to this effect being issued in 1280 and 1287. This involved providing between £300 and £400 a year.[83]

The luxury goods supplied to the household form another example of particular Riccardi expenditure in this general category, although they represent a very different household "necessity." It was in the capacity of suppliers of fine cloths, gems, and the like that the merchants of Lucca had originally become associated with Henry III, and they continued this traffic in valuables along with their money-lending and wool export. In 1284, for example, they must have made the rounds of the Paris gold- and silversmiths, for they bought there, "ad opus regis," seven gold cups, forty-nine silver cups with gilded work, thirty-two similar cups with covers, thirteen silver cups with worked gilded covers, five silver pitchers with gilded work and enamel, along with one plain pitcher, two pairs of silver bowls, and eleven gold buckles.[84]

[83] E 403/27. *C.P.R. 1272-1281*, pp. 152, 168, 210, 212, 272, 361, 367, 378, 393, 396, 419, 446. *C.P.R. 1281-1292*, p. 270. One of the leading Riccardi partners in England, Riccardo Guidiccioni, as the attorney to Columbar, appointed a London citizen, Hamo Box, to collect the prise of wine and gauges at Hull in 1287. The Riccardi evidently had a close relationship with the king's butler and acted as his attorney in his private business as well as the king's affairs. See E 159/59 m. 17d., E 159/62 m. 7, E 13/12 m. 29. Between Ascension 1278 and Michelmas 1279, they paid £308 19s. 0d. for royal wines, C 47/3/48; in 1289 and 1290, £792 6s. 11d., E 372/143 m. 35d. They also paid for some wines in Ireland, C 62/53, and in Bordeaux, *R.G.*, II, no. 1765.

[84] E 101/351/14. They presented Edward with a bill for £658 17s. 7d.

During the first seven years of the reign we find them buying jewels worth £2,085 10s. 8d., of which stones worth £216 11s. 5d. were purchased in Paris.[85] In 1281 they delivered jewels costing £112: nine square-cut balasses, four "of larger size and more rounded shape," six rubies, and five emeralds.[86] In 1290 they bought more silver vessels and gold buckles for the king in Paris.[87]

Just as Edward needed Riccardi loans to meet continual household expenses, he also frequently called upon his bankers to supply the funds which kept the king's works rising. There can be no doubt that Edward was a great builder and especially a great castle-builder. "The reign of Edward I," wrote R. A. Brown and H. M. Colvin, "marks the climax of castle-building as an exercise of royal authority on the part of the kings of medieval England.[88] His greatest building project, the chain of fortresses which ringed North Wales, is best considered as an inseparable part of war finance. But there are further important cases of Riccardi funding of the king's works.

The virtual reconstruction of the Tower of London ranks with the Welsh castles as one of Edward's major building enterprises. He converted the Tower into an up-to-date concentric fortress in the decade 1275-1285 by the completion of the inner curtain wall and the building of the outer wall with elaborate land and water entrances, a wide moat, and a wharf. As a result the present plan and appearance of the Tower are due to Edward I more than to any other English king. The cost of these major operations, along with the attention given to the domestic buildings they defended, came to approximately £21,000. Nearly a third of this sum was supplied by the king's merchants.[89] At times they were

[85] E 101/126/1. During this period the records also show them carrying cloth of gold "from the house of Luke of Lucca to the Tower, where the King was." E 101/3/15.

[86] *C.P.R. 1272-1281*, p. 425.

[87] C 47/4/5 m. 17.

[88] H. M. Colvin, ed. *King's Works,* I, p. 228.

[89] *Ibid.*, II, pp. 715 *et seq.* Giles of Audenard, keeper of the works there, accounted for £4,366 13s. 4d. in one account, E 372/120 m. 22d., and a further £1,817 6s. 8d. in 1277-1278, in a later account, E 372/121 m.

ordered to deliver lump sums for the works,[90] but beginning in July of 1278 the Riccardi were expected to provide £100 weekly, continuing until the following June.[91]

At other strategic fortresses, Edward was concerned mainly with repair or completion. He spent £500 for work carried out at Dover Castle in 1278. A knight and six men-at-arms were dispatched from Dover to London to convey the sum safely from the Riccardi to the castle.[92] At Nottingham, the most important royal fortress in the Midlands, the Riccardi were called upon for £236 15s. 5-1/2d. toward expenses incurred in 1289-1290.[93] They provided £160 for work at Windsor Castle in 1276.[94]

Other of the king's works were of a less military nature. Westminster Palace had to be altered to meet the requirements of a new household on Edward's accession, and repairs and improvements were recurrent necessities; throughout the first twenty years of the reign, the king's merchants provided funds for wages and materials.[95] But the major project at Westminster began in 1292, when the foundations for the new royal chapel dedicated

---

22d. This second account includes works at Westminster, but the only evidence of Riccardi payments for the palace works in this period names Master Robert de Beverley as the recipient. So it is likely that all of the expenditure was at the Tower.

90 Such as the 2,000 marks on 2 January 1277, *C.C.R. 1272-1279*, p. 367, or £1,000 on 16 February 1278, *C.P.R. 1272-1281*, p. 259.

91 *C.P.R. 1272-1281*, p. 273.

92 The castle was virtually complete when he came to the throne. See H. M. Colvin, ed., *King's Works*, II, p. 638. E 372/123 m. 39. The original order to the society, 16 February 1278, specified only £300. *C.P.R. 1272-1281*, p. 259.

93 E 372/143 m. 35d. The total expenditure at Nottingham during Edward's entire reign was about £1,078, H. M. Colvin, ed., *King's Works*, II, pp. 760-761.

94 *C.C.R. 1272-1279*, p. 364. *C.P.R. 1272-1281*, p. 193.

95 The Riccardi were ordered to pay £202 19s. 9d. in 1275 and 1276 (*C.P.R. 1272-1281*, p. 167) and in the latter year also received a writ of *liberate* for £37 19s. 6d. for sums delivered for these works (C 62/52). Between 1283 and 1287 they furnished £758 6s. 8d. out of the £988 11s. 8d. expended. (E 372/131 m. 26, E 372/136 m. 31d., E 101/352/2, E 101/351/16). They provided a further £250 in 1287-1288 (E 372/136 m. 31d.) and £32 in 1289 (E 101/352/15, E 372/138 m. 26d.).

to St. Stephen were laid in April. Three months later the Riccardi advanced £400 for the works; they paid £680 in August, and £275 6s. 8d. in February and March of 1293.[96] These payments probably represent nearly half of the expenditure on work completed during this time.[97] Domestic work at Langley manor in 1282-1283 and 1285[98] drew £60 and £600 respectively.

Riccardi loans were essential for all these royal activities. But the merchants provided yet another service for the crown by acting as guarantors—or at least convenient agents—for loans negotiated with others. After Edward's costly stay on the continent in 1286-1289, he borrowed 6,000 marks from his wealthy cousin, Edmund, Earl of Cornwall, and arranged for the Riccardi to act as surety for this sum. Repayment was in fact made by the merchants, who were later given an allowance in their account for 1290-1294.[99] This role of intermediary was even more prominent when Edward wanted to make contact with the other firms of Italian merchants operating in England. At times of pressing need the king sought loans from virtually all the firms in London. On several occasions the Riccardi were given the bonds for these loans with instructions to receive the money for the king; later, they would also see to its repayment. This was probably the means used to obtain a general loan of £20,300 to provide the specie needed at the outset of the great recoinage in 1279. It was certainly the case in the large loans raised during the

[96] These sums are allowed them in their account for 1290-1294. E 372/143 m. 35d.

[97] These payments total £1,355 6s. 8d., while the total cost on the chapel between April of 1292 and July of 1297 came to about £4,000. H. M. Colvin, ed., *King's Works,* I, pp. 510-512, 522.

[98] *C.P.R. 1281-1292*, p. 176. H. M. Colvin, ed., *King's Works,* II, p. 971, citing C 81/1766 no. 25.

[99] Edward issued three bonds to Edmund. The first, dated 24 February 1289, shows a loan of only 2,000 marks. *C.P.R. 1281-1292*, p. 313. The second and third, on 18 June 1290 and 13 July 1290, are in the sum of 6,000 marks; the latter promises repayment by the Riccardi. *Ibid.,* pp. 366, 374. For the allowance given to the merchants see E 372/143 m. 45d.

Welsh wars, as we will see.[100] Our evidence is much sketchier on two further cases of loans from the various Italian firms, but the procedure may have been much the same. In September of 1290 the Riccardi acted as the king's surety for a loan of £1,000 from five other companies.[101] The loans from thirteen Italian firms repaid in that same year were much bigger. The kings's debt to these companies stood at £18,900. Since most of this could be repaid from the clerical grants of a twentieth and a fifteenth from the province of Canterbury and a thirtieth from the province of York, the Riccardi were expected to provide only £2,360 9s. 9 3/4d.[102] But though our sources fail to show it, we might reasonably assume that they helped to negotiate this as other loans from their fellow-countrymen.

Although the bulk of Riccardi loans fall into only a few categories, and although the most essential services of the Riccardi are quickly outlined, it must be said again that they carried out almost any task touching matters financial. Edward often called upon them to pay the fees of important crown servants—keepers of great fortresses, justices, exchequer officials—especially during the early years of the reign.[103] When he decided to have new crowns made in 1277, the king ordered that the process of extracting the jewels from the old crowns and the melting down of

[100]The mechanisms of these loans will be more fully explained as a part of the financing of the Welsh campaigns. See Chapter IV, Section 5.

[101]*C.P.R. 1281-1292*, p. 385.

[102]E 159/63 m. 17. The wardrobe repaid £9,566 6s. 8d.; £2,360 9s. 9-3/4d. came from the wardrobe "per manus mercatorum Lukanorum"; the rest came from the three clerical taxes.

[103]Keeper of the Tower, Michaelmas term 1272 and 1278, Michaelmas and Easter terms 1276, 1277, 1279, 1285; C 62/52, E 403/52, *C.P.R. 1272-1281*, pp. 168, 203, 269, 295, 310. Constable of Corfe castle, half of 1274, all of 1276; *C.P.R. 1272-1281*, p. 168. Keeper of Dover, £154 toward his yearly fee of £300, 1279; *Ibid.*, p. 299, *C.C.R. 1279-1288*, p. 5. Justices of Jews and of the Bench, 1276, keeper of rolls and writs of the Bench, 1278, itinerant justice in Cumberland, 1278, justice *coram rege*, 1278, 1279, justice of jail delivery, 1285-1286; *C.P.R. 1272-1281*, pp. 168, 282-283, 295, 304, 308, 310. *C.C.R. 1272-1279*, p. 366. C 62/52, C 62/54, E 403/52. Chancellor of the exchequer, several barons

the gold be carried out before representatives of the society. By the "ordering of the [treasurer] and by view and in the presence of the said merchants," goldsmiths (who had been placed under oath) were to make "two, three, or four gold crowns to the king's use."[104] Much later, when the full-size bronze effigies for the Westminster tombs of his father and his first wife, Eleanor of Castile, had been completed by the London goldsmith William Torel, they were gilded with gold supplied by the Riccardi in the form of hundreds of florins.[105] The gilt which still glistens on these striking effigies in the heart of Westminster Abbey was thus coined in Italy and shipped to London in merchants' strongboxes. At the same time the Riccardi had arranged for the recruitment of four miners from Lucca who were brought to the islands of Guernsey and Jersey to prospect for veins of silver. These miners spent six and a half months in the effort and presented an account before the Riccardi when they left, presumably a rather discouraged lot![106] These few examples help to reinforce a strong impression that in almost any financial document from the first two decades of Edward's reign we will encounter the *mercatores de societate Riccardorum.*

3. REPAYMENT AND BENEFITS TO THE RICCARDI

We have considered the payments and services which were the responsibilities of the king's bankers, but the other side of the relationship is equally important. How was Edward able to maintain "the Riccardi system," and what were the inducements and benefits which attracted the firm to the royal service?

---

of the exchequer and some clerks, 1277, 1278; *C.P.R. 1272-1281*, pp. 188–189, 272, 295. Otto de Grandson, all £1,000 salary, 1285, part of the salary, 1289; E 101/351/16, E 101/352/15. Law professors and papal notaries; *C.P.R. 1272-1281*, p. 299. E 101/352/22. Cf. note 44.

[104] *C.P.R. 1272-1281*, p. 213. June 13, 1277.

[105] E 372/143 m. 35d. E 101/353/1. H. M. Colvin, ed., *King's Works,* I, pp. 481–482. Although Henry III died in 1272 and Queen Eleanor in 1290, it was only in 1293 that the effigies were completed.

[106] E 372/135 m. 35d.

It is reasonably certain that the Riccardi did not enter into their relationship with Edward because of compulsion. Although any firm of merchant-bankers had to lend money to the crown if it wished to continue doing business in England,[107] an occasional loan is quite different from the close and continuous cooperation which characterizes the arrangements between the Riccardi and the crown. The merchants no less than the king saw their relationship in positive terms.[108] The Riccardi served as crown financiers mainly because such service was highly profitable.

The acquisition of new sources of revenue, as we have seen, gave Edward the financial base for a system of regular borrowing; thus the burden of repaying Riccardi loans fell mainly on the tariff on exported wool and hides and the taxes on lay and clerical movable property. A later chapter will examine in detail the wool custom as the major means of repayment. From the combined English and Irish customs the Riccardi collected as much as £211,000 between 1275 and 1294.[109] The proceeds of taxation rank second in importance, providing only about half as much as the customs. Four secular tax grants must be considered: the twentieth for Edward's crusade in 1270; the fifteenth of 1275; the thirtieth of 1283; and the fifteenth of 1290.

Even before Edward came to the throne the merchants of Lucca had begun to receive tax proceeds. Two payments totaling 7,000 marks were made to them from the twentieth granted in support of the Lord Edward's crusade. According to the pipe roll account the Riccardi were to transfer the money to Edward for his return from the Holy Land, but this probably meant that their partners in Italy would advance an equivalent sum on his arrival there.[110]

107See the comment by R. L. Reynolds, "Origins of Modern Business Enterprise. Medieval Italy," *Journal of Economic History*, 12 (1952) p. 365.

108The Riccardi business letters, E 101/601/5, make this clear. After the break with Edward in 1294, the merchants' often-expressed wish is to establish the old relationship with the king once again.

109Chapter III, Cf. E. B. Fryde, *C.E.H.* III, pp. 456-457.

110E 372/117 m. 6d.

By the time Edward returned to England his debt to the Riccardi had grown considerably and the first grant of the reign, the fifteenth of 1275, went in large measure to his bankers. Giles de Audenard, keeper of the Tower, was appointed to supervise their collection of the proceeds from various counties. If we correlate the account of their receipts at the Tower[111] with a more comprehensive account for this tax[112] the total Riccardi receipt appears as £74,598. Some of the installments due from the counties were carted to the Tower for delivery to the Riccardi,[113] but the merchants themselves received other sums at collection centers in the shires.[114] While it is difficult to set the total proceeds of the fifteenth, Willard's figures for its assessed value come to £80,138. The amount actually extracted from the counties would, of course, be lower because of exemptions, expenses, and the like.[115] The close and patent rolls contain many orders for the issue of acquittances from the exchequer for sums paid to the Riccardi, and from those which date these payments it seems that the collection began only in the spring of 1276 and continued through 1277, with a few small sums coming in as late as 1278.[116] That the king himself had to wait until 1279 for nearly £3,000 of arrears is demonstrated by a series of stiffly-worded letters sent to sheriffs in March of that year.[117] From this single

[111] E 372/123 m. 23d.

[112] E 359/1.

[113] E.g., *C.C.R. 1279-1288*, p. 19. On the Thursday after St. John before the Latin Gate in 6 Edward I, the sheriff of Cumberland delivered £480 of the second half of the fifteenth of his county to Giles and Reiner Magiari of the Riccardi at the Tower.

[114] E.g., on Wednesday after St. Andrew, 5 Edward I, Luke Natale and Matteo Rossciompelli received £1127 6s. 8d. "good and legal sterling" for the fifteenth of Bedford and Buckingham at the priory of the canons at Dunstaple. In their receipt they promised the representatives of the Abbott of Ramsey and the sheriff of these counties to hold them free of all damage, pledging all their goods in case of default. C 47/13/1/12. Cf. *C.P.R. 1272-1281*, p. 172.

[115] *E.H.R.* 28 (1913), p. 519.

[116] *C.C.R. 1272-1279*, pp. 544, 546. *Ibid., 1279-1288*, pp. 1, 6, 12–14, 17, 19, 29–31, 72. *C.P.R. 1272-1281*, pp. 172, 209, 255, 261, 269, 300–301.

[117] *C.C.R. 1279-1288*, p. 524.

tax the Riccardi received more than their combined receipt from all other lay and clerical grants.

Three overlapping accounts deal with the next grant from the laity, the thirtieth of 1283. It was a war subsidy and the largest part of the proceeds are found in the special wardrobe account for the war years.[118] But the separate account rendered by the Riccardi,[119] and that devoted to arrears[120] must also be considered. Once the duplicated sums are eliminated, the total Riccardi receipt comes to £24,837. As was true for the fifteenth, many of the installments were evidently collected from those responsible in the cities and counties, but £2,200 from far-off Bristol were delivered to the Riccardi in London in 1284, and arrears of £1,735 were received at the Tower.[121]

The last tax on secular property used for repaying the Riccardi, the fifteenth of 1290, was coupled with a clerical grant of a tenth. Since financial reforms in that year had resulted in closer exchequer supervision over the collection of taxes, our evidence comes from special issue rolls recording the allocation of the proceeds. The amounts turned over to the Riccardi and the dates of their receipt are given below:

5 March, 1291	£2,000	E 403/1310, 1311
9 March, 1291	£1,000	E 403/1310, 1311
26 May, 1291	£1,160 12s. 1d.	E 403/1312
19 Nov., 1291	£6,000	E 403/1314
11 June, 1292	£2,000	E 403/1315, 1316

Two receipts in Ireland during 1293 and 1294 (£285 and £600 respectively),[122] bring the total to £13,045.[123]

[118]E 372/136 m. 33.

[119]E 359/4 A.

[120]E 372/133 m. 30.

[121]E 159/61 m. 1d. E 372/133 m. 30.

[122]E 101/232/10. *C.D.I. 1293-1301*, no. 113.

[123]The money received in May was actually paid to the society of the Mozzi, for the Riccardi. Baroncino Gualteri received a further £133 6s. 8d. from the tax in the city of London, E 372/140 m. 24, but by this time he was no longer a member of the Riccardi.

Much smaller amounts went to the merchants from the purely clerical taxes during the years of their prominence—the triennial fifteenth of 1280 in the province of Canterbury, and the twentieth for two years granted by this province after the second Welsh war. York gave a tenth for two years in 1280, and a triennial thirtieth in 1286, but the Riccardi received nothing from these. Our only source of information for the earlier Canterbury tax, the wardrobe accounts, indicates a Riccardi receipt of £6,642, with an additional but unspecified portion of £566.[124] From the later twentieth, we know only that the king's merchants received a part of £627 from the arrears.[125]

Over the whole period of two decades, then, the Riccardi received at least £125,018, plus some part of £1,194, out of the proceeds of taxes. This represents a little more than half of the sum collected from the customs.

The third important source from which Edward repaid his bankers was the body of revenues traditionally paid into the exchequer, i.e., the shire farms, revenues from crown lands, profits of justice in county and hundred courts, and the like. A search of the *liberate* rolls would seem to indicate that near the end of the Riccardi period the merchants were no longer collecting any substantial sums from the treasury. But this impression is misleading and reflects merely a change in bookkeeping. In the early years of Edward's reign the Riccardi received money from the exchequer when a writ of *liberate* was issued in their name. Later, because of their close association with the wardrobe, payments were sometimes made to them on a writ issued in favor of the keeper of the wardrobe. The first example of this was a £500 *liberate* in 3 Edward I,[126] but Riccardi receipt of money on wardrobe writs did not become frequent until the 1280's. At that time the developing practice of assigning block sums to the wardrobe on a single large writ (gradually expended in smaller sums noted on the

[124]E 372/130 m. 5. E 372/138 m. 26.

[125]E 372/138 m. 26. For clerical taxation in this period see H. S. Deighton "Clerical Taxation by Consent, 1279-1301," *E.H.R.*, 68 (1953).

[126]As recorded in E 403/27, the issue roll.

issue memoranda rolls) meant that the Riccardi occasionally received sums which would be charged to one of these writs; we must consequently search the issue memoranda rolls for evidence of their repayment *de thesauro*.[127] The logical step was taken in January of 1291 when the Riccardi were issued one of these large writs themselves in the sum of £10,000.[128]

Whether the *liberate* were issued in the name of the keeper of the wardrobe or the *societas*, the Riccardi found themselves involved in the system of tally-receipts,[129] the notched wooden sticks originally given to sheriffs as receipts for money paid into the exchequer. Since the reign of Henry III tallies had been issued to royal creditors in lieu of cash. In the hands of the creditor the tally became, in effect, an order for payment which he could present to a collector of royal revenues. Over the years the Riccardi were given a great many of these tallies and must have been busy at times collecting from sheriffs and bailiffs of every description; but they seem to have dealt most often with the sheriffs of Yorkshire and Lincolnshire, collection probably being the responsibility of their northern branch in York.[130]

But the tallies issued to them were not always directed at revenues in sheriffs' hands. Another source of money from the exchequer was the frequent tallage imposed on the Jews. Sums exacted from the community of the Jews of England contributed more than £8,000 to the total amount received by the king's merchants *de thesauro*.[131]

This total receipt from exchequer revenues is not easily estimated. The merchants' account for 1272-1279 lists £36,433.[132] A search of both the chancery and exchequer series of *liberate*

[127]E.g. E 403/51, 55, 57, 59, 61 (the issue roll and the issue memoranda are sewn together here), 63 66, 70, 76.

[128]C 62/67 m. 4, schedule.

[129]See Tout, *Chapters*, II, pp. 99 ff.

[130]E 403 series, *passim*. Cf. C 47/4/5/ m. 10d.

[131]E 101/126/1, E 372/130 m. 5, E 372/132 m. 1, E 372/138 m. 26. Cf. *C.P.R. 1272-1281*, pp. 51-52, *C.C.R. 1272-1279*, p. 484.

[132]A search of the series of *liberate* and issue rolls for the first seven years of the reign showed £34,342 received by the Riccardi from the treasury. This figure is corrected by the 1279 account, E 101/126/1. One

rolls and the issue rolls for the next eleven years, 1279–1290, shows that the figure fell to something more than £8944.[133] However two additional sums are obliterated in the rolls and there is no general Riccardi account to use as a check during these years. The next four years, 1290–1294, are covered in the last Riccardi account, which shows £13,989 received from the treasury.[134] However, as a result of the exchequer control over taxes instituted in 1290, we may justly suspect that a part of this receipt can be traced to the £12,160 the Riccardi collected from the 1290 tax of a tenth and a fifteenth. In England, in fact, two sums in the general Riccardi account can be linked with these taxes, the £2,000 paid to them on 5 March, 1291, and the £1,000 four days later. Thus, although the merchants received roughly £50,000 from the treasury during the entire period, we should probably deduct the £12,160 as included already in the total figure for their receipt from taxes, leaving £38,000 as a reasonable estimate for sums *de thesauro*.

The *cambium*, i.e., the mint and exchange,[135] is the fourth important source of revenue from which Edward financed the "Riccardi system," although the evidence concerning it presents serious difficulties of interpretation.[136] By 1279 the condition of

---

sum in this total is also contained in the total receipt from taxes, given above. This is the 1,000 marks received in 3 Edward I from the twentieth granted several years earlier for his crusade.

[133]This figure was obtained by correlating the chancery and exchequer series of *liberate* rolls (C 62, E 403 respectively) with the issue rolls (E 403) for these years.

[134]E 372/143 m. 35d.

[135]The term is used in the documents in both senses. Cf. Sir John Craig, *The Mint*, p. 46, C. G. Crump and A. Hughes, "The English Currency Under Edward I," *Economic Journal,* V (1895), p. 51.

[136]There is a staggering amount of exact information about the 1279 recoinage, the exchange rates, the amount of profit made, etc., although little of it sheds much light on the specific Riccardi role at the mint. A thorough study could be written by someone with a good knowledge of the technicalities of coinage, strong eyesight, and real determination. The wealth of detail is striking: vast numbers of coins are counted and weighed; barrels, cords, and horses are hired for transport; candles, copper, great

the money circulating in England clearly indicated the need for a general recoinage.[137] Considerable planning and financial expertise would be required for a project as sizable and complex as renewing the coinage of the realm, and no small profit would be realized. Thus it is not surprising to find the king's merchants given what was most likely virtual control of the *cambium*. Orlandino da Pogio and Gregory de Rokesley, a rich merchant of London and mayor of the city, were named co-keepers on 7 January 1279.[138] By spring the arrangements had been made, the dies for striking the new coins were entrusted to the keepers, and along with the other ministers of the cambium Orlandino and Gregory swore to serve faithfully.[139]

London was the center for the recoinage,[140] but the commission of Gregory and Orlandino named Canterbury as well, and

---

balances, counters, tables, benches, vessels, etc. are purchased. Workers are brought over by the score "from beyond the sea," although evidently some of them were not overly pleased with employment in the king's mints: men were paid at Dover and the Scottish border to go after workers who fled. See E 372/132 mm. 2, 2d., 3, 3d., E 372/123 m. 22, E 372/124 m. 30, E 101/288/8, 10, 11, 12, 13, 15, 18, 21, E 101/230/9, 21, 22, E 372/136, plus the K.R. and L.T.R. Memoranda Rolls, the Liberate Rolls, the enrolled wardrobe accounts and the calendars of Patent, Close and Fine Rolls. Mavis Mate has recently studied the mint as an example of maladministration: "A Mint of Trouble, 1279 to 1307," *Speculum* XLIV (1969).

137Normal wear and the efforts of clippers, counterfeiters, and exporters gradually reduced a sound coinage and necessitated a new issue. There were at least seven such cycles in the twelfth and the thirteenth centuries with recoinage in 1105, 1156-1159, 1181, 1205, 1247, 1279, 1299. Sir Albert Feavearyear, *The Pound Sterling, A History of English Money*, p. 12.

138*C.F.R. 1272-1307*, p. 106. It is clear that Orlandino was serving as a representative of the Riccardi and not as a private businessman. In a later order the former keeper, Bartholomew de Castello, is directed to deliver his office to Rokesley and the merchants of Lucca. *C.P.R. 1272-1281*, p. 301. On Rokesley see G. A. Williams, *Medieval London*, *passim*.

139E 159/52 m. 7d.

140In Edward's agreement with his master moneyer, William of Turnemire, in 1280, London is to have as many furnaces as possible while set numbers are stipulated for the other mints. E 372/132 m. 3. Cf. Craig, *Mint*, p. 41.

other *cambii* were soon operating at Durham, York, Lincoln, Newcastle, Bristol, Chester, the abbey of Bury St. Edmunds, and in Ireland.[141] Only minimal information is available on the work done in any of the provincial mints except Canterbury. Here the archbishop had rights to three of the eight furnaces, but committed them to Rokesley and Pogio for the sum of 1,000 marks to be paid to the king in satisfaction of an old debt.[142] The mint in Durham was in the hands of the bishop, and he too made some arrangement with the Riccardi.[143] Rokesley was apparently not a party to these arrangements. Their exact nature remains unclear due to the condition of the one document stating their terms,[144] but by August of 1280, and through the following year, a "James Orlandi" of Lucca was in charge of the Durham *cambium*. He seems to have operated the financial affairs there in much the same manner as Rokesley and Pogio in London and Canterbury.[145] In January of the following year the Irish *cambium* (with mints and exchanges apparently at Dublin and Waterford) was committed to Alexander of Lucca, and the profits from Dublin were soon assigned to the Riccardi;[146] but whether Alexander was a member of the company remains in doubt.

Clearly, other Italian firms were also employed. For the liaison between the mints and "the towns and places" throughout the realm, Edward used the companies of the Bardi, Circuli, and Scala. Their members were commissioned as agents to bring in old

[141]Crump and Hughes, *Economic Journal*, V, pp. 56–71, Craig, *Mint*, p. 41. Neither of these sources mention the Irish mint. See notes 151 and 162 below for the latter.

[142]E 368/53 m. 2d. The king ratified the arrangement on 13 November 1279. *C.P.R. 1272-1281*, p. 334.

[143]Dies for the new coinage were given to his attorney in November 1279. E 368/53 m. 2.

[144]C 202/H/4 no. 68. The document records the nature of the chirograph executed between the bishop and Baroncino Gualteri and Enrico da Pogio.

[145]*C.C.R. 1279-1288*, pp. 32, 33, 97.

[146]*C.P.R. 1272-1281*, p. 423. *C.C.R. 1279-1288*, p. 76.

money to the exchanges and return it in the new coins.[147] The actual process of striking the coins was likewise carried out by other foreign experts.[148]

Orlandino was nonetheless busy on mint affairs. He received his expenses when traveling between London and Canterbury, and probably collected the considerable salary of two shillings a day.[149] One of his most important functions may have been to procure the loans from foreign merchants which provided £20,300 as the main supply of silver to initiate the recoinage.[150] However our evidence allows us to do little more than speculate on the role of the Riccardi in arranging these loans. The mint accounts state only that the money was received from foreign merchants and later repaid. But the patent rolls record the king's letters obligatory as well as the orders for repayment. From these we learn that the loans were collected from numerous Italian firms. The first money to be received was £2,200 paid to the Riccardi by representatives of four firms in April of 1279. The date of 4 January 1280 is given for the receipt of the remainder of the loans, both Gregory and Orlandino being named as receivers. However, if the procedure followed during the Welsh wars is a guide, the Riccardi may well have been employed to negotiate all these loans from their fellow countrymen.[151]

147C 202/H/4 no. 62. *C.P.R. 1272-1281*, p. 320. A letter sent to Thomas Bek by Orlandino and the mayor of London apparently refers to some of these merchants and the exchange at York, but is badly faded. S C 1, XXX, no. 143.

148See the terms contracted between the king and William of Turnemire, E 372/132 m. 3.

149E 372/132 m. 3. His salary is never stated, but these were the wages which Rokesley received, and we know Orlandino was also salaried.

150*Ibid.* The total receipt of money "for making exchange" between April and November of 1279 was £28,734. Most of the £8434 which did not result from Italian loans came from the stringent campaign against Jewish money clippers. Cf. E 372/123 m. 22. *C.P.R. 1272-1281*, p. 312.

151*C.P.R. 1272-1281*, pp. 311, 358. See below Chapter IV, Section 5. Some of the money may have been collected by Riccardi agents in France. A document from this period preserved among the Chancery Miscellanea records the receipt of 3,750 marks from the Bardi, Frescobaldi, Falconieri

The recoinage was, of course, lucrative, and a constant stream of directives ordered the keepers to make payments out of the proceeds.[152] Although the position of Rokesley is unclear, it is likely that the Riccardi were given authority in the *cambium* primarily to increase the revenues at their disposal, in the same manner as their control of the customs. At times it may have been simply convenient to have the Riccardi satisfy the king's creditors or supply money to the household on its peregrinations, while collecting an equivalent from profits of recoinage in London and Canterbury.[153] Between 1279 and 1284 the keeper of the wardrobe charged himself with receipts of nearly £25,000 from these mints "by the hands of Orlandino and Gregory."[154] Since no general Riccardi account for the years of the recoinage has survived we cannot say definitely how many of the payments making up this sum represent Riccardi loans.[155] For the provincial mints and exchanges we lack any detailed accounts.

---

and Circuli of Florence by two Riccardi in Paris. C 47/13/1 no. 15. Peregrine of Lucca and his fellows loaned £200, and Theobald of Lucca and his fellows loaned £1,333 6s. 8d., *C.P.R. 1272-1281*, p. 358, but these Luchese were not members of the Riccardi company.

[152]These orders can be found throughout the calendars of the patent and close rolls for this period.

[153]In June of 1280, for example, the Riccardi were paid £123 9s. 0d. from the London mint for this sum of money given to Matthew de Columbar. He had used their advance to purchase 118 tuns of wine for the king. *C.P.R. 1272-1281*, p. 378.

[154]E 372/124 mm. 24d., 59. E 372/128 m. 32d. E 372/130 m. 5. An order sent to the keepers in June of 1279 directed them to pay Baroncino and Enrico da Pogio 6,000 marks "for the expedition of certain of the king's affairs." *C.C.R. 1272-1279*, p. 531. The mint account covering April–November in 1279 shows only £2,000 paid to the Riccardi, with an additional £1578 13s. 4d. paid on their behalf to several merchants who had loaned money to the wardrobe. *C.P.R. 1272-1281*, p. 320. Either the rest of the money was not paid to the Riccardi or they actually retained a part of the money listed in the account as paid to the wardrobe, etc., in repayment of a temporary advance.

[155]These sums entered in the enrolled wardrobe accounts are recorded by the "per manus" type of entry discussed in Chapter II, Section 4. They may have been retained by the Riccardi as repayment for loans, but one would then expect the entry in the wardrobe account to read something

It can be shown, however, that some mint revenues went directly to the Riccardi. In 1279 they were allowed £2,000 from the London profits.[156] From the Irish *cambium* they were given £500 (from Waterford) in 1282, and in 1283 were acquitted of £2,000 due from them "at the last exchange (*cambio*) of money in Ireland."[157] The Bristol *cambium* paid the merchants £500,[158] and that at York £2,000.[159]

By the time Orlandino and the Riccardi left the mint to be managed by Rokesley alone in July 1281, the main work of recoinage, and its period of highest profits, were past.[160] The firm had received at least £7,000 in the two years and through its hands had passed several times this amount in mint profits, some part of which may have been retained in repayment of current loans to the crown.

As one Riccardi advance followed another while Edward was in Gascony, he turned to the issues of Ireland for repayment of their loans and committed Gascon revenues to their charge. The proceeds of these lands form the fifth major source for funds given to the king's bankers. In mid-September of 1288 a writ of *liberate*

---

like "received from the cambium by the hands of Baroncino and his fellows, merchants of Lucca"–i.e., no mention of Gregory and some mention of the *societas*, Trying to interpret these entries by correlating enrolled wardrobe accounts and enrolled mint accounts is a frustrating and fruitless endeavor. When the time period of the two types of account coincide, the totals of payments to the wardrobe do not match; but the periods of account are usually not coincident.

156E 372/132 m. 3. E 101/126/1.

157*C.C.R. 1279-1288*, p. 164. *C.P.R. 1281-1292*, p. 57. Concerning the latter, they had paid the justiciar of Ireland £1,500 and their companions in England had paid the wardrobe £500.

158They answered for this when rendering an account for customs revenues. E 372/125 m. 1.

159*C.P.R. 1272-1281*, p. 425. This sum appears in the wardrobe account for 1281 as received "by the hands of the merchants of Lucca." E 372/128 m. 32d.

160Orlandino was given an acquittance and Rokesley took upon himself all London and Canterbury mint obligations, and the surplus left in their proceeds. E 159/55 m. 2 Cf. *C.P.R. 1272-1281*, p. 450.

was sent to the treasurer and chamberlains of the exchequer at Dublin, ordering the payment of all the money in the Irish treasury to the Riccardi. It is hardly surprising that this writ was not immediately or fully acted upon,[161] but within a year the Riccardi were receiving general Irish issues as well as the customs. In 1290 they accounted for £2,698 5s. 7d. of the custom from 16 Edward I and of the Irish issues before Michaelmas in 17 Edward I, of £1,570 10s. 6d. out of the issues of the remainder of 17 Edward I, and of £1,480 14s. 5d. of both issues and custom for this year.[162] Their general account for 1290–1294 shows an even greater levy on Irish revenues in their behalf. During these years the Dublin exchequer turned over £19,075 to the Riccardi, of which more than £13,000 were paid in 1292–1293.[163] As in the 1290 statement these sums would include customs revenues.

The receipts from Gascon revenues are much less certain, and in fact it is here that we meet the greatest gap in the series of accounts between king and banker.[164] We know that by the early summer of 1289, however, the Riccardi were collectors of the great custom of Bordeaux; some payments made by them are charged on this revenue in the same manner as orders in England on some revenue there.[165] Yet the Bordeaux customs alone were not adequate. At about the same time they had been committed to the Riccardi, Edward added an assignment of the tolls and proceeds of Marmande (*de pedagio et exitibus Marmande*) for that year.[166] Once back in England, these partial measures were

161*C.D.I. 1285–1292*, no. 814. It is one of a file of twenty-one writs from the period when Nicholas de Clere was treasurer.

162*C.P.R. 1281–1292*, p. 328.

163E 372/143 m. 35d.

164This is the gap Dr. Fryde refers to in *C.E.H.*, III, p. 457, n. 1.

165On June 13, 1289, the constable of Bordeaux was ordered to allocate to Orlandino and his fellows, "receptoribus custume regis Burdegale, omnes soluciones quas fecerunt, sive in garderoba regis sive extra, per litteras magistri W. de Luda, custodis." *R.G.*, II, no. 1030.

166*Ibid.*, no. 1721. On the inadequacies of the Bordeaux customs see J. P. Trabut-Cussac, "Les coutumes ou droits de douane percus à Bordeaux sur les vins et les marchandises par L'administration anglaise, 1252–1307," *Annales du Midi*, LXII (1950). pp. 149–150.

covered by a blanket assignment to the Riccardi of "all the proceeds of our duchy beyond necessary expenses for wages and fees." Two orders to this effect were dispatched, on 11 April and 16 May 1290.[167] But the officials in Bordeaux were as reluctant to turn over all their profits as those in Dublin, and a third order had to be sent in July of 1291. Reviewing the previous mandates, the king added that he has learned "by the report of our dear merchants" that the constable had committed the collection of the Bordeaux and Marmande custom to others, "concerning which we are greatly amazed (de quo quamplurimum admiramur)." These receivers were to be "totally removed" and the Riccardi given control.[168] Whether the merchants actually received any substantial sums in the three years before their fall from the king's favor remains uncertain. In Edward's last years the revenues of the duchy came to "rather more than" £84,000 in the money of Bordeaux, or about £17,000 sterling.[169] An issue memoranda roll for 1293 shows some payments made to the Riccardi in black *livres tournois*, in the pound of Paris, and in *gros tournois*,[170] but we would expect Gascon revenues to be in *livres bordelaises*. Beyond this we have no information. Although the Riccardi had in fact been receivers for a time, no Gascon revenues appear among the receipts charged to them in the 1290-1294 account.

A final important source of revenue remains to be noted. Fines imposed on individuals for misconduct or negotiated in lieu of some obligation were often channeled to the Riccardi. During the embargo on exports to Flanders, many merchants were fined for carrying on the profitable trade in defiance of the king's orders. More than £13,321 went to the Riccardi from their fellow-

167*R.G.*, II, nos. 1772, 1784.

168*Ibid.*, III, no. 1975.

169Powicke, *Thirteenth Century*, pp. 304–305. The exchange rate is that of 1282. Trabut-Cussac gives an even higher estimate in *Bibliotheque de l'École des Chartres,* CXIX (1961) p. 121. He thinks 100,000 *livres tournois* a conservative estimate for the four-year farm of the custom and other revenues of the duchy and the isle of Oléron in 1270–1274.

170E 403/76.

merchants between 1272 and 1279. In the same account they acknowledged the receipt of 4,000 marks by which Adam de Stratton bought his way back into the royal favor.[171] A fine of 2,000 marks for custody of certain lands was paid to the merchants in 1288.[172] In both the 1276-1277 and 1282-1283 Welsh campaigns, many of those who substituted a money payment for active service at the head of an armed band paid their fines to the king by the hands of his merchants. Approximately £1,700 came to the Riccardi from these fines.[173] Since other examples could be cited, a figure of £20,000 might be taken as a safe minimal figure for receipt from fines of all sorts.

The question of interest payments received by the Riccardi is of obvious importance, yet the evidence is most difficult to assess with certainty. No one would now accept the older view that the only compensation for loans came from the favors and considerations bestowed by the king.[174] E. B. Fryde has shown that the firm of the Bardi collected about 26 percent on its advances to Edward III.[175] But though we can be certain that the Riccardi were collecting interest on loans to other Italian firms and private individuals, it is more difficult to demonstrate such compensation in their credit dealings with the king. The detailed records for the loans made to Edward III are not duplicated in the more sparse accounts of the late thirteenth century.

We have seen that Riccardi loans were not negotiated on an

[171]E 101/126/1. C 47/4/5 m. 10d. This was the first of two times he was caught in the activities which made him infamous in his lifetime. See Powicke, *Thirteenth Century*, pp. 364-366. The payment to the king's merchants confirms the contemporary suspicion that he bought himself off, though the letters of pardon state that he had proved his innocence before the king and council. *C.P.R. 1272-1281*, p. 335.

[172]*C.P.R. 1281-1292*, p. 292.

[173]See Chapter IV, Sections 1 and 2.

[174]This is the view of R. J. Whitwell, *T.R.H.S.*, n.s., XVII (1903), pp. 184-185.

[175]E. B. Fryde, "Loans to the English Crown, 1328-31," *E.H.R.* LXX (1955), pp. 209-210. This may have been enough profit to cover the overhead expenses of all the Bardi establishments in England.

individual basis and that the merchants were constantly paying and receiving in the king's name. Thus we would expect to discover interest payments at the periodic general accountings. Our sample is limited to the three cases for which these audits survive, the "view of account" in 1276 and the accounts in 1279 and 1294. Only in the last of these can any specific compensation be found. In this account the Riccardi were given an allowance of 5,000 marks "for the praiseworthy service done for the king and the labors undertaken for the king on this side of the seas as well as beyond the seas." Yet even this sum fails as a convincing case of interest for general Riccardi loans, for, despite the rhetorical flourish about services on both sides of the seas, the money seems to have been generous repayment for their gift-giving at the papal court and their financing of the English ambassadors there.[176]

It would be strange indeed if the Italian merchants, who were notoriously sharp businessmen, dropped any interest charges to the king while deeply engaged in financing the operation of his government at home and abroad. The loans which cost Edward III 26 percent could hardly have gone free to his grandfather. That we cannot pinpoint this interest reflects not only contemporary fears of ecclesiastical censure, but also the nature of the extant accounts, which were drawn up from a mass of vouchers, receipts, etc., and condensed into brief statements. Payments coming to £126,816 are credited to the Riccardi in 1279, for example, with only the following explanation: "in payments made by the merchants to the king's treasurer in the wardrobe, and to diverse persons for divers royal works as well in Wales as in England, and in other expenses of the king . . . as appears in their roll of particulars."[177] By the standards of the accounts this is even a bit verbose. It is possible that if we had the full "particulars" they would contain some royal "gifts" or simply might not add up to the stated total. Though this cannot be proved, the nature of the accounts would make it very easy to write in compensation of any desired amount.

[176]E 372/143 m. 35d. See notes 47 and 48. [177]E 101/216/1.

Statements of the king's indebtedness to his bankers further reinforce the probability that some interest was charged. In these letters obligatory the promised date of repayment is never far in the future and thus is unrealistic if not impossible. When a "view" was held in January of 1276, the Riccardi payments were found to exceed their receipts by £13,333. This sum was duly promised to them by a fortnight after the following Easter, i.e. within three months.[178] In December of 1279, after a general account of that summer, the date specified for repayment of £23,000 was the following Michaelmas.[179] In January of 1293, Edward promised to repay Riccardi loans for household expenses totaling £10,000 within two months.[180] It seems hardly possible to take such repayment dates seriously. They may well represent a practice, current among medieval lenders, of securing a formal date for repayment well in advance of the actual date agreed upon by both borrower and creditor. Ecclesiastical censure could then be avoided by collecting legitimate "damages" for nonpayment on the date in the formal contract.[181]

If the Riccardi business letters, which are extant for 1295-1303, were also available for the years before their break with the king, the question could be settled beyond doubt. But in those letters which have survived there is one relevant reference, an estimate of the debts owed by the king's brother Edmund, Earl of Lancaster. In 1295, his debt stood at 30,000 marks. The bulk of this debt was made up of a loan of 25,031 marks advanced in 1293 while Edmund was on the king's service in France. Thus the Riccardi thought this debt should go onto Edward's own account with them and after noting the sum of 30,000 marks they stated that if the "damages" are added it would come to 40,000 marks. This represents an in-

[178] *C.P.R. 1272-1281*, pp. 131-132.

[179] *Ibid.*, p. 355.

[180] C 81/7 no. 597. *C.P.R. 1292-1302*, p. 59.

[181] Raymond de Roover, *The Rise and Decline of the Medici Bank*, pp. 10-11. T. P. McLaughlin, "The Teaching of the Canonists on Usury (XII, XIII and XIV Centuries)," *Medieval Studies* 1 (1939), pp. 140-143.

terest charge of no less than 33-1/3 percent over a period of two years.[182]

Since the Riccardi were constantly receiving the king's revenues and meeting his expenses, it would have been impossible to say at what time any particular expenditure was repaid. Thus interest was probably not charged at a certain annual rate, but as a flat rate on the amount owed them at the end of any period of account. Since they considered the debt of Edmund as an item on the king's account it is possible that they received as much as a third on the balance owed them. This is as close to an estimate as we can come.

Yet the privileged status of the king's merchants was a bonus received in addition to any interest. Because of their royal patron, the Riccardi could not only escape most of the disabilities facing alien merchants but could reap many positive rewards as well. One important case in point is the collection of debts through exchequer machinery. In Michaelmas term of 1274, the barons of the exchequer were instructed to aid "Luke of Lucca" in recovering debts owed him within the realm, so far as was just, by hearing and terminating the pleas concerning these debts at Luke's request.[183]

This privilege was not the sole preserve of merchants who were the royal bankers; any Italian who loaned the king money might receive the right to use the exchequer's process.[184] However, the Riccardi received special favors at the exchequer by the king's command. In Trinity term of 1277 Edward noted that since they were bound to the king for goods and sums of money he wished to show them grace concerning the debts owed them. Thus the barons were instructed to summon all Riccardi debtors before them and give aid and counsel in the recovery of the sums due.[185] Again in 1285-1286 a general summons of those owing money to the bankers was prefaced

[182]E 101/601/5, p. 26d.

[183]E 368/48 m. 2d. E 159/49. Cf. *Select Cases in the Exchequer of Pleas*, Selden Society 48 (1931), pp. cxii-cxiii.

[184]See Whitwell, *T.R.H.S.*, n.s., XVII (1903), pp. 203-204.

[185]E 368/50 m. 5d.

with the statement that "special grace" was to be shown to the merchants who were attending the king's affairs. In all counties in which debts were owed to the Riccardi—either debts for which they had recognizances "or that they can otherwise establish (aut aliter de iure constare possint)"—the sheriffs were to receive instructions under the exchequer seal to distrain the debtors to satisfy the merchants or their certified attorney without delay.[186] When several years later the treasurer, John Kirkby, died owing money to the Riccardi, the king ordered these debts to be levied from Kirkby's goods, "as if they were debts owed the king himself."[187] In a similar case in 1279, the Riccardi were linked with the king as the first creditors to be satisfied from the goods of John le Gross who had died in their debt.[188]

Protections, trading licenses, and safe-conducts were often given to the Riccardi in England, Ireland, and Wales when they sent their agents there during Edward's campaigns.[189] Although the documents sometimes state that they were going on the king's affairs, we may be sure this would in no way preclude private business. During the first Welsh campaign the Riccardi made use of a journey to Conway to buy wool from the abbot of Aberconway and transport it back to Chester under a safe-conduct.[190] Occasionally, a ship laden with Riccardi goods was covered with the king's protection. When the "Saint Katherine" coming from Ireland with a cargo of leather owned by the members of the company put into Portsmouth and was forcibly unloaded against their will, firm orders were sent from the throne to the bailiffs of the port and the sheriff of Cornwall to set things right.[191]

[186]E 159/59 m. 23. E 368/59 m. 7. [187]E 159/63 m. 15.

[188]E 159/53 m. 1d. Whitwell, *T.R.H.S.*, n.s., XVII (1903), pp. 205, 206 n. 1.

[189]*C.P.R. 1272-1281*, pp. 29, 213, 369. *Ibid. 1281-1292*, pp. 27, 39, 154, 197, 218, 322, *C.D.I. 1285-1292*, no. 1140. *C.C.R.V., p. 234.*

[190]*C.P.R. 1272-1281*, p. 235.

[191]E 159/66 m. 26. The king gave the sheriff general instructions to protect and defend all Riccardi goods and chattels in his county "as if they

At various times the Riccardi were exempted from murage, stallage, and lastage in various parts of the realm.[192] When they were with the king in Gascony the merchants were freed from contributions, tallages, loans, or other actions whatsoever in the cities of the duchy "even as familiars of our household are free (tanquam familiares hospicii nostri sint liberi et quieti)." They could be summoned in a legal action only before the seneschal of Gascony and the constable of Bordeaux. Furthermore, all officials in the duchy were ordered to maintain, protect and specially defend the merchants, and their goods.[193] In England, licenses were issued in their favor allowing them to sell cloth not meeting the assize requirements, and pardons were handed to them when they were found violating the standards.[194] Dealing with the Flemish contrary to proclamation, and the fine for this traffic, could be forgiven.[195] A conviction of coin clipping in Ireland may have directed the royal wrath less at the merchants than at their judges.[196]

Trading and lending opportunities must have been multiplied by the contracts and prestige accruing to the merchants of the king. Useful channels of information were also opened: as collectors of the custom the Riccardi would have complete figures on the wool exports of friends and rivals alike; a share in the direction of the mint and exchange would provide valuable information on the timing, rates, and progress of the recoinage.

Since the Riccardi moved in the circles of the great men of the day, they personally became men whose influence was

---

were our very own." For another case see *C.P.R. 1292-1301*, p. 11. In 1293 a ship called "La Bonegayne" from Winchelsea, belonging to Geoffrey le Banwic of that city, carried Riccardi goods to Flanders and back under a safe conduct.

[192]See the orders in May of 1283 (*C.P.R. 1281-1292*, p. 63), June of 1285 (*Ibid.*, p. 170), September of 1291 (*Ibid.*, p. 446), and April of 1292 (*C.C.R. 1288-1296*, p. 229).

[193]*R.G.*, II, no. 1463.

[194]*C.P.R. 1272-1281*, pp. 300, 337, 356. *Ibid. 1281-1292*, pp. 27, 37, 109. *C.C.R. 1272-1279*, p. 437. *Ibid. 1279-1288*, p. 1.

[195]C 202/H/2 no. 18. *C.P.R. 1272-1281*, pp. 125, 532-533.

[196]See Chapter I, Section 4.

sought by others. Through them one might be able to gain some favor from the king or his ministers, if the proper sum were offered. For example, at the request of Labro Volpelli of the company, in 1292 the prior of Lewes, who had been a frequent seller of wool to the Riccardi, was granted a respite of three years on a debt of 2,000 marks owed the king. The prior apparently paid handsomely for this service by the king's merchants.[197]

4. THE SCALE OF THE TRANSACTIONS

In discussing the respective obligations and benefits of the king and his merchants, we have obtained some impression of the scale of the transactions for certain periods. But in order fully to assess the importance of the Riccardi to English government finance it is necessary to attempt a more comprehensive and a more quantitative analysis. The formidable problems such an effort entails have already been seen. Not only are the explanations of figures in any single account often vague, but there is the yet more serious obstacle of correlating the information scattered through accounts for various revenues and the records of the wardrobe and the rolls of the exchequer. Often the periods covered by these accounts do not coincide, and a sum found in one document may be partly included in one found in several other accounts. In other words, there are many pieces to the puzzle and they often overlap.[198] Tout stated the confession of every student of medieval English finance when he wrote, ". . . when all safeguards are considered, the extreme difficulty of getting at the bottom of the con-

[197]See note 108 of Chapter I. For other cases see S C 1, X, nos. 84, 85, *C.P.R. 1272-1281*, p. 371.

[198]Wardrobe accounts are based on the regnal year which began on the feast of St. Edmund, king and martyr, 20 November, and closed on the following 19 November. Exchequer accounts, however, are based on the exchequer year which ran from Michaelmas (29 September) to Michaelmas. The special Riccardi accounts show varying dates. Thus the chance of confusing overlapping of important periods of account is great.

fusions and intricacies of medieval finance will be only too likely to plunge one attempting the rash task into a sea of personal errors for which he can only ask indulgence."[199]

For our particular "rash task" we should turn first to the wardrobe documents. The central role of the wardrobe in Edwardian financial administration and the close cooperation of the Riccardi in its operations place the wardrobe accounts in the first rank of our evidence. If we had the large body of documents from which the enrolled accounts were compiled, many of the uncertainties surrounding Riccardi transactions would disappear. However, we can profitably use the summary accounts placed on the pipe rolls. Two basic types of entries can be found in the receipt section of these accounts. One simply lists a sum "from the merchants of Lucca (de mercatoribus lukanis)," often with the additional phrase "as a prest (de prestito)" or "as a loan (de mutuo)" and perhaps "on various occasions (per diversas vices)." Although we might wish that a few details and some specific dates were given, the meaning is clear; a certain sum of money has been advanced to the wardrobe by the king's bankers. Much more troublesome are those entries which record the receipt of a sum from some specific source of royal revenue "by the hands of the merchants of Lucca (per manus mercatorum lukanorum)." What does it mean when the wardrobe receives money from the customs or a tax or the mint "by the hands of the merchants of Lucca"? We can quickly reject one possibility. It is most unlikely that the Riccardi were merely agents of transfer, nothing more than the means by which customs receipts or tax proceeds were hauled from the place of collection to the current location of the wardrobe. Ordinary wardrobe machinery and personnel were quite sufficient to handle carting and hauling. The Riccardi were not given control of the wool custom, the mint, and much of the proceeds of taxes in order merely to carry them to the king as the money was slowly collected. Instead we can be sure that money collected "per manus mercatorum lukanorum"

[199]Tout, *Chapters*, II, p. 87.

stayed in those hands, that it was retained by the Riccardi as repayment for their loans. Advances from the merchants to the wardrobe are thus charged on the revenues in their keeping.

Yet an explanation of *per manus* entries cannot stop here. Were the sums being repaid for past advances or for loans made during the period of wardrobe account in which they stand? In other words, when the receipt portion of a wardrobe account for any regnal year contains only *per manus* entries from the Riccardi, does this mean that during this time period the merchants made no loans to the wardrobe, and that they were simply collecting money in repayment of loans recorded in previous accounts? Over the whole period when they were the king's bankers the wardrobe receipt from them *de mutuo, de prestito*, etc., is nearly balanced by wardrobe receipts "by their hands." Would this not indicate simply a series of loans and their later repayment? Attractive as such an analysis is, the answer to both these questions must be negative. At least in some cases the *per manus* entry must record repayment of loans made within the period covered by the account in which it is found; in some cases such entries must record both the fact that loans have been made and the means by which they were repaid. That is, at least some *per manus* entries are actually nothing other than more informative types of the usual note of explanation, showing both the loan itself and the revenue to which it was charged.[200] Unless this were the case we would have to interpret the two enrolled wardrobe accounts for the period of the 1282-1283 Welsh war as showing virtually no Riccardi loans, although we know from other evidence that the Riccardi were lending so much for the war effort that it was putting a severe strain on the firm. From the few particular accounts which have by chance survived it is clear that the

[200]An exception would be the series of loans collected from the several Italian firms in England during Edward's second war in Wales. In the 1276-1277 and 1287 campaigns, however, similar loans did not enter into wardrobe accounting and so present no problem in our evaluation of Riccardi participation in wardrobe finance. Cf. note 36 of Chapter IV.

Lucchesi loaned more than £4,000 into the wardrobe and paid out several thousand more for its wartime needs.[201] Since the enrolled wardrobe accounts for the war years show only the *per manus* type of receipt involving the Riccardi, in this case these entries must be interpreted as covering large Riccardi loans advanced during the war. Moreover, both the preliminary "view of account" in 1276 and the subsequent general accounting of 1279 show that no great backlog of wardrobe indebtedness had been building up before the second war in Wales. When the campaign began the Riccardi were certainly not owed the huge sums listed as received "by their hands" in the two wardrobe accounts for the war. Again, it appears that these entries must be read as indications of current loans for the conquest of Wales. They are charged on revenue sources in Riccardi hands because there had been an opportunity to decide this matter of bookkeeping by the time the accounts were enrolled.

The table on the following page shows the Riccardi contribution to wardrobe finance and the division between the two types of entries. From these figures it is apparent that at a minimum one pound in six came to the wardrobe as Riccardi loans, counting only the *de mutuo* entries. If all the *per manus* sums also recorded Riccardi loans, a maximum figure of one pound in three is obtained.

It is arguable that the larger figure comes closer to the mark. If we compare the wardrobe statistics with those obtained from non-wardrobe sources, it becomes immediately obvious that the total of *de mutuo* entries cannot represent the total Riccardi advances to the wardrobe. In their various accounts the merchants were given allowances for approximately £203,267 loaned to the wardrobe. Not only is this considerably more than the total of *de mutuo* entries, it does not include any allowances for the enormously heavy Riccardi expenditure for the wardrobe in Gascony, 1286-1289, when the king's obliga-

[201] See below, Chapter IV Section 2. These surviving documents are, of course, only a small sample. Riccardi support for this campaign was undoubtedly substantial.

Table II Riccardi Contribution to Wardrobe Finance

Regnal Year	Total Receipt (£)	Receipt Involving Riccardi *de mutuo*, etc.	*per manus*	Source
57 Henry III– 2 Edward I	31,457	9,097	666	E 372/121 m. 22
2–3 Edward I	17,817	2,966		E 372/119 m. 22
4 Edward I	16,231	11,665		E 372/123 m. 23
5 Edward I	35,714	24,476		E 372/123 m. 23
6 Edward I	19,316	18,233		E 372/123 m. 22d.
7 Edward I	30,920	15,312	400	E 372/124 m. 24d.
8 Edward I	23,942		7,704	E 372/124 m. 30d.
9–10 Edward I	50,943	2,240	8,000	E 372/128 m. 32d.
10–13 Edward I (Special War Acct.)	102,641	10,000	48,899	E 372/136 m. 33
11–12 Edward I	101,953	1,333	33,509	E 372/130 mm. 5, 5d.
13 Edward I	40,699		10,242	E 372/136 mm. 31, 31d.
14 Edward I	35,413	11,985		E 372/136 mm. 31, 31d.
15–16 Edward I	77,339	25,523		E 372/136 mm. 31d.
17–18 Edward I	140,900	783	39,000	E 372/138 mm. 26, 26d.
19 Edward I	62,045	6,667		E 372/138 m. 25
20 Edward I	33,154			E 372/138 m. 26
21 Edward I	34,872	10,000		E 372/139 m. 6
22 Edward I	65,850	8,896		E 372/144 mm. 20, 21
	921,156	159,176	148,420	
		307,596		

tion to the company mounted to £103,733.[202] A figure in the range of £300,000 might thus accurately represent total Riccardi advances to the wardrobe.

Moreover, a figure on this order of magnitude seems reasonable when we use a completely different approach to a quantitative evaluation of Riccardi services. Important as the wardrobe was in Edward's financial scheme and in his utilization of the *Societas Riccardorum*, the merchants nonetheless sometimes operated entirely outside of the wardrobe accounting system. We must therefore try to obtain at least some notional idea of their total expenditure in the king's name. The most convenient way to arrive at such a figure is to rely on the series of accounts between the king and his bankers: the two general accounts covering all receipts and expenditures in 1272-1279 and 1290-1294, and the four customs accounts for 1279-1290. The aggregate expenditure listed in these accounts comes to roughly £392,284.[203] (See table on following page).

But although a useful indication of the scale of Riccardi expenditure, this cannot be a complete figure. We might suspect that there were transactions between 1279 and 1290 which were not charged on customs revenue received during those years; and we should note that Irish customs do not even figure in the accounts during these years not covered by general accounts.[204] Moreover, even in the more comprehensive general accounts some loans may be missing. The 1290-1294 account omits a loan of 25,031 marks to the Earl of Lancaster for his diplomatic mission to the French court in 1293-1294. Adding this sum gives a revised minimum of £408,972, or slightly more than £18,500 a year on the average for the entire period when the Riccardi were royal bankers. A figure of this magnitude tal-

[202]See the general accounts for 1-7 Edward I (E 101/126/1) and 18-22 Edward I (E372/143 m. 35d.) and the customs accounts for the intervening period (E 372/124 m. 1d., E 372/125 m. 1, E 372/133 m. 32d., E 372/134 m. 3).

[203]See E. B. Fryde, *Cambridge Economic History,* III, p. 456.

[204]The Riccardi control of Irish customs was not continuous while they were the king's bankers. See below, Chapter III, Section 3.

Accounting Period	*Type of Account*	*Riccardi Expenditure*	*Source*
20 November 1272–29 September 1279	General	£201,478	E 101/126/1
19 May 1279–13 April 1281 (England) 4 May 1275–29 September 1280 (Ireland)	Customs	26,328	E 372/124 m. 1d.
12 April 1281–29 March 1282	Customs	9,309	E 372/125 m. 1.
29 March 1282–14 April 1286	Customs	41,319	E 372/133 m. 32d
14 April 1286–1 June 1290	Customs	14,604	E 372/134 m. 3.
1 June 1290–7 August 1294	General	99,246	E 372/143 m. 35d
		£392,284	

lies well with the total of £401,000 obtained by adding the major categories of royal repayment to the Riccardi examined in this chapter, including the customs, lay and clerical taxes, sums *de thesauro*, recoinage proceeds, and fines, but excluding the sums from Ireland and Gascony, which remain problematical.

If we had certain statistics on the average annual income of the English government between 1272 and 1294 it would be possible to give a fairly precise estimate of what Riccardi loans meant to crown finance. However, the irregular and incidental nature of much of the royal income make constructing such annual figures hazardous. Perhaps the safest course of action is to measure the minimal annual figure of £18,500 against the average annual receipt of the wardrobe in this period, which was about £41,416. By doing so we can see that each year the king owed his bankers on the average nearly half as much as the receipts accounted for by the principal agency of government finance.

The meaning of these figures, however, must be kept in mind. Although King Edward's aggregate obligation to the Riccardi was undoubtedly as high as £408,972, this does not mean that the Riccardi had loaned this full sum, for an indeterminate amount of interest would be included. Likewise this vast sum does not mean that the king was falling progressively and hopelessly into debt. Repayment came at a sufficient rate to maintain his obligation at a manageable and fairly constant level; it stood in 1294 at about the same level as in 1279. In both cases the debt outstanding after a general accounting had been held was certainly less than the revenue which Edward could count on receiving in any ordinary year. Using the Riccardi did not put an intolerable strain on the king's resources.

The attempt at an overall quantitative evaluation of the role of the Riccardi encounters all of the expected pitfalls of medieval accounting and yields figures which can be only rough approximations. Yet the result helps to substantiate the impression gained from more limited and qualitative evidence. For more than two decades the smooth functioning of the government of Edward I and the achievement of the king's aims rested in no small degree on the employment of the *Societas Riccardorum* in a sophisticated financial system. During these years the crucial problem of royal finance had been solved.

APPENDIX THE RICCARDI vs. JOHN OF BERWICK

The accounts between king and banker covered transactions so numerous and sums so vast that we would expect at least a multitude of disputes and misunderstandings, if not a welter of charges and countercharges between royal officials and members of the company. A system involving much money and complicated record-keeping is an invitation to peculation. Yet surprisingly few cases appear in the records, outside of the Irish disputes.

The most notable instance in England occurred in 1287, while Edward was across the Channel in Gascony.[1] It created something of a stir, for the treasurer and barons of the exchequer, the justices of both king's bench and common pleas, and other members of the king's council were called together by the regent, Edmund, Earl of Cornwall, to hear the evidence. The case was initiated by John of Berwick, a royal clerk and keeper of the queen's gold. Berwick charged that the Riccardi had not answered for a sum of 500 marks he had paid to them in 1284 for the queen's account. But since he could not at first produce their letter of receipt for this sum, the queen's records being on the continent, a hearing was delayed. When this letter was recovered the parties again appeared and the Riccardi request for a delay was denied because of the privileged status of the queen. After inspecting the letter, dated 10 December 1284, they acknowledged that it was genuine but said that they had already been acquitted in an accounting with the queen's officials, a claim which Berwick denied. To counter his evidence

[1] The dispute is recorded on two K. R. Memoranda Rolls, E 368/58 mm. 41, 41d., and E 368/60 m. 22d. The Riccardi letter of receipt and the king's writ are entered on both Memoranda Rolls, E 159/60 m. 3, E 368/60 m. 3. For the royal order concerning the hearing of the case see C 47/34/5 no. 10.

of their receipt the merchants produced a writ from the king stating that Edward understood that they had been charged with the same sum twice and that a careful search of the documents should be made. When the rolls were searched and only one sum of 500 marks was found, received in August of 1284, Berwick triumphantly called them once more to account. But the Riccardi again countered, charging that since the accounting with the queen's officials, Berwick had come to them on 10 December 1284 and said that his own account was soon to be heard and he had lost their letter proving that he had paid them the 500 marks. He pleaded with them to provide another and save him from ruin. They did so "incautiously and not believing any loss would come to them," especially since other important men had also spoken to them on Berwick's behalf. When they had related their version Berwick's response was to ask whether they be allowed to assert this "by their simple word, without other evidence (per simplex verbum suum absque alia evidenci ratione)." Once again the officials searched the rolls of account and the particular documents from which they were compiled; but though they searched diligently they had to admit that "the simple truth was not at all apparent (pura veritas nullomodo apparet)." It was provisionally decided that since the merchants had executed the recognizance the queen should have an allowance of 500 marks in her debt to them, but that if it were later learned from the auditors of the accounts that the sum was being counted twice, then the money would be returned to the Riccardi and their letter cancelled. The final solution is not apparent and was probably achieved only after the king and queen returned to England.[2] Yet the case is nonetheless illustrative of the kinds of difficulties which could easily arise.

[2] No disgrace or royal displeasure seems to have fallen on the Riccardi or on Berwick as a result of this dispute. In fact, the merchants continued to deal with Berwick on the queen's behalf. See E 101/352/7, E 159/59 m. 6d.

Chapter III The Control of the Customs, 1275–1294

1. ESTABLISHING THE 1275 CUSTOM

The creation of a viable customs system has been hailed as the outstanding contribution to English government finance in the reign of Edward I.[1] Yet we have seen that the proof of this evaluation is not to be found solely in the significant increment these duties brought to the royal revenues. Even more important were the possibilities presented by using this steady source of funds as security for loans negotiated with firms of Italian merchant-bankers. For nineteen years, 1275-1294, the export duties on wool formed the principle means of repaying the continuous advances made to Edward I by the Riccardi of Lucca.

Edward's grandfather, King John, first established customs duties throughout the realm; but his two experiments were short-lived.[2] The significant step towards the Edwardian custom was

[1] Powicke, *Thirteenth Century*, p. 628.

[2] Between 1202 and 1206 John collected a fifteenth of the value of all imports and exports. While the levy may originally have been aimed against French merchants, it was charged on all foreign merchants by 1204, and possibly on English merchants as well. A treaty with Philip Augustus apparently ended the profitable duties in 1206, for one clause of the treaty specified free trade between the kingdoms. Even less is known about John's second custom, charged on woad and grain. Custodians were set over coastal districts at Michaelmas 1210, and one partial account shows that the duties were collected into 1211. See the discussion of John's tariffs by Sidney Painter, *The Reign of King John*, pp. 138-139, N.S.B. Gras, *The Early English Customs System*, pp. 48-53, A. L. Poole, *Domesday Book to Magna Carta*, p. 93. Gras prints documents relating to the earlier duties on pp. 217-22. Only Painter discusses the later custom.

taken in the period of readjustment after the defeat and death of Simon de Montfort. In order to facilitate the restoration of foreign trade, Henry III in February of 1266 granted the Lord Edward full control and supervision over "all stranger and oversea merchants" coming into the realm and staying there with their merchandise.[3] Upon consultation with the merchants Edward utilized his control to obtain a "reasonable portion" of the goods of these merchants imported or exported, "whereby the merchants will not be grieved immoderately." The arrangements were confirmed by King Henry in a letter patent dated April 2.[4]

The comprehensive tariff thus established came to be known as the "new aid."[5] It was collected on all wares exported or imported, presumably by aliens and denizens alike, on an *ad valorem* basis. There is no evidence of the involvement of a parliament or great council in the establishment of the tax and the conclusion is that the grant was simply negotiated with the merchants. Neither the original agreement nor any accounts are extant, but we know that the duties were in fact collected. In February of 1267, two men were appointed to supervise the accounts of the collectors who were agents directly appointed by Edward.[6] However, the custom was soon farmed to Florentine merchants for 6,000 marks a year.[7]

Opposition to the "new aid" arose almost at once. The towns objected to a violation of their liberties and at least two of them, London and Beverley, obtained exemptions, the former by a "gift" of 200 marks, the latter through the influence of the archbishop of York.[8] Loss of the revenue from London commerce

[3] *C.P.R. 1258-1266*, p. 551. The grant is dated 12 February, 1266.

[4] Rymer, *Foedera*, I, 1, p. 468. *C.P.R. 1266-1272*, pp. 575-576.

[5] The "new aid" is discussed by Gras, *Early English Customs*, pp. 53-58, Powicke, *Thirteenth Century*, pp. 619, 628-29, Grace Faulkner Ward, "The Early History of the Merchant Staplers," *E.H.R.* 33 (1918), pp. 305, 313-315.

[6] *C.P.R. 1266-1272*, p. 129. Gras, *Early English Customs*, p. 54.

[7] *Liber de Antiquis Legibus*, p. 109. The names of the Florentine merchants are not given.

[8] *Ibid.*, pp. 109-110. *C.P.R. 1266-1272*, p. 223. Gras, *Early English Customs*, p. 55.

was, of course, a serious blow. The bishop of Durham and the countess of Aumale opposed Edward's agents to the extent that the king ordered his bailiffs in York and Northumberland to give aid to the harassed collectors.[9]

In addition to the resistance within the realm, the custom provoked complaint and retaliation abroad. It was probably one of the factors behind the seizure by the countess of Flanders of all the goods of English, Irish, and Gascon merchants within her territory.[10] In response to the milder reaction of St. Louis, Henry III suspended the custom for a time in May of 1267, in order to allow French merchants to state their objections to the duties at the next fair of St. Giles, Winchester, then four months in the future.[11]

The custom was eventually renewed, for in May 1270 it was again farmed to Florentines for a period which lasted to at least 24 December 1272.[12] During the following several years the gen-

[9]*C.P.R. 1266-1272*, pp. 1-2. Gwyn Williams estimates that Londoners handled a third of the wool exported from England in the early fourteenth century, plus a quarter to a third of the wine. But in the late thirteenth century the city had not yet become the hub of the traffic in wool. Boston, for example, was more important until 1304-1306. *Medieval London*, pp. 106, 110, 113-114.

[10]Powicke, *Thirteenth Century*, p. 621, notes that while she was collecting the long overdue pension owed her by Henry III, it is difficult not to see in her flagrant action some resentment against the English customs policy.

[11]*C.P.R. 1266-1272*, pp. 140-141. Gras, *Early English Customs*, p. 55.

[12]*C.P.R. 1266-1272*, p. 442. Gras, *Early English Customs*, p. 55. The Italians are "Diutautus Gwillelmi, Hugh Pape, Hugelin de Palesho, Gerard Pape, James Demaci and Bencivenna Jacobi." They may have named Englishmen in the ports to collect for them. A John Clement of Ipswich was then collector in that port and was later accused of holding back some of the money. E13/9 m. 2d. The original grant was to run for one year from 22 May 1270 "and three weeks after," but was extended on several occasions. The first of these was to continue the assignment until the quinzaine of the Assumption (in late May), and was negotiated for 2,000 marks. However, the Lord Edward soon decided he was being cheated of half the true value of the lease for this length of time. Just before sailing from England on his crusade, he revoked the agreement and gave the lease for the extended time to the firm of Peter and William

erally inadequate evidence on the "new aid" fails almost completely and we are on sure ground again only in March of 1275. At this time Lucasio Natale and his fellow merchants of the Riccardi received a commission to collect the duties until a week after Easter.[13]

It was during his unhurried return to England after his crusade that this firm emerged as Edward's bankers, lending money not only to the king but also to his agents who were carrying on the process of government in his absence. More than £31,000 had come from Riccardi coffers to further the king's business and satisfy his creditors in this short time.[14] The possibilities repre-

---

Beraldi (or Beraud) of Cahors, apparently for 4,000 marks. *Ibid.*, p. 463. The calendar gives a figure of 40,000 marks, and it was probably on this basis that Powicke decided that the reference to a "new aid" meant the twentieth of 1269-1270 granted for Edward's crusade. *Thirteenth Century*, p. 281 and note 4. But this tax is consistently termed "the twentieth" or even "the twentieth in aid of the Holy Land" in the documents. E 372/117 m. 6d. *C.P.R. 1266-1272*, pp. 416, 419, 421-423, 439, 448, 493, etc. The fact that the lease for this "aid" begins when the previous lease of the 1266 custom expires and refers to the same firm can hardly be a coincidence. The figure of 40,000 marks would be impossibly large for this custom and is probably a typographical error for 4,000 marks. Edward had originally granted the extension for 2,000 marks and revoked it because he was "manifestly deceived of more than half the just price." Which group of merchants held the "new aid" in the next six months is not apparent. During Edward's absence Walter Giffard, archbishop of York, Roger Mortimer, and Robert Burnell, the men "supplying the place of Edward, the king's son," leased the custom to Duitautus and his associates from 4 December 1271 to Christmas 1272. Edward confirmed this on 24 January 1272. *C.P.R. 1266-1272*, p. 617. A mandate for all persons to lend aid and counsel to the collectors was issued not long thereafter. *Ibid.*, p. 630. The Florentines evidently were to answer to Edward for the forfeitures of merchants violating the customs regulations, for by November of 1272 they had not yet answered for this profit and Edward wanted the money levied for his use. *Ibid.*, p. 717.

[13] *C.P.R. 1272-1281*, p. 84. One piece of evidence indicates that the duties were collected during this time. On 5 October 1273, the collectors of the "new aid" in London and Southampton were given special instructions concerning Rouen merchants who had been released from the obligation to pay duties at the request of Philip III of France. *C.C.R. 1272-1279*, p. 33.

[14] Tout, *Chapters*, II, p. 4. *C.P.R. 1272-1281*, pp. 131-132.

sented by such financial resources were not lost on the king and his advisers. If his subsequent action is a guide to his intentions at this stage, Edward, having found that he could work conveniently and profitably with the Luchese merchants, was seeking a financial base on which he could regularize and continue the relationship.

The traditional revenues which had been available to his father or grandfather were not well suited to such an end. Drafts on the exchequer could hardly be considered ideal security. The pressing demands of government expenses continually outpaced the king's income as a landlord and a feudal lord. There would be no guarantee that the exchequer could honor these drafts without unsatisfactory delay. Although the new taxes on personal property brought considerable returns—and would prove to be one of the most important means used to repay Riccardi loans—at the beginning of the reign no one could foresee the frequency of these grants to Edward I. On the contrary, the memory of the thirty-two years, 1237-1269, when Henry III had been refused a single grant on temporal goods must have raised doubts in the minds of calculating creditors. Direct taxes were not only infrequent in incidence, their assessment and collection were laboriously slow.

During the two-year period of the king's return from crusade when the Riccardi loaned £31,052, writs of *liberate* directed the exchequer to repay only £5,213 6s. 8d. of this total. The merchants had to wait at least a year to collect on two of the writs totalling £1,046.[15] From the twentieth of 1269-1270, granted

[15]The dates and amounts of these writs, with the sources for the writs on both series of *liberate* rolls and on the issue rolls are as follows:

28 January 1273	£500	C 62/49 m. 1
		E 403/21A m. 1
		E 403/1230 m. 1
18 and 23 April 1273	£1,000	C 62/49 m. 2
		E 403/21A m. 1
		E 403/1230 m. 1
7 May 1273	1,000 marks	C 62/49 m. 3
		E 403/21A m. 1
		E 403/1230 m. 1

for the support of Edward's crusade, the Riccardi were repaid a further £5,226.[16] From the biennial tenth of 1272, a tax for the same purpose imposed by the pope, they received 9,000 marks.[17] Thus drafts on the exchequer and the proceeds of taxes provided only about half of the sum needed to repay the Riccardi in this period. A new revenue source was needed if employment of merchants on so grand a scale was to continue.

The flourishing foreign trade offered a tempting solution to this need. Duties tapping this source, moreover, would provide excellent security for loans. They could be collected continuously according to an exact schedule of charges in a relatively small number of ports. The royal creditors could place their agents in

---

22 May 1273	1,000 marks	C 62/49 m. 3 E 403/21A m. 1 E 403/1230 m. 1d.
6 July 1273	1,000 marks	C 62/49 m. 4 E 403/23 m. 1 E 403/1232 m. 1
23 October 1273	£1,000	C 62/49 m. 3 E 403/23 m. 1 E 403/1232 m. 1
24 April 1274	1,000 marks	C 62/50 m. 3 E 403/25 m. 1 E 403/1233 m. 1 E 403/1234 m. 1
15 October 1274	70 marks	C 62/50 m. 6 E 403/27 m. 3 E 403/1235

Those writs delayed more than a year were the last of the writs for £1,000 and that for 70 marks.

16E 372/117 m. 6d.

17The Riccardi had loaned Edward 8,000 marks on the security of the tenth and were given this amount out of the proceeds of the tax. *C.P.R. 1272-1281*, p. 53. Cf. *C.C.R. 1272-1279*, p. 33. The Issue Roll for 3 Edward I shows this sum plus an additional 1,000 marks given to the Riccardi as a prest, for which they were held to answer to the king. E 403/32. In their 1272-1279 account the merchants are charged with £8,000 from this tax. E 101/126/1. Some of this may have been received after 1275.

these ports as supervisors.[18] Yet it was apparent that the "new aid" could not fulfill these needs. The comprehensive duties had aroused considerable opposition at home and abroad; exemptions and temporary suspensions had been allowed; and the revenue was valued at a farm of only £4,000 annually.

The conditions under which the Riccardi held the "new aid" underscore the fact that a new custom duty was in fact being planned. In their first account of general receipts and expenses, rendered in 1279, a receipt of £2,000 is listed as profit "from the new aid for one year (de novi auxilii per unum anum)."[19] Yet, in the letter patent of 27 March 1275, which announced the appointment, the expiry date is set at a week after Easter in that year.[20] This would limit the Riccardi term to only twenty-five days. Since it is hardly likely that collection of the 1266 custom would have continued after the new system was introduced in June, the one-year term could not have begun in March. We may assume, instead, that the Riccardi had been collecting the "new aid" for nearly a year before this letter patent was issued, extending their grant while the new custom was being arranged. The parliament which would discuss the custom was originally summoned for February of 1275, and later prorogued to the following April.[21] The letter of 27 March was thus probably intended to continue the Riccardi collectorship until the parliament could approve the new customs system. The suspiciously round sum of £2,000 indicates that the merchants held the custom at farm. The low amount of the lease shows that they

[18]Robert L. Baker, "The English Customs Service, 1307-1343: A Study of Mediaeval Administration," *Transactions of the American Philosophical Society*, n.s., 51 (1961), p. 11. Baker discusses the credit usefulness of various sources of government revenue in his unpublished dissertation "The Administration of the English Customs Service, 1307-1343," pp. 89-90. (Firestone Library, Princeton University.)

[19]E 101/126/1.

[20]Gras, *Early English Customs*, p. 55 and n. 6. *C.P.R. 1272-1281*, p. 84. It is stated that the Riccardi are to collect the custom on all goods coming into the realm. Omission of any mention of exports may be due to the current embargo on the export of wool and other merchandise to Flanders.

[21]*Parliamentary Writs*, I, p. 1.

were making an immense percentage of profit. In short, the appointment as farmers of the "new aid" appears to have been an interim measure designed to give the king's chosen firm of bankers a profitable "retaining fee" for their future services, while at the same time helping to pay the bill for past advances.

While returning from the Holy Land Edward found that conditions were favorable for the establishment of a new custom. Wool, the major English export, was bringing high prices and could bear the charge of a duty.[22] Moreover, in the current economic war between England and Flanders the king had at hand a most useful means of preparing the minds and purses of wool growers and exporters for just such a duty.

The quarrel[23] had its origin in the continued delay of the English government in paying Countess Margaret of Flanders her promised annual fee of £600, which stood in arrears from the period of the barons' war. The countess, ageing but still formidable, collected the debt in 1270 by expelling all merchants of English dominions from Flanders and seizing their goods. When news of this action reached the Lord Edward on his way to the Holy Land, he hurried off recommendations for action to the king and council. By royal order all Flemings were to be arrested and all wool export prohibited until a parliament could discuss the matter. In the assembly held after the Translation of St. Thomas (13 October), it was ordained that all merchants—Flemish excepted—could export wool so long as they swore that the wool was not going to Flanders and that they personally had

[22] Eileen Power, *The Medieval English Wool Trade*, p. 77.

[23] This discussion of the Anglo-Flemish dispute is based on the following sources: H. Heben "Une guerre économique au moyen age; l'embargo sur l' exportation des laines anglaise (1270–1274)," *Études d'histoire dédiérs a Henri Pirenne*; A. Schaube, "Die Wollausfuhr Englands vom Jahre 1273," *Vierteljahrschrift für Social-und Wirtschaftsgeschichte*, 6 (1908), pp. 44–52; *Chronica Maiorum et Vicecomitum Londiniarum*, in *Liber de Antiquis Legibus* (Camden Society no. 34); Powicke, *Thirteenth Century*, pp. 621–23. A paper on this topic was read by Richard Bowers at the Fifth Biennial Conference on Medieval Studies, Western Michigan University, 21 May 1970, and should be published soon.

no dealings with the Flemish.[24] A system of licenses soon developed and no doubt made its contribution to the treasury.[25] It clearly did not bring Flanders to her knees. The looms were kept busy with wool passing indirectly to Flanders through "neutral" ports, as well as that shipped directly, and illegally, from England. The English government was not over-zealous in enforcing the regulations.[26]

This state of affairs changed dramatically when Edward took the reins of government into his own hands. Strict enforcement of the embargo was demanded of the king's officers. The special passes to privileged Flemish merchants were revoked, and they were given until Christmas to leave the realm.[27] A fleet was gathered from the Cinque Ports under the direction of the warden, Stephen de Penchester, and sent to sea against the flagrant smuggling.[28] Special inquisitions were launched, and the Hundred Rolls show that among the questions put to the jurors in

[24]The London Chronicle gives a clear outline of this stage of the quarrel. *Liber de Antiquis Legibus*, pp. 126-127. Cf. *C.P.R. 1266-1272*, pp. 462, 486.

[25]Power, *Wool Trade*, p. 76. For the licenses see *C.P.R. 1266-1272*, pp. 553-557, 558-567, 593-595, 685-687, 688-693, 698-699, 702-704, 712-713, *Ibid., 1272-1281*, pp. 13-27, 51-52, 54-55, 64-65, 67-68.

[26]Heben, *Études a Henri Pirenne*, pp. 13-15. *C.P.R. 1266-1272*, pp. 599-600, 625, 687-688, 702, 706. *Ibid., 1272-1281*, pp. 106, 114, 125, 146, 165, 185, 199. Cf. *Rotuli Hundredorum* I, pp. 385-386, 404 ff. For special favors allowed contrary to the regulations see *C.P.R. 1266-1272*, pp. 524, 526, 557-558, 647, 659.

[27]Heben, *Études a Henri Pirenne*, pp. 15-16. Power, *Wool Trade*, p. 76. *Liber de Antiquis Legibus*, pp. 159-160.

[28]*Liber de Antiquis Legibus*, p. 161. "Hoc anno, ante festum Sancti Michaelis et post festum . . . homines de Cinque Portibus in manu valida et armata cum navibus et galeis pluribus navigaverunt in mare et omnes quas invenerunt velificantes cum lanis versus Flandriam arestaverunt, et omnia bona Flandrensium in mare inventa ceperunt." Cf. *C.P.R. 1272-1281*, p. 12, where orders are sent to the barons and bailiffs of the ports of Dover, Winchelsea, Rye, Romney, Hythe, Hastings and Sandwich. They are to do what is enjoined on them by the constable of Dover who has instructions concerning the king's affairs touching the matter of the countess of Flanders.

London during the inquest of 1274 one asked for the names of violators of the wool embargo.[29]

Edward had no doubt achieved one of his objectives when shortly before returning to England he met Guy de Dampierre, son of Countess Margaret, at Montreuil-sur-mer and received his pledge on behalf of his mother to pay the damages owing to English merchants.[30] But the king was not merely recovering the £4,755 his merchants were owed in compensation for the seizures.[31] The sudden and strict enforcement of the embargo must have impressed on both alien and native merchants who had been busily engaged in evading an ill-enforced law that a new and moderate custom charged on normal trade would not be a bad substitute for the dangers of inquests and fines. The embargo can best be seen, in other words, as an instrument forged primarily with a new custom in mind; it provided Edward with the leverage he needed to assure the cooperation of wool growers and merchants.[32]

The outline for the customs administration found on the fine roll speaks of the custom "grante par touz les granz del realme e

[29]*C.P.R. 1272-1281*, pp. 68-69, 71, 86. *Rotuli Hundredorum*, I, pp. 385-386, 404 ff.

[30]The treaty is printed in *Foedera*, I, ii, pp. 513-514. Cf. *C.P.R. 1272-1281*, pp. 60, 187.

[31]Edward even granted Count Guy, six years later, £1,000 "in part subvention of the money in which the count was bound to the said merchants for the Flemish arrest." The Riccardi were ordered to pay this sum to proctors of the English and Irish merchants in November of 1280, out of the profits of the mint in their keeping. *C.P.R. 1272-1281*, p. 400. The king could afford to be generous. His bankers probably collected fines equal to three times the sum owed by the Flemish, and the custom would bring in twice the Flemish debt annually. See note 43, and Table I.

[32]Additional pressure seems to have been applied to the great Italian merchant-banking companies so important in the wool trade. A usury investigation was conveniently conducted while the custom was being planned, and several pardons were issued in late May and early June of 1275, suspiciously close to the establishment of the custom in mid-May. *C.P.R. 1272-1281*, pp. 91-93, 95, 128.

par la priere des comunes de marchanz de tot Engleterre."[33] But a draft of a letter patent preserved among the chancery files gives even more weight to the merchants. The grant had been made by "the community of merchants exporting wool and hides from our realm of England and our land of Ireland" and the great men had given their "benificent assent" to this grant.[34]

The text of the Irish grant of the custom reinforces the idea of the prior discussion with merchants. The great lay and spiritual lords and the commonalty of the realm have made the grant "at the instance and request of merchants." The lords of Ireland therefore made a similar grant "at the request and instance of the said merchants."[35]

In the words of Eileen Power, "It is quite clear that the tax had been negotiated with [the merchants] before the magnates were called in, and indeed negotiations must have been going on for some time, for it is certain that foreign merchants, too, must have been consulted."[36] Consultation with foreign merchants, and with the Italians in particular, would have been quite important, for the Italians held a predominant position in the wool trade of late thirteenth century England.[37] We do not know what form

33The original is on the Fine Roll for 3 Edward I, m. 24d. It is printed by Gras, *Early English Customs*, pp. 233-234, and calendared in *C.F.R. 1272-1307*, p. 47.

34C 202/H/2 no. 8.

35Several copies of the form of the Irish grant have been preserved. One was entered in the "Liber A," a contemporary register of documents considered to be of value. E 36/274 folio 191, m. 230d. There is another among the chancery warrants, C 47/10/13 no. 15, but it is so faded and the parchment so blackened that is is barely legible, even under untraviolet light. The grant is printed by Stubbs, *Select Charters*, pp. 443–444, and is calendared in *C.F.R. 1272-1307*, p. 60. Eleven lords individually made the grant to the king.

36Power, *Wool Trade*, p. 76.

37*Ibid.*, pp. 51-55. Adolf Schaube's study of wool export in 1273, based on the export licences, showed that foreign merchants were responsible for 65.1% of the trade, with 24.4% due to Italians alone. *Vierteljahrschrift für Social-und Wirtschaftsgeschichte*, 6, p. 68. But, as we will see below, the large number of sizable fines paid for illegal export casts serious doubt on the utility of these figures.

the consultations with foreign merchants took, nor what role the Riccardi may have played in them. On later occasions the king made contact with the entire Italian community in London through his merchants from Lucca.[38]

Although we know nothing about these negotiations, there is no doubt that the king employed the Riccardi in the enforcement of the embargo. This is a matter of significance in view of the important part played by the embargo in bringing about the 1275 custom.

The merchants of Lucca had, of course, violated the wool regulations along with the others, and the Hundred Rolls show that London juries were well aware of this fact. But royal pardons were not long in forthcoming.[39] Far from being prosecuted, the king's bankers profited from the violations of others. In obedience to a royal order five firms of their fellow-countrymen transferred £6,216 5s 0d. into Riccardi chests as fines, paying 10s. a sack for their illegally exported wool. Similar royal orders were sent to other merchants, for the total Riccardi receipt from these fines may have exceeded £13,000.[40]

A more active assignment was given to the king's merchants in April of 1274. In each of fifteen countries Lucasio was to conduct an inquisition, acting with a *clericus regis*, determining the names of offenders against the embargo and securing their arrest.[41] One merchant alleged that he had shipped his goods from

[38]Notably during the Welsh wars. See Chapter IV, Section 5.

[39]*Rotuli Hundredorum*, pp. 404 ff. *C.P.R. 1272-1281*, p. 125. A specific fine is entered on the pipe roll for the Riccardi, but it was soon pardoned. See the London membranes of E 372/120 and E 372/122. *C.C.R. 1277-1279*, p. 532.

[40]They acknowledged receipt of £13,321 15s. 0d. from fines and amercements on various merchants in their account covering 1272-1279. E 101/126/1. Although much if not all of this sum was probably made up of fines paid for violations of the embargo, only the five fines mentioned above can be definitely identified as belonging to this period. Four of them are on the London membrane of the pipe roll for 4 Edward I, E 372/120. Acquittances in the form of letters patent were issued for three fines, including one which is not included on the pipe roll. *C.P.R. 1272-1281*, pp. 91-92.

[41]*C.P.R. 1272-1281*, p. 48. *C.C.R. 1272-1279*, p. 86.

Hull before the prohibition, only to have them seized when the ship put into Sandwich. The case was investigated by Lucasio in association with John de Oketon, a clerk who had been a sheriff of York and a justice. After an inconclusive first investigation at Hull, they were ordered to summon a jury in that port to determine the facts of the case.[42] Edward clearly suspected that much of the wool laden at Hull and other Humber ports found its way to Flanders, for in late May he ordered Lucasio or his attorney to seize all wool ships found "in the Humber and at sea in the northern parts" bound for the continent. All the king's bailiffs were directed to lend their aid.[43] In carrying out this assignment the assistance of the fleet from the Cinque Ports evidently was necessary.

If the strict enforcement of the embargo and fines of 10s. a sack for violations gave Edward the leverage needed to establish new duties, the idea of paying a new custom was made more palatable by the sensible limitations on the size of the charges and their incidence. The rates established in 1275 were 1/2 mark (6s. 8d.) on each sack of wool or 300 woolfells, and 1 mark (13s. 4d.) on every last of hides. Thus only the major exports were taxed and there was no levy on imports.[44]

From the government's point of view the new duties avoided the defects of those levied since 1266. It would be easy to control collection on such bulky exports as wool and hides. Moreover, no exceptions were allowed, and the king was authorized to place collectors within as well as without liberties in the realm of England, the land of Ireland, and in Wales and the Welsh marshes. Thus London, which had escaped the 1266 duties, was now brought within a customs system. All these arrangements received formal approval in the first parliament Edward held after his coronation.

The administration of the customs was a model of simplicity.

[42] *C.P.R. 1272-1281*, pp. 50, 66.

[43] *Ibid.*, Powicke, *King Henry III and the Lord Edward* p. 616.

[44] A sack of wool was that quantity which weighed 364 English pounds. The last of hides was a measure of 200. Baker, *T.A.P.S.* 51, pp. 5, 7. Woolfells were the skins of sheep with the wool still attached.

Wool and leather were to be exported only through designated customs ports, ideally one for each county. In these ports two substantial citizens ("des plus leaus et plus pussaunz") were to be chosen by the community to act as collectors. They were given one foil or face of the so-called cocket seal used to attest payment of duties by exporters. The second foil of this seal was held by a controller named by the king. Two additional men were selected locally to keep watch on the other ports of the county, allowing no export of wool or leather without a sealed clearance. To provide time for this machinery to be established, all export of wool and hides as prohibited until the coming Trinity (9 June).[45]

The Riccardi were soon given an active part in setting up the machinery of collection. On 24 June Edward directed Lucasio to travel to "various places in the kingdom" with a clerk, Leoninus, son of Leoninus, on "business relating to the custom." At the same time Lucasio's attorney Bartolomeo Bandini was to accompany the clerk Ralph de Besages on a similar mission.[46] Although the assignments are not specified, it is likely that they concerned selection of local collectors in the ports. A few days earlier the sheriff of Gloucester had been notified that a Riccardi attorney, Guido of Lucca, was to accompany him when he elected the two townsmen in Bristol by oath of twelve good and lawful men. Their instructions to cause similar elections to be held in all the

[45]*C.F.R. 1272-1307*, p. 47. Gras, *Early English Customs*, pp. 223-224, The calendar obscures the important fact that men were sworn in all ports to watch for illegal export, while the seal was kept only in chief ports. Edward clearly granted that forfeitures resulting from violations of the custom should be paid to the lord of any liberty in which collectors were placed. C 202/H/2 no. 8. E 36/274 m. 230d. *C.F.R. 1272-1307*, pp. 47, 60, 114. When a writ *de intendendo* was issued for the Riccardi on 12 October 1275, they were given power of inquiry and arrest concerning concealment. *C.P.R. 1272-1281*, pp. 106, 144. In 1284-1285 the Riccardi accounted for some profits received for transgressions, but the sums are insignificant. E 372/133 m. 32d.

[46]*C.P.R. 1272-1281*, p. 97.

ports of the county probably refer to choosing men to guard against any illegal export.[47]

Establishing the customs administration had taken slightly longer than estimated and once in operation it probably required some adjustment. In May 1276, Donatus of Lucca and Ralph de Besages, Janian of Florence and William de Stainton were given orders summarized in their commission only as furthering "the business of the new custom, in divers places within the realm." Both of the Italians were Riccardi agents; Donatus had been named the society's collector at Sandwich and Janian of Florence can probably be identified as the "Janyn Tedaldy" who collected for the Riccardi in London.[48]

We may conclude from the evidence on the background and establishment of Edward's 1275 custom that it was created with the Riccardi in mind, that Riccardi involvement was the king's intention from the outset. The royal agent holding one foil of the cocket seal (the "un ke sera assigne par le rei" in the Fine Roll outline for the custom) would thus refer not to a salaried English official in each port, but rather to a Riccardi factor. Edward did not suddenly shift from a previous plan of centrally appointed controllers to a system based on the Riccardi.[49] From the time he returned from crusade the company was involved in the royal regulation of foreign trade and the profit derived from this control. The Riccardi farmed the "new aid"; they helped prepare the way for its replacement by the inquests concerning violations of the Flemish embargo and by collecting fines from the violators; they were employed in creating the administration of the new custom in the ports; finally, they had this custom almost entirely

47*C.F.R. 1272-1307*, p. 61. As early as 10 May the exchequer officials were told that the sheriffs in various counties were supervising the selection of men to serve with Riccardi attorneys in the customs ports. The names were to be enrolled by the treasurer and barons. E 368/48 m. 10. E 159/49 m. 34.

48*C.P.R. 1272-1281*, p. 141. *C.F.R. 1272-1307*, pp. 46-47.

49This is the suggestion of Baker, *T.A.P.S.*, 51, pp. 10-11. His views are more fully stated in his unpublished thesis, "The Administration of the English Customs Service, 1307-1343," p. 20.

in their hands for nineteen years, collecting its revenues to repay their advances to the king.

The merchants' official appointment as collectors of the custom in England and Wales is found in an entry on the Fine Roll, dated 21 May 1275.[50] But this formal commission does not determine the date on which the Riccardi were actually given their collectorship. A writ of aid, dated 19 May, ordered all bailiffs to aid the Riccardi who have been named receivers in England and Wales.[51] The grant of the custom for England was made by 10 May,[52] that for Ireland was dated 25 May.[53] A second writ of aid was issued on this last date, notifying the Irish bailiffs that the Italians were to be king's receivers.[54] The commissions to the Riccardi were thus made at the time of the grant of the "nova custuma" or slightly thereafter. Such commissions could hardly have been issued before the grants of the custom were formally approved. The evidence indicates that an agreement between the king and his bankers must have preceded the grants in Parliament by a considerable time.

It is significant that in these grants no term is set, that there is no idea of a farm involved, that no one loan is being negotiated on the security of the new duties. As duke of Aquitaine Edward was familiar with the farming of the customs of Bordeaux by the seneschal, and had himself used them to obtain a loan from King

[50]*C.F.R. 1272-1307*, pp. 45-46. The appointment is twice entered on the roll under this date. A draft copy of the grant was found misplaced in a file of documents from the reign of Edward III by Dr. E. B. Fryde, who called it to my attention. C 202/H/8 no. 26.

[51]C 202/H/2 no. 10. It is quite clear that Luke and his fellows have already been appointed. "Cum constituerimus Lucam de Luka mercatorem de Luka et socios suos custodes et ballivos nostros. . . . " This writ is calendared in *C.P.R. 1272-1281*, p. 90.

[52]C 202/H/2 no. 8, C 202/C/1 no. 67, cited by Powicke and Fryde, *Handbook of British Chronology*, p. 507.

[53]See note 35.

[54]*C.F.R. 1272-1307*, p. 60. *C.D.I. 1252-1284*, no. 1117. The fact that the outline for the customs administration was sent with this writ further links the Riccardi with the controllers mentioned in this document.

Louis for his crusading effort.[55] But something quite new and different was being attempted here, an experiment which would prove highly successful. Having created a customs system, Edward was now turning it over to a firm of merchant-bankers with the understanding that they would provide cash at his request. The foundations for "the Riccardi system" had been laid.

2. CUSTOMS PORTS AND PERSONNEL

We can draw up a list of the ports in which Italian and English collectors were placed to receive duties and issue sealed clearances. Although the most important English ports were consistently ports in the customs system, there was never any set number of them and slight variations occurred from year to year. The enrolled customs accounts provide the best evidence, since between 1279 and 1290 customs revenue is itemized under the constituent ports. From these accounts the basic list of customs ports in England includes the following: Newcastle (Northumberland), Hull (Yorkshire), Boston (Lincolnshire), Lynn and Yarmouth (Norfolk), Ipswich and Dunwich (Suffolk), London, Sandwich (Kent), Shorham, Seaford, Chichester, and Winchelsea (Sussex), Southampton (Hampshire), Weymouth (Dorset), Exeter (Devon), Haverford (Pembroke), Bodmin (Cornwall), Bristol (Somerset).

Though the original outline for the customs administration called for one main port in each county, it was obviously decided to include all the major centers for wool export along with other ports at intervals on the coast. As a result, some coastal counties had more than one customs port, and Durham had none. Considerations of control necessitated the establishment of customs ports on both coasts although Southampton was the only southern coastal city through which an appreciable amount of wool passed.[56]

[55] *C.P.R. 1266-1272*, pp. 24, 396. *Foedera*, I, i, p. 485. Powicke, *Thirteenth Century*, p. 281.

[56] Baker, *T.A.P.S.*, 51, p. 5.

In a number of instances the same collectors served several adjacent ports. Ipswich and Dunwich, for example, apparently formed one area of responsibility. Revenue from these ports is listed as a single sum in the accounts, often including duties paid for exports from Orford as well. Occasionally when only one or the other of the ports is listed there is no significant drop in the revenue collected. In the years for which information is available the same collectors operated in both ports.[57] Thus this stretch of coastline must have been served by a single two-foiled seal kept by two local collectors and one Riccardi agent.

The ports of Shoreham, Seaford, and Chichester are almost invariably named together in the enrolled accounts and once again the revenue is given as one sum. In the four years for which customs particulars have survived for more than one of these ports, the same Italian collector acted for the Riccardi in all of these ports, but they had different pairs of English collectors.[58]

The entries for Newcastle in the enrolled accounts regularly include some note concerning adjacent ports. Between 1279 and 1281 the revenue includes sums paid "for wool exported at

[57]Both ports are listed under a single sum of revenue in enrolled accounts covering 1279-1280, 1282-1286, 1287-1290. Orford is also mentioned in 1284-1286 and 1287-1288. The names of collectors are available for 1282-1284. E 372/124 m. 1d. E 372/134 m. 3. E 372/133 m. 32d. Cf. E 122/50/2 and E 122/50/7.

[58]There are particulars for Shorham and Seaford in 1285-1286 (E 122/135/2 and 2A); in 1284-1287 (E 122/135/3 and 3A); for Chichester, Seaford, and Shorham in 1288-1289 (E 122/32/2, E 122/135/4 and 4A); and for Chichester and Seaford in 1290-1291 (E 122/32/3, E 122/135/4B). During the course of the latter year Riccardo Honesti, who collected for the Riccardi, was replaced in both ports by an agent of the firm whose name appears as Rokjohan Canel'. When the customs administration was originally established, separate Italian collectors were named by the Riccardi for these three ports. *C.F.R. 1272-1307*, pp. 46-47. It is interesting to note that one of the local collectors at Shorham, John le Blak (or Blake), is known to have been a representative in the Easter parliament of 1275 at which the custom was discussed. Hilary Jenkinson "The First Parliament of Edward I," *E.H.R.* 25 (1910), p. 235. In November of 1289 he was exempted from assizes, juries and recognizances while attending to the custom. *C.P.R. 1281-1292*, p. 327.

Carlyle, Corbridge, Pembroke, and the Scottish marches for the same time (pro lanis transmittes apud Karl [egion] Corbrigg Pembroke et marchiam Scotie per idem tempus)";[59] in 1282-1286 duties are shown "from nearby ports [for wool] sent to Scotland (de portibus contiguis transeuntibus usque in Scotiam)."[60] These additional duties are listed separately in 1286-1290 as custom paid on wool sent from nearby ports to various destinations.[61] From these entries we can see that the small amounts of wool and leather shipped into Scotland or sent from Wales and the marches received their clearances at Newcastle.

The Cinque Ports may have been considered as a unit in the customs administration, with the many "member" ports and their "limbs" paying export duties through the port of Sandwich. Among the major member ports, Sandwich was the only one which appears in the accounts from 1279 to 1290, the period when individual customs ports are listed, and it is the only one to which a Riccardi controller was originally sent in 1275.[62] Local collectors were chosen in others of the Cinque Ports,[63] but they probably worked in conjunction with a Riccardi agent at Sandwich. Seaford would have been an exception to such an arrange-

[59] E 372/124 m. 1d.

[60] E 372/133 m. 32d.

[61] E 372/134 m. 3.

[62] *C.F.R. 1272-1307*, pp. 46-47.

[63] On 10 June 1275 exchequer officials were ordered to enroll the names of local collectors. The list includes collectors for Folkstone, Hythe, Romney, Fordwich, and Sandwich. E 368/48 m. 10. E 159/49 m. 34. A year later the bailiffs and barons of Sandwich, Dover, Hythe, Romney, Winchelsea, Rye, Hastings, and Pevensey were ordered to obey Luke of Lucca and Donatus Lambard, king's merchants, and Ralph de Droxford, king's clerk, keepers and bailiffs of the custom. But the writ gives no clue as to what this might mean for the administration of the customs. *C.P.R. 1272-1281*, p. 149. Some actual collecting was apparently done at Romney, for a roll of particulars covering 14-19 Edward I was sent to the exchequer. The total custom came to only 64s. 3-3/4d. E 122/147/11A. This is not mentioned in the enrolled account for 14-18 Edward I, but the merchants might have answered for even so small a sum as this in the account for 18-22 Edward I. We have only the overall totals for this account in the general account covering these years.

ment since, as we have seen, it was associated with two ports not belonging to the federation.

If the effort to sort out the customs ports for any particular period results in some uncertainty, we may take comfort from the fact that it confused contemporary exchequer officials as well. When the sheriff of Hereford was solemnly ordered in April of 1293 to have the collectors from the city of Hereford before the barons of the exchequer on the morrow of the Nativity of St. John the Baptist, he replied that there were no collectors in Hereford, nor anywhere else in his county.[64]

Evidence on customs personnel, like that on customs ports, is not complete. But we do know the names of most of the Riccardi controllers sent to the ports to begin collection in 1275. Donettus del Pape held the foil in Newcastle, Janian Theobaldi in London, Henry of Lucca in Boston, John Monsyre in Ipswich, Theobald Janiani in Hull, Mamettus Reinerii in Southampton, Guy Fornery in Shorham, Philip of Lucca in Yarmouth, James Janiani in Lynn, Hugh Donati in Chichester, Donatus of Lucca in Sandwich, Salomen of Lucca in Exeter, and Guydocus of Lucca in Bristol.[65] The list shows that at the outset the Riccardi drew upon the firms of their fellow-countrymen in order to staff the customs ports; several of the names can be identified as members of other Italian companies active in England.[66] This may have been a temporary measure, but we do not know exactly how long any of these collectors remained in their assigned ports. By the 1280's, when

[64] E 368/64 m. 65.

[65] *C.F.R. 1272-1307*, pp. 46-47, 61. Except for Guydocus, the names appear in a list of writs of aid dated 21 May. But a similar writ had been issued two days earlier for Janian Theobaldi who had at that time been named collector by the Riccardi in London. The draft of this writ has been preserved. C 202/H/2 no. 10. Cf. *C.P.R. 1272-1281*, p. 90. The names in this list have been spelled as in the calendar.

[66] James Janiani was a member of the Frescobaldi. *C.P.R. 1281-1292*, p. 311. Though it cannot be demonstrated, Theobald Janiani was probably also a member of this firm. Hugh Donati was one of a group of Florentines who farmed the Irish custom in 1282. Donnettus del Pape was also a Florentine, and one of the association headed by Diutautus Guillelmi which collected the "new aid" while Edward was on crusade. See note 12.

the evidence from customs particulars becomes available, the personnel representing the merchants of Lucca had changed almost completely. Throughout the period 1285-1294 the Riccardi agents are invariable described as being from Lucca (*de Luk'*).

The series of these particular accounts from the individual ports is incomplete, but does show that some of the Italians were collectors for nearly the whole period in one port or another. "Forner de Luk,' " for example, kept the foil at both Shorham and Seaford in 1285-1286, at Southampton in 1287-1288 and again in 1289-1290. If he may be identified, as seems reasonable, with the "Guy Fornery" appointed to Shorham in 1275, his association with the customs would cover at least fifteen years.[67]

Yet the Riccardi did not maintain representatives in all of the ports throughout the nineteen years of their control of the customs. Predictably, it was in the smaller ports that they relied on the local collectors without supervision, for it was here that they would run the least risk of loss. In February of 1278 the sheriff of Devonshire, along with selected men in the ports, was ordered to collect the custom in his county, turning over the proceeds to the Riccardi "who are unable to attend to the collection in that county at present."[68] Moreover, in the customs account for the tenth through fourteenth regnal years the merchants answer for receipts in six ports in which "they did not have custody . . . but did receive the proceeds by the hands of those deputed by the king's mandate." In each case the Riccardi received the money from the local collectors and accounted for it at the exchequer.[69]

67E 122/135/2 and 2A. E 122/136/2. He could not have continuously kept the seal in Shorham 1275-1285, for a Peter Jordani of Lucca represented the Riccardi there in 1282. *C.P.R. 1281-1292*, p. 19. The English collectors likewise tended to hold their positions for a number of years and often kept the job in the family when they stepped down. Those in Yarmouth in 1286 were still acting in 1293, while the Seaford collectors in 1285 remained until at least 1291. See E 372/134 m. 3 and E 122/148 nos. 1, 2, 3 for Yarmouth; E 122/135 nos. 2A, 3A, 4A and 4B for Seaford.

68*C.C.R. 1272-1279*, p. 442.

69E 372/133 m. 32d. E 372/134 m. 3. E 352/79 m. E 352/82 m. 19. These ports and the years when the Riccardi did not keep custody in their hands include the following: Winchelsea, 1279-1283; Bodmin, 1278-1284;

The collectors may have been chosen by the port communities, but it is likely that some were elected by the Riccardi themselves.[70] This was the case in Lynn in the early 1290's when Henry of Weymouth and Alan of Lindsey were chosen "by the king's merchants of Lucca on the king's behalf."[71]

This list could be extended by other evidence. There were no Riccardi agents in the Cornwall ports, for example, between 1285 and 1293,[72] and at Bristol the period of Riccardi absence can be extended from 1285 until the Riccardi fell from royal favor in 1294. Here they named Emeric de Pomeroy to hold their part of the cocket and all apparently went well. But when Emeric died his wife Matilda kept this seal, and kept using it, largely to her own profit, "to the manifest damage of the king," and "against the peace." She was not called to account until 1299.[73]

Exeter, 1278–1283; Weymouth, 1282–1283; Bristol, 1278–1283; Haverford, 1279–1283. The periods of time during which the Riccardi assigned local Englishmen to act for them in these ports might be extended through the years 1290 to 1294 in some cases, but since the customs account for those years does not itemize revenue by ports, merely giving yearly totals, information on collection on individual ports is not available.

[70] The sections of the account for Bristol revenues makes a point of stating that the collectors were appointed by the king and not by the merchants ("deputati fuerunt custodes per regem et non per mercatores"), implying that this was not always the case. E 372/134 m. 3. An order found on the King's Remembrancer Memoranda roll for this period strengthens the view that the Riccardi named some of the collectors. The keepers and collectors of the custom named by Baroncino and his fellows, merchants of Lucca, were to account before the exchequer officials at a set date. E 159/57 m. 3d. This could refer to Italian collectors in ports which the Riccardi retained in their immediate control, but coming just at the time the society was relying on local collectors in some ports, it may well refer to these Englishmen.

[71] E 368/63 m. 42d.

[72] E 372/134 m. 3. E 122/39/3 and 4.

[73] The Riccardi were informed of the fraudulent use of the cocket (after their fall) by letters from the mayor of Exeter and the sheriff of Devon. Federigo appeared before the treasurer and barons of the exchequer to urge that Matilda be arrested. She was seized, as were all her goods and chattels. When she gave an accounting (for the period 18–27 Edward I), it appeared that she had paid the Riccardi £49 13s. 10d. in 1291 and 1292,

Though it is not unexpected to see the Riccardi resorting to locals in secondary ports, it is more surprising that some of the rolls of customs particulars from important ports show no Italian names among the collectors. In the rolls for both Newcastle and Boston in 15-16 Edward I only two men account, and they were obviously Englishmen. Another Newcastle roll shows that in 16-17 Edward I the Riccardi added an English agent of the company in that port, and the third name appearing in 21-22 Edward I can also be linked to the company.[74] Yet the general Riccardi customs accounts for this period show nothing unusual; the merchants account for the revenue from these ports as before, with no explanatory notes or comments in the documents.[75]

The most puzzling piece of evidence on customs personnel is a commission, issued in May 1277, which named Janian of Florence and Hugh de Dignineton collectors of the custom throughout the realm.[76] The writ certainly does not mean that the Riccardi had lost control of the customs system, nor can it even be connected with those ports from which they had withdrawn their

---

but owed them a further £55 6s. 8-1/4d. Since Riccardi debts were at this time in the king's hands, this became a debt owed the crown. Edward seems to have been even more incensed by the fact that despite the prohibition of wool export Matilda used the seal to allow merchants to ship wool abroad and pocketed the duties. E 368/70 mm. 29d., 72d., and schedule between mm. 30 and 31. For the original accounts from Exeter see E 122/40/1A, 3, 4, 5.

[74] For Boston see E 122/5/1 and 2. For Newcastle see E 122/105/1 and 2, E 122/148/4. The Riccardi agent, Roland Trentacost, is not identified with the company in any way in the roll, but a slightly later reference in the King's Remembrancer's Memoranda Roll shows that he was "ad custodiam coketti apud Novum Castrum super Tynam per societatem Luk' deputatus." He may not have been a wise choice. In Hilary term 23 Edward I he was accused of exporting wool after the prohibition and was convicted by a jury and fined 40s. Orlandino da Pogio and Federigo acted as his pledges. The jurors did not believe his claim that he had sold the wool before the prohibition was declared. E 159/68 m. 33. E 368/66 m. 31.

[75] E 372/134 m. 3 deals with 15 and 16 Edward I. The later years fall into the last period of account in which information on individual ports is not given. E 372/143 m. 35d.

[76] *C.P.R. 1272-1281*, p. 210.

controllers, beginning in 1278.[77] The appointment of Hugh, a *clericus regis*, to act with an Italian in collecting royal revenues suggests that he was to function as a controller.[78] Janian, though not from Lucca, had been a Riccardi agent two years earlier and may still have been in their employ. At this time the chief representative of the Riccardi in England, Lucasio Natale, had just gone abroad,[79] the first of Edward's wars in Wales was being fought, and the Riccardi were undoubtedly busy in the king's service. Thus it is likely that Janian, acting for them, was temporarily placed in overall charge of collecting the customs and that he was given the official sanction of a royal commission, along with the watchful assistance of a royal controller.

Such a controller had been assigned to work with the chief Riccardi members one year earlier. This was John of Droxford, who would later rise to high household and exchequer rank and achieve the administrator's prize of a bishopric.[80] However, in both instances the controller's role was either of little importance or of short duration, for no orders to the Riccardi included his name nor did he account with the merchants at the exchequer.

3. THE IRISH CUSTOMS

A list of Irish ports in which customs dues were collected is more clear-cut than one for England, at least in the early years of

[77]Their account for 1275-1279 lists revenues from the custom for this period without any break at 1277. The average sum for these years is, in fact, higher than that for the succeeding four years. E 101/126/1. See Table I. If the Riccardi temporarily lost control of the customs we would expect some new commission to be issued for them before 1279 when the detailed accounts show they had controllers in most ports and received the revenues in the remainder. No such order can be found.

[78]As constable of Orford Castle Hugh had aided in Edward's vigorous measures against Flemish merchants. He worked with Luke Natale in the investigations concerning the embargo in the counties of Norfolk and Suffolk. At the time he received the customs commission he was also conducting an investigation of the Jews of England. *C.P.R. 1272-1281*, pp. 44-45, 48, 240.

[79]*Ibid.*, p. 196.

[80]*C.P.R. 1272-1281*, p. 144. See Tout, *Chapters*, II, pp. 16-17.

the reign. The same ports appear in customs accounts between 1275 and 1280. A few of these can be traced into 1282, but from this time we have no separate customs accounts and cannot determine whether changes were made. For the first years of customs administration, however, the following ports had collectors: Drogheda, Ross, Waterford, Cork, Youghal, Limerick, Dublin, Galway, Wexford, and five Ulster ports–Dundalk, Carlingford, Strangford, Carrickfergus and Coleraine. Apparently the only addition to these ports was made in 1278-1279 when Dingle in County Kerry received collectors.[81]

Yet the Riccardi control of the Irish customs followed an uneven course, and the firm did not enjoy continuous control of the customs administration. The original commission named Bonasius Bonante and his fellows, merchants of Florence, as well as Luke and his fellows.[82] Although the exact relationship between the Florentines and the Lucchesi is elusive, they seem to have been in some type of partnership. Collectors appointed by the Lucchesi held the foils in Ross, Waterford, Drogheda, and the Ulster ports, and the Florentines collected in Dublin, Wexford, Youghal, and Galway.[83] As we have seen, this arrangement was brought to an abrupt halt in March of 1277 when Bonasius was killed by "malefactors and disturbers of the king's peace." Since an accounting had not yet been held for customs revenues, the justiciar was ordered to seize all the Florentines' goods and to collect the debts owed them. Only later did the king relent and allow their possessions to be returned on the condition that they find sureties to guarantee an account.[84] Before Bonasius was killed he had turned over £100 of customs revenue to the Riccardi agents in Ireland, and they later accounted for a further £72 "received of

[81] *C.D.I. 1252-1284*, p. 415.

[82] *C.F.R. 1272-1307*, p. 60. Little information is available on Bonasius. In November of 1273 he had loaned the king £1,000 and the exchequer was ordered to repay it. E 403/1238.

[83] E 101/230/5 mm. 1, 7. Yet when an accounting twice a year is specified in September of 1276, only the Riccardi are mentioned. *C.P.R. 1272-1281*, p. 161. This would indicate that the primary responsibility went to the merchants of Lucca.

[84] *C.C.R. 1272-1279*, pp. 375-376.

the goods of the same Bonasius after his death. . . ."[85] Whether these obligations were an established feature of the shared customs control or the result of some specific transactions between the Italian companies does not appear. Six years later, when Bonasius' accounts were being audited, it was provided that his expenses as a collector were to be written off according to the discretion of his executors and the Riccardi.[86]

Robert de Ufford, the justiciar, had been ordered to take measures to carry on the customs administration in the ports formerly controlled by the Florentines, "that no damage be done to the king."[87] It seems likely that in Limerick and Galway the local collectors continued, without their Italian counterparts. In Youghal, Hugh Donati, a Riccardi collector in Chichester in 1275, appears as one collector. The arrangement in the remaining ports not under Riccardi supervision cannot be determined, but one by one they slipped into the control of the merchants of Lucca. By Michaelmas 1278 the entire system in Ireland was once more under the watchful eyes of Riccardi appointees.[88]

At this time the troubles which would plague their Irish operations had already begun. In September 1276 the firm was ordered to send to Dublin all the revenue they had received or were about to receive, there to be placed under their seals "in safety." The assurance of safe-keeping in sealed bags could hardly have been comforting, for the money was to be delivered in whole or in part to the justiciar and treasurer for the furthering of unspecified "important business."[89] Yet their worst fears were not con-

[85]E 101/230/5 m. 1.

[86]*C.C.R. 1279-1288*, p. 169.

[87]*C.C.R. 1272-1279*, p. 375.

[88]The Riccardi accounted for Limerick from 20 March, Youghal and Wexford from 5 April, Cork from 2 July, Dublin from 15 August, and Galway from 29 September. E 101/230/5 m. 1. Hugh Donati does not seem to have been working for the Riccardi at this time; the Riccardi accounts never mention the names of their own collectors. On 26 June 1278 a writ of protection was issued in favor of Percival Gerarduci and Bendino Panici and their fellows, merchants of Lucca "for as long as they engaged in the collection of the king's new custom in Ireland." *C.P.R. 1272-1281*, p. 273.

[89]*C.P.R. 1272-1281*, p. 161.

firmed, for it seems that an equivalent sum was later returned to them. Repayment may have been delayed as long as two years, for in February of 1278 the officials of the Dublin exchequer and the Justiciar were ordered to restore all the customs money to the Riccardi. At this time the officials were also warned to cease interfering with the receipt of the custom.[90]

For their part the Riccardi could not claim a clean slate. The measure of Irish wool which made up a sack was heavier than that used in England, and on this pretext they had been collecting disproportionately high customs. Merchants complained that though heavier the sack of Irish wool was equal in value to the sack of English wool; yet they had to pay 10s. duty instead of 6s. 8d. In November of 1276 Edward ordered the justiciar to see that standard rates were charged.[91] The indictment and conviction of the Riccardi in Ireland for clipping the king's coin came shortly after this.[92]

It is tempting to connect these illicit activities with their loss of control over the Irish customs after Michaelmas, 1280.[93] However, a more probable reason for the change can be found. The instances of friction between the Irish officials and the merchants of Lucca appear as symptoms of a basic antagonism which would make an effective administration of the customs very difficult.

[90]See note 110. *C.C.R. 1272-1279*, p. 441. Some further orders may have been necessary. A document preserved in the Chancery Files and calendared in *C.D.I. 1252-1284* no. 1615 (dated only 6-7 Edward I), ordered the justiciar and treasurer to pay over to Percival and his fellows, merchants of Lucca, by the hands of those through whom they had received it, all money from the custom on hides. To hasten action it was added that "the king marvels that he has had to send so many mandates on this subject." The reference to hides may be shorthand for the new custom in its entirety, or may indicate that the Irish officials had previously returned only the duties on wool and were trying to keep those on leather.

[91]*C.P.R. 1272-1281*, p. 172. For a case of extorting extra customs in England see *Ibid.*, p. 338.

[92]Chapter I, Section 4.

[93]E 101/230/6 m. 1. E 101/230/7 m. 1. A general account of the Irish customs was ordered on 10 June 1280, and on 29 June John de Fifhide was ordered to provide collectors in all customs ports. *C.P.R. 1272-1281*, pp. 354, 384 some of these collectors accounted in E101/230/5 m. 8.

The corruption and intimidation revealed four years later in the administration of Stephen de Fulburn, Bishop of Waterford and treasurer, must have been present at this time as well. If the Riccardi and the Irish administration were unable to work together, the king may well have decided that the Irish customs could be dropped from those sources of revenue committed to Riccardi control. They could be repaid by means which would cause less trouble.[94]

But it was not long before the intense strain of financing his second war in Wales brought the king's decision once again to divert the flow of Irish customs to his bankers. Not only the customs duties but also the profits of the mint were to go to the Riccardi, who would lend equivalent sums for the war effort. The orders were issued 4 April 1282, from Devizes. Although the Justiciar and exchequer officials were instructed to pay the revenues to the Riccardi, there is no indication that the merchants were personally to collect in the ports.[95]

The documents show that one large payment was made to the Riccardi pursuant to the king's command. This was the sum of £1,500 turned over to them at Dublin on 10 June 1282. But the Irish officials proved reluctant to let the money go. On the morrow of St. Bartholomew the Apostle (25 August), Walter, deacon of Waterford, collected £200 from the Riccardi in the name of Fulburn and by his order. The bishop himself claimed £600 on the vigil of All Saints (31 October) and took the remaining £700 on the Thursday following (5 November) Only the last sum is known to have been spent for the Welsh campaign, going for wine and food sent to the king's army.[96]

[94] For the charges against Waterford see *C.D.I. 1252-1284* nos. 2332-2338.

[95] *C.C.R.V., 1277-1326*, p. 213. The exchequer officials were to send the king letters received from the merchants testifying the amount they had received. On the basis of these accounts between the king and his bankers could be adjusted.

[96] E 101/230/5. The Riccardi received a letter of acquittance for the £1,500 on November 5. One copy of the letter was given to Bendino Panici to keep in witness of the transactions; the other was sent to his associate Riccardi members in England.

Before the Irish officials had reclaimed all the revenues they had turned over to the Riccardi, the king decided to try to simplify the administration of the customs in Ireland by resorting to a farm of the revenues. A group of Florentine merchants headed by Hugh Pape, James Donati, Hugh del Post, Thorisianus Donati, and Hugh Donati were given complete control of the seals in return for the payment of £1,000 each year into the Dublin exchequer. The term of the grant was set for five years.[97] Only five months had elapsed since Edward ordered the revenues to be delivered to the Riccardi.

No arrangement for the administration of Irish customs pleased the king for long. The five-year term promised to the Florentines was quickly cut to two years. This sudden end to the farm indicates that Edward had learned that he was being cheated. An overview of the customs and other revenues in Ireland, made in 1284, set the yearly value of the customs at 2,000 marks "for which sum it can be committed to farm."[98] At All Saints (1 November) 1284, the collection of the duties was once again committed to the king's bankers. The conduct of Bishop Fulburn came under scrutiny and the king's experiments with the Irish customs came to an end.[99] From this time until the summer of 1294 the Riccardi kept the customs seals in Ireland.

[97]The appointment was first made 24 September 1282 without mention of the duration of the grant or any arrangement for a farm. Two days later these were specified. *C.P.R. 1281-1292*, p. 36. E 101/230/7 m. 2. *C.F.R. 1272-1307*, pp. 169-170. Although Hugh Donati had served the Riccardi at one time, the group of Florentines was acting without any connection with the Luchese society. In their account for the farm they speak of their dealings with the Riccardi in terms of transactions with another firm. E 101/230/7 mm. 1, 1d.

[98]*C.D.I. 1252-1284*, no. 2329. M. D. O'Sullivan makes the plausible connection between the lease of the customs for 500 marks less than its true value and the thoroughly corrupt administration of Stephen Fulburn, bishop of Waterford, who was both Justiciar and Treasurer. "Italian Merchant Bankers and the Collection of the Customs in Ireland, 1275-1311," *Medieval Studies Presented to Aubrey Gwynn, S. J.*, pp. 172-173.

[99]E 101/230/7 m. 1d. For the investigations of Waterford see *C.P.R. 1281-1292*, p. 127, *C.D.I. 1252-1284*, no. 2332 ff.

4. CUSTOMS REVENUE

The complete series of accounts of customs revenue kept between the king and his bankers allows us to determine with some precision the amount of money which the society collected from the customs in England. This information is summarized in Table I.[100] During the nineteen years of their control the Riccardi rendered six accounts, for periods ending in 1279, 1281, 1286, 1290, and 1294. With the exception of the first account, all these were enrolled on the pipe rolls. The accounts which cover 1279 to 1290 not only give total receipt but also itemize the revenue collected each year from the various ports. The first and last accounts, however, are not concerned solely with the customs; in presenting general Riccardi receipt and expenditures in 1272-1279 and 1290-1294 they give only lump sums for customs revenue. This is broken up into yearly figures in the 1290-1294 account, but not in that for 1272-1279. In neither case is the distribution of the revenue among the various ports outlined.

In the first five years of their control the Riccardi collected an average of approximately £10,367 annually. This figure dropped to about £8,900 for 1282-1287, but rose to nearly £11,323 in 1289-1294. For the entire nineteen years the annual average stands at £9,950.

Between 1275 and 1280 the evidence on the Irish customs revenues is just as complete as that given by the English accounts. The total sums collected by the Riccardi in Ireland appear in their account of the English custom on the pipe roll. In addition, since the particulars on which this enrolled account is based have been preserved, we have the customs revenue itemized according to the ports as well as to the amounts paid into the Irish exchequer. The Riccardi regained control of the Irish customs in 1284, but our evidence becomes once more available only in 1285. Six rolls of

[100] The statistics on wool export taken from these accounts are printed in E. M. Carus-Wilson and Olive Coleman, *England's Export Trade, 1275-1547*, pp. 36-38. In the introduction to this book they argue that despite smuggling the figures are reasonably accurate.

receipt of the Dublin exchequer show the customs collected in Michaelmas terms of 1285-1289, 1290-1291, and 1292-1293, and a similar printed document covers the period July 1291 to May 1292. We can supplement these documents with the enrolled Treasurer's account for 1285-1291. This information is summarized in Table II.

If we consider the 1,000 marks sent for Welsh works, the missing year 1284-1285, and the gap from Michaelmas term 1293 to July of 1294, it is certain that the total amount of customs revenue received by the Riccardi in Ireland would exceed £22,000. From the combined English and Irish accounts we can see that the overall Riccardi receipt from the customs was at least £211,000.

We may feel certain that when the merchants of Lucca charged themselves with these receipts they actually did collect at least the amount stated. But might they not have collected much more and kept the difference without the king's knowledge? There was certainly no one in a customs port who would have a burning desire to see that the royal government was never cheated. The wool exporter would hardly object to paying the collectors a substandard rate which would find its way into the collector's pocket and never onto the account roll. The unpaid local collectors would be anxious to please their friends and business associates and might not find some material reward for their service objectionable. For the Italians holding the other half of the seal, an undervalued return of the port revenues would give them immediate profit without diminishing the king's debts to them which were being repaid by the customs revenue.[101] We have no real evidence of false returns, but in hunting for corruption the argument from silence is not very powerful.

Yet if some extra profit was being made there were strong factors at work to keep it within bounds. The customs formed the base for a system highly profitable to the Riccardi. They would be unwise to risk their profits and privileges as the king's bankers by flagrant abuse of the opportunities it presented. The

[101] See Baker, *T.A.P.S.*, 51, pp. 11-12.

risk of detection would be too great. Through the collection of the "new aid" and the system of wool export licenses which preceded the 1275 custom, Edward and his advisers must have had some idea of what could reasonably be expected from the customs. Moreover, it is significant that the duties show a definite increase during the period of Riccardi controllership. An increase in the amount of wool exported from England probably could not be foreseen by the government and so provided an opportunity for undeclared profit by the collectors. The increase could, of course, have been actually a more substantial rise than the collectors reported, but we do know that they did not annually report the figure from the previous year and stow the difference in their strong boxes.

The honesty of the collectors may have been as much a worry to the society as to the king. Several years after they were deprived of the customs the Riccardi discovered that one of their agents, Cionello Ghirardinghi, had been pocketing sums ranging from 50 marks to £100 on each account. The Lucca partners hoped that the London agents could check their customs accounts, which had been seized by the government along with their other records, and set the exact date of each account. Then they could charge the offender interest on the sums fraudulently retained.[102]

Aside from any question of false returns, the revenue from the customs duties was not the sole advantage the Riccardi gained from holding the seals. As one of the great Italian firms dealing in wool they must have found the detailed information available on the exports of rival firms of real value to them. Whenever the Riccardi shipped out their own wool the duty could be simply, and legitimately, entered on the roll as if it were paid in cash. Often they must have been able to convince the local collectors working with them to overlook their wool export altogether.[103] Finally, as collectors their agents would be in a position to expect

[102] E 101/601/5, undated letter, p. 45.

[103] The series of customs accounts from individual ports (E 122) does, however, show many instances of the customing of Riccardi wool.

a constant supply of small additional fees, gratuities, and the like to lubricate the process of customs transactions.[104]

The government probably expected, and in general disregarded, these fees and gratuities, but the cocket fees charged for affixing the customs seal were occasionally written into the receipt portion of an account. The sums involved were very small. Between 1282 and 1286 the Riccardi accounted for £69 12s. 0d. from this source; in 1286-1288 the amount was £44 0s. 11d.; and in 1288, £17 19s. 3d.[105] Cocket profits are mentioned only in the accounts which deal solely with the English customs; in other years and in Ireland the fees may have simply been allowed as added profit.

In ports where weighing rights were not the prerogative of some lord, the Riccardi may have collected tronage fees for the weighing of wool prior to export. If so, they were not obligated to report this profit, for the accounts make no mention of tronage fees. Yet in one case we know they were to answer to the exchequer. In the spring of 1291 the king recovered from John of Brittany the fee of a halfpenny a sack of wool weighed on the king's beam at the fair of St. Botolph, Boston. He then allowed the Riccardi to begin collecting this fee, with the instructions that they were to account for it at the exchequer.[106]

Maintaining agents in the ports involved a certain amount of expense, and the Riccardi were given allowances for the costs they incurred. Information available from 1279-1294 shows an annual average allowance of £279. Until 1282 it seems that a set sum of £276 was given them. In the latter half of the period of

[104]See Baker, *T.A.P.S.*, 51, pp. 9-10.

[105]E 372/133 m. 32d. E 372/134 m. 3. In 3 Edward II the Frescobaldi of Florence, who were the king's bankers at that time, asked to have the wages and expenses for collecting that had been allowed the Riccardi. The rolls were searched and these allowances are cited. The Frescobaldi were given expenses on the basis of these figures. E 159/83 m. 52. Easter Recorda. Dr. E. B. Fryde supplied this reference.

[106]E 368/62 m. 45d. The date is 23 June 1291. The king's beam at the Boston fair may have been used for other purposes than determining the customs owed on wool, etc., but this seems to have been one of its functions. As a custom port Boston is regularly called St. Botolph in the enrolled accounts and in the particulars.

Riccardi control, however, allowances were probably more directly related to actual expenses. The annual figures for 1290-1294 show the slight variations we would expect, and the totals for 1282-1286 and 1286-1290 cannot be neatly divided into the set figures of the previous years. In Ireland the merchants received £400 to cover their costs in the five years 1275-1280, but this was soon increased to a fixed allowance of £120 each year. (See Table III.)

Riccardi control of the customs came suddenly to an end in the summer of 1294. In a laconic order sent 29 July, the king ordered "his dear Orlandinus de Podio and associates, the king's merchants of Lucca" to give up the cocket seals without delay to men assigned to collect in the various ports.[107] So important had been their control of the customs that it is this order which marks the collapse of the system of government finance based on the Riccardi, as well as the beginning of the failure of the merchants' fortunes in England.

[107] E 159/68 m. 82d.

Table I Riccardi Customs Receipt in England, 1275-1294[108]

23 May 1275 - 19 May 1279	£43,801	18s.	9d.	E 101/126/1
19 May 1279 - 19 May 1280	8,108	13	5	E 372/124 m. 1d.
19 May 1280 - 13 April 1281	8,688	19	3-1/2	*Ibid.*
Various ports, 1279-1283[109]	409	7	8-1/2	E 372/134 m. 3
Easter 1281 - Easter 1282	8,411	19	11-1/2	E 372/125 m. 1
Easter 1282 - Easter 1283	8,604	19	3	E 372/133 m. 32d.
Easter 1283 - Easter 1284	10,273	13	3-1/2	*Ibid.*
Easter 1284 - Easter 1285	9,098	7	0	*Ibid.*
Easter 1285 - Easter 1286	8,094	13	6-1/2	*Ibid.*
Easter 1286 - Easter 1287	8,023	6	10-3/4	E 372/134 m. 3
Easter 1287 - Easter 1288	8,960	3	10	*Ibid.*
Easter 1288 - Easter 1289	9,976	6	1-3/4	*Ibid.*
County of Cornwall, 1285-1289	55	0	0	*Ibid.*
Easter 1289 - Easter 1290	10,358	3	2-1/2	*Ibid.*
Easter 1290 - Easter 1291	11,315	0	14-1/2	E 372/143 m. 35d.
Easter 1291 - Easter 1292	10,222	2	8	*Ibid.*
Easter 1292 - Easter 1293	12,908	11	8	*Ibid.*
Easter 1293 - Easter 1294	11,811	3	5-1/2	*Ibid.*
Total	£189,167	2	3-1/2	

108Since the deductions made from the king's debt to the Riccardi were based on the totals given in the accounts, these figures are presented here uncorrected. The occasional deviation between them and the result obtained by adding the composite sums is never more than a few pounds. Whenever the pipe roll was not legible, the corresponding chancellor's roll was used.

109Winchelsea, 7-11 Edward I; Exeter, 6-11 Edward I; Weymouth 10-11 Edward I; Bristol, 6-11 Edward I; Bodmin, 6-12 Edward I; Haverford, 7-11 Edward I.

Table II Riccardi Customs Receipt in Ireland, 1275-1294

4 May 1275 - 29 Sept. 1280	£5,171	18s.	6-1/4d.	E 101/230/5 m. 1
4 May 1275 - 11 April 1277	1,000	0	0	*Ibid.* E 101/126/1
(1275 - 1280)[110]	1,392	2	6	E 101/230/5 m. 1 E 372/124 m. 1d.
29 Sept. 1285 - 29 Sept. 1286	675	0	0[111]	E 101/231/6 no. 1 mm. 17, 18
29 Sept. 1286 - 29 Sept. 1287	1,202	19	10-1/4	*Ibid.*, no. 2 m. 7
29 Sept. 1287 - 29 Sept. 1288	1,208	11	10-1/4	*Ibid.*, no. 3 m. 5
29 Sept. 1288 - 29 Sept. 1289	1,311	16	1-1/4	*Ibid.*, no. 4 m. 4
29 Sept. 1290 - 29 Sept. 1291	1,587	13	4-3/4	*Ibid.*, no. 5 m. 5
5 Aug. 1285 - 2 Aug. 1291	2,997	1	4-1/4[112]	E 372/139 m. 8
July 1291 - May 1292	1,560	16	0-3/4	*C.D.I. 1285-92*, no. 1112
29 Sept. 1292 - 29 Sept. 1293	1,343	7	10-3/4	E 101/232/5 m. 13
9 June 1292 - 24 June 1294	836	18	2-1/2[113]	E 372/139 m. 8
Total[114]	£20,268	5	9-1/4	

[110]The pipe roll gives this sum with the confusing note "de alio tempore," but the particular account shows that it was received by the merchants from the Dublin exchequer. In E 101/230/14 m. 1 we find that £725 10s. 10d. were paid to the Riccardi as part of 2,088 marks 2s. 6d. (equal to £1,392 2s. 6d.) received at the exchequer from the custom. This possibly represents a repayment of those sums from customs revenue which the particular accounts show were paid into the Dublin exchequer by the Riccardi between 1275 and 1280–£392 11d. 8d., £57, and £578 6s. 8d.–plus the duties collected by the Itish administration in the ports which had been held by Bonatius and the Florentines, during the interval between Bonatius' death and the acquisition of the seals for these ports by the Riccardi. As we have seen, they did not control Cork, Youghal, Limerick, Dublin, and Wexford for varying lengths of time, each a period of about a year. Judging from the accounts, these ports might have brought in a total of £475 to £500 a year. Thus the total of the revenues collected there plus the sums paid into the Irish exchequer could be £1,392.

[111] The reason for this low sum is that 1,000 marks were sent by the Riccardi during this period for the work on Welsh fortifications. A writ of *allocate* for this amount was sent to the Irish exchequer on 12 June, 1286. *C.D.I. 1285-1292*, no. 248.

[112]This figure is made up two sums from the Treasurer's account for these years which are not found in the particular rolls of receipt.

[113]This sum appears on the Treasurer's account, but not on the particular rolls of receipt.

[114]This total does not, of course, include the missing year, 1284–1285, nor the period from Michaelmas term 1293 to July of 1294.

Table III Allowances for Customs Expenses in England

11 May 1279 - 13 April 1281	£552	0s.	0d.	E 372/124 m. 1d.
Easter 1281 - Easter 1282	276	0	0	E 372/125 m. 1 E 352/74
Easter 1282 - Easter 1286	1,131	13	11	E 372/134 m. 3
Easter 1286 - Easter 1290	1,083	19	11-1/2	*Ibid.*
Easter 1290 - Easter 1291	282	5	11-1/2	E 372/143 m. 35d.
Easter 1291 - Easter 1292	284	14	0	*Ibid.*
Easter 1292 - Easter 1293	283	11	11	*Ibid.*
Easter 1293 - Easter 1294	287	7	9	*Ibid.*
Total	£4,184	13	6	

Allowances for Customs Expenses in Ireland

1 August 1275 - 29 Sept. 1280	400	0s.	0d.	E 372/124 m. 1d.
1 Nov. 1288 - 1 Nov. 1289[115]	120	0	0	C 62/65 m. 2
1 Nov. 1289 - 1 Nov. 1290	120	0	0	C 62/67 m. 5
1 Nov. 1290 - 1 Nov. 1291	120	0	0	C 62/68 m. 4
1 Nov. 1291 - 1 Nov. 1292	120	0	0	C 62/69 m. 2

[115] The writ orders this payment "as has been done in previous years."

Chapter IV The Welsh Wars

War was the chief emergency confronting medieval kings and war imposed the most sudden and severe strains on the royal finances. The latter part of Edward's reign would bring warfare on several fronts; in the first half of the reign it was limited to Wales. But even this earlier campaigning consumed royal treasure at an alarming rate. Warfare began in Wales soon after Edward returned from crusade, when in November of 1276 the uneasy truce in Anglo-Welsh relations (dating from the 1267 Treaty of Montgomery) was ended by Prince Llywelyn's refusal to do homage. Edward's decision to "go upon him as a rebel and disturber of our peace"[1] launched the first of several campaigns which would result in the complete conquest of Wales. Since one of the purposes of Edward's special relationship with the Riccardi was to provide cash for fiscal emergencies, we should find significant Riccardi support for the financing of the first war in 1276-1277, the second in 1282-1283, and the suppression of the revolt of 1287.[2]

Although the rising cost of warfare seems to be one of the more persistent phenomena of European history, there are clear and

[1] *C.C.R. 1272-1279*, p. 359.

[2] The importance of the Riccardi in the Welsh Wars has been briefly discussed by T.F.T. Tout, *Chapters in the Administrative History of Medieval England,* II, pp. 29, 112-113, J. E. Morris, *The Welsh Wars of Edward I,* p. 140, and E. B. Fryde, *Cambridge Economic History of Europe,* III, p. 456. By the time of the 1295 Welsh rebellion the Riccardi were no longer king's bankers.

identifiable reasons why Edward I should feel the pinch in his Welsh campaigns. Perhaps most important is his "marked tendency to put warfare on a paid basis," to replace the feudal quota with the paid retinue, and to supplement that with large levies of foot soldiers drawn from the shires and marches. As Sir Maurice Powicke has observed, "the king was no longer content to rely upon the feudal host. He needed longer and more competent service; he wished to combine cavalry with crossbowmen and archers, and sometimes with masses of infantry, under trained and trusted captains. He had to plan in terms of campaigns, not of martial demonstrations."[3]

Edward thought it necessary to resort to paid cavalry, not only because the feudal forty-days' service expired all too soon, but also out of a desire to achieve something like effective organization and subordination of command. Even though he might summon men to serve him in arms on the basis of their feudal obligation, he often found it convenient to pay them wages once their feudal service had expired, and sometimes even from the outset of a campaign. The first and last summons of the 1282-1283 war, and the only summons for the war against Rhys ap Maredudd, were "affectionate requests" for service *ad vadia nostra*, addressed largely to those who would serve as bannerets. The earls stood on their dignity and refused to accept pay. Not only was it degrading, but it would also tend to lessen the king's dependence on their unpaid cooperation. But lesser men willingly pocketed the king's coin when it was offered, and large bodies of paid cavalry would be found serving in all the Welsh campaigns. Many barons led contingents of horse much larger than their feudal retinues, and they were supplemented with mounted Gascon mercenaries.[4]

To this traditional core of the army Edward I added large numbers of foot soldiers, with archers now predominating over spearmen. They were predominantly Welsh or marcher foot, although English levies from neighboring shires were also summoned. In

[3] *Thirteenth Century*, p. 543.

[4] Michael Powicke, *Military Obligation in Medieval England*, pp. 96-103. John E. Morris, *The Welsh Wars of Edward I*, pp. 68-71.

mustering these communal troops Edward introduced the systematic use of the commissioners of array. His decision to allow foot soldiers "to share the place of honour with cavalry" has been termed a military revolution.[5]

When to these forces we add the king's household knights and consider the close administrative supervision of the household exercised by its wardrobe clerks,[6] we can see that the Edwardian army could be highly effective. Michael Powicke's evaluation is that "the army of Edward I achieved a balance between contractual, feudal and communal troops which exceeded anything achieved before or after," and Sir Maurice Powicke labeled the army of 1277 "the best controlled, as it was the best led, that had been gathered in Britain since the Norman Conquest."[7]

But if effective, it was also highly expensive. Bannerets received 4s a day, while other mounted men might draw daily wages ranging from 2s. to 6d., depending on the quality of the armor and mounts with which they fought. The footmen naturally served for less, but still had to be given 2d. a day. Moreover, they had to be paid every three or six days, since they bought their own supplies out of their salaries, with the crown acting as middleman. For the same reason the various workmen employed with the armies were paid as frequently. The numbers of foot fluctuated widely, the men often serving short terms, but as many as 15,000 might be in the royal pay in times of great activity.[8]

The emphasis on pay was not the only cause of financial stress. In both the first and second wars the king's plan featured an irresistible advance of the main force, hewing roads through the Welsh forests, building strong bases of operation, supplied with great quantities of matériel by sea as well as by land. Although an operation on a smaller scale, the suppression of the 1287 revolt

5See Michael Powicke, *Military Obligation*, Chapter VII. The quotation is from p. 118.

6See Tout, *Chapters,* II, Chapter VII, Section VI.

7Michael Powicke, *Military Obligation*, p. 97. F. M. Powicke, *Thirteenth Century*, p. 411.

8Morris, *Welsh Wars*, pp. 49–54, 92–93. F. M. Powicke, *Thirteenth Century*, p. 411.

was characterized by overwhelming military strength in proportion to the threat it had to meet. This care and thoroughness, as well as the determination to carry out the plan, stood in contrast to earlier English campaigns in Wales, but the effort was bound to be costly. The most eloquent testimony to this determination, and the price unavoidably attached to it, are the massive castles erected on the sea borders of North Wales as insurance against the success of any future Welsh rising.[9]

The need for the ready cash the Riccardi could supply was intensified by the suddenness with which the wars broke out both in 1282 and again in 1287. It was with complete and bitter surprise that the king received the news that Dafydd, the brother of Prince Llywelyn, who had been a much favored English ally in the first war, had opened hostilities against him with a night attack on Hawarden castle.[10] If Edward harbored any hopes that this would be war on a small scale they were quickly quashed, for new castles at Flint and Rhuddlan were soon under assault, and Llywelyn had joined his brother in arms.[11] Likewise, the rebellion of Rhys ap Maredudd in 1287 came at a time when the king felt that affairs in Wales were well settled—so much so that he had turned to continental business which had been postponed for years and had crossed over to Gascony. Rhys had been outstanding among the loyalist Welsh lords throughout two wars. But now, chafing under what he considered the intolerable restrictions of English shire jurisdiction and the dominant position of

[9] See J. G. Edwards, "Edward I's Castle-Building in Wales," *Proceedings of the British Academy* 32 (1946). Even more detailed information is available in H. M. Colvin, ed., *The History of the King's Works,* I, Chapter V (by R. A. Brown), Chapter VI (by A. J. Taylor) and II, Appendix C.

[10] This attack, in fact, surprised Prince Llywelyn as well. He wanted no war with Edward, but realized he would have to lead his people or be supplanted by Dafydd. See J. G. Edwards' Introduction to *Littere Wallie Preserved in Liber A in the Public Record Office*, pp. lxi–lxix.

[11] Morris, *Welsh Wars*, pp. 152–153. Powicke, *Thirteenth Century*, pp. 420–422, writes "Edward never acted more quickly and strenuously than he did when he heard of this rebellion. He could not gauge the extent of the danger, for he could not, as in 1276–1277 methodically prepare his way for his main attack. He had been taken by surprise and would run no risks and brook no delays."

Robert de Tibetot as Justiciar, he broke out in revolt on 8 June 1287.[12]

The need for ready cash in the wars is obvious. A preference for salaried troops, a strategy of bringing overwhelming force to bear on the enemy, the need to react quickly in the face of sudden risings, a program of massive castle-building–all required a steady flow of silver to Wales. It was the great advantage of the "Riccardi system" that it assured the flow of cash necessary for the success of these ambitious undertakings.

Since the wardrobe was the arm of English government mainly concerned with war finance, the evidence concerning the role of the Riccardi is to be found primarily among wardrobe records.[13] From the enrolled wardrobe accounts the Riccardi contribution to the financing of the wars can be assessed in broad terms, and where the particulars on which these accounts are based have survived, somewhat fuller information may be obtained. Orders and acquittances in the form of letters close or patent fill in some gaps. The evidence for the financing of these campaigns is less complete than we might wish; we cannot chart the incidence of every source of royal income to determine precisely how much revenue the king could spare for Wales at each particular stage of a campaign. But the surviving documents for the first two wars show convincingly, if generally the importance of the credit structure based on the Italians; for 1287, when a more quantitative analysis is possible, this importance is confirmed.

1. THE FIRST WAR, 1276-1277

The wardrobe account for 5 Edward I, a period conveniently coinciding with the duration of this war, is particularly sparing in

12 Morris, *Welsh Wars*, pp. 205-206. Powicke, *Thirteenth Century*, pp. 438-439. D. L. Evans, "The Later Middle Ages (1282-1536)," *A History of Carmarthenshire*, ed. Sir John E. Lloyd, pp. 203-204.

13 Wardrobe accounts present serious difficulties of interpretation, as Tout noted, *Chapters*, II, p. 85. He speaks of "the bewildering and varying number of accounts, the feeling that you have never got even all the recorded facts before you" and the "complicated system of short term loans and their continued renewal and occasional repayment. . . ."

the explanations attached to its composite figures. Nonetheless, the contribution of the merchants of Lucca is readily seen in broad terms. Thomas Bek, keeper of the wardrobe, acknowledged a receipt of £22,476 from the Riccardi between 20 November 1276 and 20 November 1277.[14] This sum must be seen in relation to the total amount of war expenses entered in this account —more than £20,220[15]—as well as the cost of the war to the English government, calculated by J. E. Morris to be £23,149.[16] The Riccardi advances during this period thus represent a greater sum than the wardrobe spent on the campaign, and fell only slightly under one estimate of the total cost of the war.

The enrolled wardrobe account for 6 Edward I shows, moreover, that the financial strain imposed by this war continued to be felt well beyond its conclusion in November of 1277. The very moderate wardrobe expenses in the account for the postwar period, the sixth regnal year (20 November 1277 to 20 November 1278), were met only by borrowing from the Riccardi a further £18,233 5s. 6d. out of the total receipt of £19,316 7s. 3-1/2d.[17] This brings the Riccardi contribution to £40,709 5s. 6d. out of a total wardrobe receipt for this period of £57,030 4s. 1-1/2d.

It must be emphasized that in both of these documents the figures represent Riccardi advances for all the normal expenditures met by the wardrobe, as well as for the special needs of a period of war. The extant "rolls of particulars" for this war give information on the specifically military employment of only a small portion of this money. But they do help to illustrate the ways in which many of the Riccardi advances were utilized. For example, in July, while cutting his way through the coastal forests of North Wales, Edward ordered his merchants to pay 2,000

[14] E 372/123 m. 23.

[15] Tout found that in this account war expenses could be separated from ordinary *mises* and that the former came to over £20,200. *Chapters,* II, pp. 112–113.

[16] Morris, *Welsh Wars*, p. 140. This figure, of course, can be only a rough approximation.

[17] E 372/123 m. 22d. Cf. Tout, *Chapters,* II, p. 113.

marks to certain paymasters in charge of the wages of troops in Carmarthenshire and Cardiganshire.[18] Evidently their requirements at this time were greater than had been expected, for the Riccardi provided £2,000 to one of them, Ralph de Broucton, as appears in his account. This money was paid in four installments, three of which were made in London by either Orlandino da Pogio or Reiner. The fourth and largest payment, of £1,433, was made by Orlandino and Riccardo Guidiccioni at Bristol.[19] These leading members of the Riccardi were probably on their way to the war zone; we know that Orlandino and other representatives of the company actually accompanied, or followed, the armies into North Wales. As good businessmen, they used the opportunity to purchase wool from the abbot of Aberconway and even got a royal safe-conduct for conveying it back to Chester.[20] Several months earlier the merchants had delivered £1,000 to the household at Basingwerk, near the site where Flint castle was being built.[21]

Their partners in England were meanwhile directed to collect funds in some convenient location to serve as a war chest. A writ sent to Enrico da Pogio and his fellows in York notes that they were awaiting delivery of 1,000 marks from another group of Italians led by Hugolino da Vicio. The Riccardi were to deliver the money to Boston or some other center where they might bring together the funds to be sent to the king in Wales, "so that

[18] *C.P.R. 1272–1281*, p. 218.

[19] E 101/3/20. *Ministers Accounts for West Wales, 1277–1306*, Part I, pp. 4, 7, Myvanwy Rhys, ed.; the dates are not given for any of these payments. Broucton's total receipt was £6,303 4s. 6-3/4d. See the payments made for war expenses by him in J. G. Edwards, ed., *Littere Wallie*, pp. 196 ff. In mid-November of 1277 the constable of Bristol Castle, Peter de la Mare, was ordered to deliver to the Riccardi without delay all the king's money in his keeping. But we know neither how much he could provide nor when it was turned over to the merchants. *C.P.R. 1272–1281*, p. 235. *C.C.R. 1272–1279*, pp. 235, 408.

[20] *C.P.R. 1272–1281*, p. 235. The safe-conduct for twenty sacks of wool was dated 15 November 1277.

[21] C 47/4/1 p. 37d.

the king may have the same whenever he thinks fit to send for it."[22]

Beyond these few instances we can seldom trace any details concerning Riccardi advances in the war years. Yet is is clearly the war costs which loom largest in the wardrobe expenditure for this period[23] and it is certain that the advances from the merchants were arranged to help meet these requirements. The increased scale of Riccardi activity during the first war can be seen from the more general royal accounts with the company as well as the wardrobe records. Since a "view of account" covered the first four years of the reign up to Hilary (13 January) 1276,[24] and a second account included the entire period up to Michaelmas (23 September) 1279,[25] it is possible to make a rough comparison between the four years before the war and the three years covering the war and its financial aftermath. In the first period, Riccardi receipt is given as £41,206 6s. 1d., against an expenditure of £54,539 12s. 9d. When these sums are deducted from the inclusive 1279 account, the receipt for 1276-1279 is £139,272 6s. 6-1/2d., the expenditure £146,938 8s. 10-1/2d. In the war period Riccardi activity thus jumped to three times its peacetime level.

To ask how Edward repaid Riccardi aid in this or any of the wars poses two questions. We would like to know first of all how much of the king's money was actually available for their war expenditures. Then we would ask how the king satisfied them for the remainder of their payments, either by additional allowances on the revenues in their hands, or out of other royal funds. If we

[22] *C.P.R. 1272-1281*, p. 215. Earlier, in June of 1277 writs of aid were issued for several Riccardi members "appointed to do certain arduous business in the realm." *Ibid.*, p. 213. Some of the Riccardi payments were independent of wardrobe accounting. This was the case with 1,000 marks paid to Roger Bigod, Earl of Norfolk and hereditary earl Marshal, during the early stages of the war. The order came to them by letter patent. *C.P.R. 1272-1281*, p. 195.

[23] As Tout noted, the wardrobe receipt for this year was more than double that of the preceding year. *Chapters*, II, p. 112.

[24] *C.P.R. 1272-1281*, pp. 131-32.

[25] E 101/126/1.

could answer both these questions fully it would be no task to draw up complete balance sheets for the Riccardi role in each war, a feat which would no doubt have astounded the clerks who penned the original accounts. But the job which would have seemed dubious and very difficult to them is impossible for us. It would require evidence giving the exact date and amount of every payment of customs duties in each port, every installment of a tax, as well as the exact date and amount of every payment made by the merchants to a long list of wardrobe clerks, castellans, paymasters, and the like. It need hardly be added that such evidence is not available.

Yet we do know the allowances given to the merchants as a result of war finance, and also the payments made to them out of other royal revenues. We can thus show in rough outline the means by which Edward ultimately financed the war expenditure handled by the Riccardi, though we cannot graph its progress according to the incidence of royal revenues and the expenditure by the royal bankers.

As was true for Riccardi expenditure, repayment of their loans for the first war remains most obscure; no detailed account can be reconstructed. Since custom duties and the proceeds of taxes were the most important royal revenues used to repay the Riccardi throughout the period during which they were king's bankers, the charge of Riccardi services in 1276-1278 would presumably fall most heavily on these sources. At this time the customs brought in about £10,950 annually.[26] From the only tax being collected during the first campaign, the fifteenth of 1275, the merchants were given £74,599 between 1275 and 1279.[27] Yet there were many charges on these revenues, and we cannot determine what portion went for Riccardi war expenditure, nor even for their total expenditure in the war years. The general account between the king and the company drawn up in 1279

[26] See Chapter III, Table I

[27] E 372/123 m. 23d. E 359/1. We shall see below that the Riccardi repaid a series of loans negotiated with other Italian societies from this tax.

deals with receipts and expenditures in block sums for the entire period, 1272-1279, without any subtotals for the war years.[28]

During the campaign and the following year of financial recovery the exchequer paid the merchants £10,000. But again no sums are linked to their war expenditure.[29]

One type of Riccardi receipt which can without much doubt be classified as repayment for this war is the series of fines for service due from those who had not fulfilled their feudal obligation. But these fines provided only £656 13s. 4d.[30]

2. THE SECOND WAR, 1282-1283

The costs of the second Welsh war were even greater than those of the first, and the Riccardi correspondingly extended greater and more diverse financial services to the crown.[31] Once again the wardrobe accounts are our major source. However, the unprecedented magnitude of the receipts and expenditure now controlled by wardrobe personnel led to the creation of a special war account beginning on Palm Sunday (22 March) 1282, and closing about 20 November 1284) In this period of two and one-half years the account lists £101,621 as received for the prosecution of the war.[32] Yet this does not exhaust the wardrobe war receipt, for the ordinary wardrobe account for 11 and 12 Edward I is

[28] E 101/126/1.

[29] E 403/37, 38, 39, 40, 41. Of this money £2,000 came from the most recent tallage on the community of Jews in England. See *C.C.R. 1272-1279*, p. 408.

[30] E 101/126/1.

[31] Tout and Whitwell have noted the importance of leading Riccardi partners at this time. Tout describes Orlandino da Pogio's services both in this war and the 1277 campaign as "indispensable. . .sometimes receiving, more often lending, the sums needed for the daily expenses of that wandering royal household which was also an army mobilized for service." *Chapters*, II, p. 29. Whitwell similarly notes that Baroncino Gualteri was constantly by Edward's side, at Devizes, Worcester, and Rhuddlan. *T.R.H.S.* n.s. XVII (1903), p. 184.

[32] E 372/136 m. 33. E 101/4/2. The account is printed as an appendix to the *Chronica Johannis de Oxenedes* (Rolls Series), pp. 326–336. Requests for money from the Riccardi were not limited to war purposes, of course.

totally separate from this special account and contains further receipt and expenditure for Wales. It is worth noting that the aggregate receipt into the two accounts comes to £204,573 18s. 1d., although this was not, of course, all devoted to war finance.[33]

A considerable percentage of the receipts listed in these accounts involves the Riccardi: £39,196 19s. 3-1/2d., or nearly two-fifths of the sums making up the special fund for the war; plus £33,405 14s. 6d. in the regular wardrobe account. Once again it is instructive to note Morris' estimate of total war costs, which he set for this campaign at £60,046, or if the cost of works under progress at the castles is added, £98,421.[34]

In both accounts, however, we can observe Riccardi activity only at second half. Their advances are set down in several large sums, each charged on some major source or royal revenue, such as the customs, the mint, or a tax.[35] It is stated that the wardrobe has received the sum of money from this source "by the hands of the merchants of Lucca." Actually, we can be reasonably certain that the sums listed as wardrobe receipts from revenues wholly or partly in Riccardi hands represent an accumulation of numerous short-term advances by the merchants which were only later charged to these revenues as the money became available. In other words, what the accounts show is the repay-

---

For an example of a large nonmilitary payment in the second war, see *C.P.R. 1281–1292*, p. 83. The Riccardi are ordered to pay 3,000 marks to two emissaries being sent to the court of "Almain."

[33] The regular account is E 372/130 mm. 5, 5d. E 101/351/10 is a particular roll of receipts. Both of the wardrobe accounts were originally enrolled on the Pipe Roll for 18 Edward I, but were vacated "quia melius alibi in rotulo xix rotulo compotorum." Tout notes that never again would the volume of wardrobe transactions become so great until the stormy years of crisis after 1295. *Chapters*, II, p. 115.

[34] Morris, *Welsh Wars*, pp. 196–197. F. M. Powicke's estimate is much lower. He suggests a cost of more than £60,000, including the work on castles, *Thirteenth Century*, p. 422.

[35] An exception is the series of loans from numerous Italian companies which will be discussed in Section 5 of this chapter.

ment of sums originally advanced by the society when and where the money was needed.[36]

Although specific Riccardi loans are submerged in these block sums charged to major revenue sources, the better documentation for the second war allows a closer look at their essential services than was possible for 1276-1277. Two Riccardi loans reached the wardrobe at Chester at the time the main English force was opening the campaign. On the Sunday before St. Lawrence (9 August) Eliseo delivered £3,000 from the company and about the same time the Riccardi in Ireland sent £500.[37] Yet the intense military preparations and the hiring of troops proved so costly that by the end of the month Edward was again calling upon his bankers. The account of a paymaster provides an unusual wealth of detail. Vincent de Hilton, whom the king wanted to undertake the mission, was in Carmarthen when Edward's order reached him. After he found the king at Langernum, he traveled on to meet Riccardi agents in London. When Hilton presented the king's request to Baroncino Gualteri and Reyner Magiari, they provided £833 6s.

[36] A note in the entry relating to customs receipts helps to make this clear, although it is not involved with war finance. While the entry indicates that the wardrobe collected £22,916 from the customs by the hands of the Riccardi, the note explains that about £3,000 is in repayment for sums expended by the merchants several years earlier: for jewels bought in France and England; for the household of Alfonso, the king's eldest son; and for a loan to the wardrobe. E 372/136 m. 33. E 101/4/2. This note was added, it seems, not because it was unusual for Riccardi payments to be charged to future royal revenues, but because these payments had been made under the aegis of the former keeper, Thomas Bek, and not William Louth, the present keeper. It was probably also considered important to indicate that these sums appearing in a war account had been spent for other purposes. The accounts for the war were enrolled six years after the end of the campaign, so there was ample time to arrange the bookkeeping.

[37] *C.P.R. 1281-1292*, p. 33. Riccardi funds literally prepared the king for war. A roll of wardrobe necessary expenditure records the repair of Edward's armor, crossbows, and tents, along with the costs of transporting these to Chester. At the same time the Riccardi met the charges for shipping under armed guard £4,000 from London to Chester and £1,900 from London to Devizes. There is no indication in this document that these sums are Riccardi loans. Their costs came to £221 4s. 3-1/2d. E 101/351/9.

8d., hired four packhorses along with baskets, canvas, and cords, and paid the wages of two mounted guards and four footmen to act as escort. After a seven-day trip to Bristol the money was transferred to a boat and shipped to Carmarthen at the king's expense. When the shipment was delayed for four days at the port of "Krokerspulle" three men were set as a watch throughout the night. What is most significant about this payment is the speed with which the king could summon cash when his merchants were far from the scene of action. The entire process—the summoning of Hilton to the king's side, his trip to London, and the return with the treasure—took only forty-five days.[38]

As the fighting dragged on month after month Edward became convinced that a winter campaign, however difficult, was necessary and that he would need mercenaries from Gascony. The English defeat at the Menai Strait in November put a spur to his determination; the difficulties were overcome and a large corps of knights and crossbowmen was brought to Wales. These soldiers, who "both fought and swaggered as befitted the forerunners of d'Artagnan," were all well paid. Their special weapon was the crossbow and they came prepared to use it; 70,000 bolts were shipped over with them in twenty-nine barrels and twelve baskets.[39] Naturally the employ of such specialists was expensive, the cost coming to £7,618 2s. 10d. Of this the Riccardi furnished £3,884 15s. 7d. Apparently this was all paid in England, but nearly one-third of the sum went to a merchant of Piacenza who had supplied a loan to the king's recruiters in Gascony.[40]

[38] C 47/2/4. This information comes from the account of Walter of Nottingham.

[39] Morris, *Welsh Wars*, p. 189, citing E 101/4/6. He notes that William de Monte Ravelli was an important Gascon banneret and "one of Edward's favorite Gascon leaders of mercenaries." *Welsh Wars*, p. 72. In July the Riccardi were ordered to provide for Monte Ravelli materials for beds and robes for six knights, or to give him enough to make the purchases himself. *C.C.R. 1279-1288*, p. 214.

[40] Morris, *Welsh Wars*, pp. 186-189. Powicke, *Thirteenth Century*, p. 427. E 101/3/27. All of the Riccardi payments are listed in sterling, and payments made on the continent are usually given both in the particular currency used and the sterling equivalent. The recruiters were Antony Bek

Paid English troops no less than foreign mercenaries received their wages from the Riccardi. John de Maidstone, a paymaster and victualler with the king's armies, received £666 13s. 4d. out of his total receipt of £2221 12s. 8-3/4d. from the Riccardi.[41] They also made prests totaling £1225 6s. 8d. to seventeen barons and knights who served in Wales.[42] A further £500 was loaned to William de Beauchamp, Earl of Warwick, by royal order[43] and 1,000 marks was paid to the marshal, Roger Bigod, Earl of Norfolk, "in recompense of his damages and of his services in the last army in Wales."[44]

Although the evidence on specific transactions is spotty there can be no doubt that Riccardi loans were critical. At one point Louth was unable to obtain a needed loan from some other merchants at Boston Fair. He turned to the Riccardi, who sent as much money as they could, along with a letter to the king describing their arduous efforts.[45] The king's merchants dispatched £2,600 for the war chest along with £400 from the Mayor of London, Henry le Waleys, who had dipped into his own coffers and convinced his friends to contribute as well. This service by Waleys, and his prompt provision of an escort for the money, drew fulsome praise from the Riccardi.[46]

---

and John de Vescy, who had been sent to negotiate a marriage between Edward's daughter and a son of Pedro of Aragon. Edward used Gascony as a source of provisions as well as mercenaries. A king's clerk, Pontius Amati, was dispatched for this purpose, drawing his funds not only from the wardrobe, but, as we would expect, from representatives of the Riccardi in both London and Paris. His total receipt came to £438 6s. 8d. *R.G.*, II, p. 218. C 47/3/17.

41 E 101/4/5A.

42 E 372/138 m. 26d. These payments by the Riccardi in 1282–1283 are listed in the expense section of the enrolled wardrobe account for 1290, presumably as prests outstanding at the end of Louth's last account.

43 *C.P.R. 1281–1292*, p. 17. Not only did the king order the loan, he stood surety for its repayment, should the earl fail to do so at the appointed time.

44 *Ibid.*, p. 149.

45 See note 178 of Chapter I. It was at this time that the abduction of their chief representative in Ireland was brought to the king's attention.

46 S C 1, XIX, no. 73. Cf. *Foedera*, I, ii, p. 644.

Yet their provision of crucial loans for Edward's campaign meant a severe strain on their resources. In a letter to the king they commented on the many orders for payments sent to them. These orders, they said, "thanks to God have been paid up to the present and will continue to be paid, if in our power." But they complained of the covert attempts of rival companies to harm them by persuading the king of France and the count of Flanders to request loans at this difficult time.[47] Although we would expect the Riccardi always to represent their services as possible only through heroic effort, it seems that in 1282-1283 they actually were hard pressed. Before and after the war, in 1281-1282 and again in 1283-1284, their non-royal loans brought recognizances before the exchequer totaling more than £2,500. In 1282-1283 the amount is negligible.[48] This was the only time the king's bankers felt it necessary to suspend private loans; it provides eloquent if indirect evidence of the Riccardi role in financing this campaign.

Though the king was making frequent and heavy demands on his merchants, it is also true that he was channeling much revenue in their direction during these years of the second war. In again asking how the Riccardi were repaid we come to much surer ground than was possible in the first war.

Since tax proceeds were clearly the most important revenue used for repayment, it will be useful to consider the wartime grants in some detail. The heavy expenditure of the first war had led to a request for a clerical grant in 1279. In response, the province of Canterbury agreed in 1280 to a fifteenth for three years, and the province of York granted a tenth for two years. From the outset it was decided that a substantial part of this money would be paid to the Riccardi, but the specific amounts and the arrangements for their collection were altered several times. A set of undated minutes and three sets of orders (dated 2 May 1282, 18 October 1282 and 2 March 1283) indicate the

[47] The original letter has been preserved. S C 1, XXXI, no. 44. It is partly illegible, but is printed in calendar form in *C.D.I. 1285-1292*, no. 166.

[48] E 159/55, 56 and 57.

successive plans of collection. In the end the proceeds of the fifteenth in the bishoprics of Canterbury, Rochester, Chichester, London, Norwich, Ely, Winchester, Bath and Wells, Exeter, and Salisbury were to be delivered to the society of the Riccardi at London.[49] By the time the money was actually coming in it was badly needed for the second Welsh war. The language in the orders sent to bishops and collectors reflects the fact that, as usual, the collection went distressingly slowly. The king was "greatly astonished" at the delays and urged speed "so that damage shall not be incurred for want of the levying of the said money."[50] Yet a sufficient amount of the clerical grant was received by November of 1284, a year after the end of the war, that the merchants of Lucca could record a receipt of £4,883 16s. Od. from the ten dioceses instructed to pay the proceeds of the tax to them.[51]

The continuing drain of war costs, and Edward's reluctance to ask for yet another grant, led to an effort to raise funds by the method of negotiation. The "begging tour" of John Kirkby is best known,[52] but even earlier the king had dispatched pairs of clerks throughout England to visit towns seeking loans. In September Kirkby was sent before the Cistercians meeting at Oxford, the Augustinians at Northampton, the Benedictines at Reading, and the Praemonstratensians at an unspecified location.[53] In the special war account the monies from lay and religious, from towns and counties, including sums from eight bishops "quasi de dono," are lumped together under the heading of a subsidy for the war.[54] The Riccardi were collectors of this subsidy in Lon-

[49] *C.C.R.V.*, pp. 218–220, 249, 255, 278. Of the remaining bishoprics in the southern province, the treasurer of Lichfield was to receive the Lincoln grant at Lichfield; the proceeds from Worcester and Hereford were to be paid into the wardrobe at Chester; and "a safe place" was to be chosen for the deposit of the St. David's and Llandaff monies. The tenth from the northern province was to be paid to the constable of Nottingham castle.

[50] *C.C.R.V.*, pp. 255, 278.

[51] E 372/120 m. 5. E 101/351/10.

[52] Powicke, *Thirteenth Century*, pp. 505–506.

[53] *Ibid.*, pp. 220, 226–227, 237.

[54] E 372/136 m. 33. E 101/4/2.

don and realized £4,000 from the city. A series of original royal letters obligatory[55] gives the information about the London subsidy and also shows that the merchants received the proceeds in eight other towns. These royal letters specify payment in two installments. The burgesses of Southampton, Reading, and Winchester paid the first half at the Nativity of the Blessed Virgin (8 September); those of Norwich and Lynn at Michaelmas (29 September), and the townsmen of London, Dunwich, Ipswich, and Bury St. Edmunds at the Elevation of the Holy Cross (14 September). All the letters are dated 18 October and specify the completion of each grant at All Saints of that year (1 November). Only London is mentioned by name in the wardrobe account of the receipt of the subsidy. However, since the total subsidy from the other towns would come to only £1,661 13s. 4d., and the account shows that the Riccardi were paid £5,702 6s. 8d. (in addition to the £4,000 from London), we may assume that not only were the second installments from the eight towns collected but that other portions of the subsidy also went to Edward's bankers.[56] Two entries in the "Liber A" confirm the latter. On 2 February 1283 and again on 11 November Baroncino Gualteri and Reiner Magiari received sums which came to a total of £661 6s. 8d. from the Cistercian order in Wales, nearly the whole of the 1,000 marks pledged by these religious to Kirkby at the Oxford meeting.[57]

When Edward finally summoned a parliament to meet in January of 1283, the results of his request for a subsidy from both lay and clerical subjects alike were substantial, but not what he had hoped. The laity gave the king a thirtieth, but the clerical grant was not forthcoming until after the conclusion of the war. In place of the requested triennial tenth, the southern province gave a twentieth for three years, and the York grant of a thirtieth for

[55] The original drafts are preserved in the chancery files C 202/H/2 nos. 51-52, 56-59, 65-67. They are printed in *C.C.R.V.*, pp. 241-242, and *Parliamentary Writs*, I, pp. 386-387.

[56] E 372/136 m. 33. E 101/4/2.

[57] Printed in J. G. Edwards, ed., *Littere Wallie*, pp. 147-149, nos. 260, 263.

three years was delayed until 1286.[58] Because of these delays in the clerical taxes, only the revenue from the lay thirtieth figures in the Riccardi receipt listed in the two wardrobe accounts for the war years. Of the £37,432 16s. 1d. paid into the special account from this tax, £15,602 3s. 1-1/2d. were accounted for by the merchants of Lucca who as central collectors at the Tower of London received the money from the regional collectors.[59]

Tax proceeds, then, brought approximately £30,188 to the Riccardi for the period of the second Welsh war. This was about one-third more than the customs, which stand second in importance. The special enrolled war account shows allowances of £22,916 5s. 5d. given the merchants out of customs duties received between March of 1282 and November of 1284.[60]

The profits of the recoinage put £8,698 11s. 4d. into Riccardi hands in 1282-1283. Since this appears in the regular enrolled wardrobe account, and not the special account for the war, it is not certain whether or not it went for war finance.[61] The special war account, however, does contain one sum from mint profits. This involves a discharge for £678 10s. 9d. which the wardrobe had advanced to the society and Gregory de Rokesley as a prest for the beginning of the recoinage in 1279.[62]

The Issue Rolls show that about £3,000 came to the Riccardi from the exchequer during the second war, though each payment is said to be for household expenses or some other nonmilitary purpose.[63]

Fines for service are not mentioned in either of the wardrobe

[58] H. S. Deighton, "Clerical Taxation by Consent, 1279-1301," *E.H.R.* 68 (1953), pp. 166-167.

[59] See note 54 Cf. the Riccardi account for this tax, E 359/4A.

[60] E 372/136 m. 33. E 101/4/2. It is not specified whether this revenue came from England alone or included Irish customs receipts. But in April of 1282 Edward sent an order to the Dublin exchequer instructing the officials there to pay all issues from the customs and the exchange to the king's merchants so that the monies could be sent to him "in whole or in part as shall seem most expedient." *C.C.R.V. 1277-1294*, p. 213.

[61] E 372/130 m. 5. E 101/351/10.

[62] E 372/136 mm. 16, 33.

[63] E 403/47, 48.

accounts, yet we know that the merchants received a large number of them. They were instructed to collect certain of these fines not long after the war began.[64] From the acquittances entered in the "Liber A" or placed on the Close and Welsh Rolls, we can construct a list of the fines paid to the Riccardi. The names include the bishops of Exeter, Chichester, and London, the abbots of Bury St. Edmunds and Petersborough, and the countess of Aumale. The revenue comes to £1,048 6s. 8d.[65]

3. CASTLE-BUILDING

In the war of 1282–1283 the Welsh lost their independence, but not their spirit of resistance, a fact underscored by the revolts of 1287 and 1295. It was necessary not only to provide for law and administration, as was done in the Statute of Rhuddlan, but also to secure the military conquest by building a series of strong fortresses, several of which were joined to fortified boroughs settled with Englishmen. Furthermore, many of the earlier crown castles had suffered damage and stood in need of repair. A policy of energetic castle-building was essential. As R. A. Brown and H. M. Colvin note, "Others had penetrated into Wales, and some of them had built castles in the hope of holding what they had gained. But the siting of these castles had not been determined by any general strategic plan, and most of them were the private strongholds of independent Marcher lords. Edward I not only penetrated further: he determined to impose English rule on the Welsh by maintaining permanent royal garrisons on native soil. To house those garrisons new castles were needed, castles capable of resisting any army a Welsh prince might muster."[66] This policy

64 *C.P.R. 1281–1292*, p. 29.

65 E 36/274 mm. 256d., 257, 264d. E 159/59 m. 27, -61 m. 4, -65 mm. 11d., 4d., 25d., -67 mm. 24, 51, 39. *C.P.R. 1281–1292*, pp. 29, 107. *C.C.R. 1279–1283*, pp. 398, 405. *C.C.R.V.*, pp. 2, 3, 208, 212, 287, 340, 347, 352, 406.

66 H. M. Colvin, ed., *King's Works*, I, Chapter V (by R. A. Brown), Chapter VI (A. J. Taylor), II, Appendix C. Figure 25 (I, p. 183) shows the regional distribution of workmen impressed for the works in North Wales.

was initiated immediately after the first war; the walls and towers of Flint and Rhuddlan began to rise, and works were being pushed forward at Builth and Aberystwyth. In the years following the second war the new castles at Conway, Caernarvon, and Harlech were going up together, the first two standing alongside towns fortified with stone walls. As J. G. Edwards has shown, most of these works were basically completed in five to seven working seasons. It required a large force of both skilled laborers and common workmen, who were brought to the sites from even distant shires; as many as 2,700 were at work in the period after the second war. Since they were paid not only while on the job, but also while en route, Edwards reasons that the king could assemble his castle-building force only by tapping the labor market over the greater part of England.[67] He puts the total cost of these works at £80,000 "as a safe notional figure," while a more recent estimate sets the figure as high as £100,000, "an outlay such as a modern government might devote to building a fleet of nuclear submarines."[68] Not all this money was spent while the Riccardi were the king's bankers; the last of the castles, Beaumaris, was begun after their relationship with Edward was broken, and work on some fortresses dragged on for decades. Yet this great undertaking helps to explain the heavy expenditures during the war years and the need for the financial aid of the Riccardi.

From the very outset the merchants were involved,[69] and since

---

The overall plan of the works is attributed to Master James of St. George, who came to Edward from Savoy where he had directed important works for Count Philip, Edward's cousin. In England he eliminated the keep or great tower in favor of a concentric plan with emphasis on the gatehouse. *Ibid.*, pp. 203-204, 229-230.

67 Edwards, "Castle Building," *Proc. Br. Acad.*, 32 (1946) *passim.*

68 R. A. Brown, *King's Works*, I, p. 228.

69 In June of 1277, just before work was begun on Flint and Rhuddlan, Luke and his fellows were ordered to pay 40 marks to Master Robert of Belvoir (de Belvero), one of two clerks sent by the king to collect masons and carpenters, "as many as he can get, and in whatsoever works or service they may be, and to conduct them whither he has been enjoined." *C.P.R. 1272-1281*, p. 214. Cf. *King's Works*, I, p. 309. In 1278-1279 Baroncino

the wardrobe was the most important single source from which the requisite funds were drawn[70] we may be sure that at least some of the many Riccardi payments to Louth in the period of castle-building were used for that purpose. Several such payments can be traced.

In 10–12 Edward I two *clerici regis* received a total of £3,940 "as well from the wardrobe as from the merchants of Lucca," the money going for castles in West and North Wales.[71] Two years later a knight, John Bouslard, collected £200 from the Riccardi "for the works in Wales."[72] Another payment, amounting to £1,000, went to Robert de Beauver as treasurer of Wales and Adam de Whetenhale as chamberlain of Wales.[73] Edward ordered this payment on 18 September 1288, while in Gascony; Louth, as keeper of the wardrobe, communicated the order to the Riccardi members who were with the king on the continent, and they in turn relayed it to their fellows in England. Payment was made less than three months after the royal order, on 29 September.[74]

Irish revenues were the second major source of funds for the

---

received £100 from Ralph Sandwich out of the proceeds of the vacant archbishopric of Canterbury "ad constructionem castri de Lampadervar." E 368/52 m. 12. Cf. C 62/56 m. 3 for the writ of *allocate* to the keepers. Lampadervar is Llanbadarn, the modern Aberystwyth.

[70] Edwards, *Proc. Br. Acad.*, p. 64.

[71] E 101/351/7. Master Walter de Nottingham received £804 8s. 4d. for the king's castles in West Wales. Master Richard de Abingdon received £3135 6s. 8d.

[72] E 372/136 m. 31d. E 101/352/2.

[73] E 372/136 mm. 30, 31d. This is mentioned in Beauver's account and in the wardrobe account for 15–16 Edward I. E 372/136 m. 31d. The former account shows that total receipts for the castles in this period came to £1849 13s. 9d.

[74] E 368/76 m. 15. The fact that the date of the order fell in 16 Edward I but payment came at the beginning of 17 Edward I caused trouble for Beauver and Whetenhale seventeen years later, well after the Riccardi failure. The £1,000 appeared twice, in rolls for each of these regnal years, and suspicious exchequer officials summoned the two men to explain. They were saved by Frederico of the Riccardi, who came to the exchequer, examined the books of his society (by this time in the king's hands), and explained the duplication in the royal records.

castles,[75] and in this connection it is significant that in June of 1285 the Riccardi were directed to deliver all the present and future revenue from the Irish customs in their keeping to Richard de Abingdon, who was then the king's receiver in Wales, "for the welling of towns, castles and other the king's works there."[76] Within seven months he had received 1,000 marks from the merchants, the money going for the works at "karnervan, conewey, cruk, et hardelagh (Caernarvon, Conway, Cruk, Harlech)."[77]

On occasion the Irish revenues may not have reached the works in time to meet costs, for in 1288 the Riccardi advanced £200 to Beauver, with the condition that the money be restored to them out of the first receipts from the proceeds of Ireland. Such delays perhaps influenced the arrangement made in the following year by which 4,000 marks of Irish revenues would be indirectly channelled to the Welsh castles. This sum was turned over to the members of the Riccardi operating in Ireland, the London members of the firm acting as security. From the latter the barons of the exchequer were to draw 4,000 marks for the Welsh works—not, however, in one lump sum, but from time to time as the progress of the works required.[78] By this convenient arrangement the building force could be supplied with funds which would not have to be shipped with care and cost from Ireland.

Finally, the Riccardi provided half of the £199 1s. 7-1/2d. expended on the building of the town wall at Aberystwyth when this was undertaken in 1280.[79]

The castles and walled towns constructed in Wales have been described as a great "medieval state enterprise." Certainly the fact that Edward could "raise great stone fortresses by threes and fours in five or six seasons" is a witness both to his determination and to the financial strength the Riccardi helped provide.[80]

[75] Edwards, *Proc. Br. Acad.*, p. 64.

[76] *C.P.R. 1281-1292*, p. 170. For the writ of *allocate* to the treasurer and barons of the Irish exchequer see *C.D.I. 1285-1293*, no. 248.

[77] E 372/131 m. 26d. E 372/136 m. 33.

[78] E 159/61 mm. 5d, 14d.

[79] H. M. Colvin, ed., *King's Works*, I, p. 304.

[80] The quotations are from Edwards, *Proc. Br. Acad.*, 32 (1946), pp. 16, 65.

4. THE WAR AGAINST RHYS AP MAREDUDD, 1287

The castle-building was in full progress when the rebellion of Rhys ap Maredudd began in 1287. Although the fighting would not approach the level of the first two wars, this was not at first evident to a nervous regent, Edmund, Earl of Cornwall. The serious view the king's cousin took of the revolt is shown by the size of the forces which were directed to converge on Dryslwyn Castle, the seat of Rhys's power. A six-week campaign, involving nearly 24,000 men in all, ended in the capture of Dryslwyn and broke the back of Rhys's effort. When he began the fighting anew several months later, local forces were sufficient to handle the threat. After hiding in the hills for several years Rhys was captured and hanged in 1291.[81]

But in 1287 the uneasiness of the Earl of Cornwall must have been greatly increased by the fact that the wardrobe, the usual agency for war finance, was traveling with the king on the continent. Wishing to act with great speed and to crush Rhys with overwhelming force, the earl decided to replace the feudal levy with paid cavalry, and to put large bodies of infantry into the field.[82] With so much of the royal revenue being directed towards Gascony, the exchequer would have found itself hard pressed to meet such sudden and heavy demands of war.[83]

Thus within a month of Rhys's outburst the regent turned to the merchants of Lucca to finance his campaign. A letter of 6 July ordered them to provide the paymasters of horse and foot with "all funds, either our money in your possession, or money provided as loans for our business, or money procured in any other way."[84] Later orders directed the merchants to pay certain specific sums for war expenses to the king's captains and officials.[85]

[81] Morris, *Welsh Wars*, pp. 204, 207, 217. Sir John Lloyd, ed., *A History of Carmarthenshire*, pp. 205-206.

[82] Morris, *Welsh Wars*, p. 207. Powicke, *Thirteenth Century*, p. 439.

[83] Tout, *Chapters*, II, pp. 116-117.

[84] The original letter is preserved among the Ancient Correspondence, S C 1, vol. XIII, no. 63. It is quoted in the enrolled Riccardi account for the war, E 372/132 m. 1, and printed in calendar form in *C.C.R.V.*, p. 309.

[85] *C.C.R.V.*, pp. 316-19.

The troops were in the field quickly, converging on Rhys from Chester, Gloucester, and Hereford. With equal speed the Riccardi sent out their own tiny band of representatives, who must have been most inconspicuous and inconsequential among the masses of men in the medieval panoply of war.[86] In the closing days of July, Francesco Malisardi of the company was at the regent's side in Hereford where he was supplying funds to the paymasters of the forces gathering there. On 24 July he delivered £300 to William de Rye and Elias de Ford, on 25 July £300 to John de Monte Alto and Vincent de Hilton, and on 27 July £400 to Walter de Pedwardin and Master Thomas de Cantock. It may have been at about this same time that Riccardo Guidiccioni, one of the chief members of the firm in England, paid the £21 15s. required for the wages of footmen being sent from Gloucester. He also provided £100 to Vincent de Hilton for wages in West Wales.[87]

Riccardo, however, left it to lesser members of the company to follow the armies into the battle-zone. Only a small effort of imagination is needed to picture Francesco and Salomen shepherding the casks and bags of silver pennies on packhorses, while nervously scanning the surrounding hills. By 18 August they had reached Dryslwyn and paid £500 to Monto Alto and Hilton and an equal sum to Rye and Ford. On 28, 29, and 31 August and on 1 September further payments brought the total to £2,131 13s. 4d. There was much for them to see when not counting out coins: the castle was surrounded by the regent's army, Richard the Engineer had a large stone-throwing machine in operation (his supplies bought with Riccardi money), and a mine was being dug beneath the defenders' walls—a mine which unhappily for the sappers brought down the wall on their own heads. But by 5 September the castle was taken and most of the troops retired on Carmarthen, where they received back wages and were dismissed.

86 For all the payments which follow see E 372/132 m. 1. E 101/4/16, 17, 18. *C.C.R.V., p. 310.* Cf. Morris, *Welsh Wars*, pp. 212–213.

87 The former sum was paid to a clerk, Stephen de Hovedan. Fifteen years later he was questioned by exchequer officials about this sum and said that he received it from the Riccardi at Gloucester. E 368/74 m. 15.

The Riccardi paid for what seemed to be the closing expenses of the war. Salomen dispensed the money for the wages paid at Carmarthen on 13 September; Rye and Ford received £200, and £1,033 6s. 8d. went to Monte Alto and Hilton. Two months later, on 12 November, Riccardo Guidiccioni paid to Rye and Ford the £509 15s. 7d. which represented the "surplus" of their expenses over receipts. An order of 14 November requested the Riccardi to pay specified sums to thirteen lords and knights who had led contingents of horsemen; the list includes £300 to Edmund Mortimer, £200 to William Beauchamp, £120 to Roger Mortimer, £100 to John de Warenne, and lesser sums to commanders of smaller troops. Some of the contingents, however, must not have been up to full strength, because six of the commanders later returned a part of the wages to the Riccardi, £256 13s. 4d. in all.[88] At Dryslwyn the Riccardi began providing money for the repair and rearmament of the castle; of the £1,936 5s. 1-1/2 d. spent before 1289 by the keeper of the castle, Alan Plukenet, Riccardi representatives furnished £718 13s. 4d.[89] They also provided £100 out of £169 spent on new works and repairs needed at Carmarthen.[90]

But the fighting was not yet over; Rhys was still at large, and he renewed hostilities in November. Although this outbreak was suppressed by local forces, the funds had to be provided by the regent. In early December Robert de Tibetot, justiciar of South Wales, relieved Dinefwr castle, which had been besieged by Rhys, and by the end of the month he was prepared to lay siege to Emlyn castle, which Rhys had seized. Once again Richard the Engineer's war machine was hauled into a threatening position and its stone ammunition piled up in abundance. It seems that

88 The order for payment and the schedule listing the recipients and the amount each was to have were copied into the Riccardi account for the war. E 372/132 m. 1. They are also in *C.C.R.V.*, pp. 316–317. The returned sums are in the Riccardi account and also are listed among the wardrobe receipt "by the hands of the Riccardi" in 1289–1290. E 372/138 m. 26d.

89 E 372/134 m. 1d.

90 E 372/134 m. 2d. This payment was made 14 April. E 372/133 m. 28.

after this show of force the garrison opened the castle gates without a struggle.[91] Francesco and Salomen may have missed the military spectacle this time, but they provided £200 toward its cost, which eventually came to £554. The Riccardi money was on the scene about a week before the "siege" began. After the castle was surrendered Tibetot drew a further £60 from the merchants "ad municionem castri de Dynavor."[92]

The accounts of Peter de la Mare, constable of Bristol castle, provide a significant postscript to the financing of this campaign. We learn that he supervised the shipment of 2,850 marks of Riccardi money from Bristol to Carmarthen by water, and the carting of 3,160 marks of their money overland to London.[93] This means that the Riccardi had sent more than £4,000 beyond the sum actually required for the war. Had the suppression of the rebellion proved to be a longer or more costly operation, the Riccardi funds would have been available.

The actual cost of the campaign is probably not far from Morris' estimate of £10,606.[94] Out of this total no less than £8,288 can be traced to the Riccardi. They provided the wages of cavalry, infantry, and workmen, plus a significant part of the costs of taking Dryslwyn and Emlyn castles.[95] Furthermore, two years after the war had ended they repaid £639 12s. 6d. in small loans which the treasurer had obtained from various other Italian companies for the war chest.[96]

In the case of the 1287 campaign we can be reasonably certain

91 Morris, *Welsh Wars*, pp. 215–16.

92 E 372/133 m. 28. E 372/134 m. 2d. His total receipt for this purpose was £111 8s. 8d.

93 E 372/133 m. 29.

94 *Welsh Wars*, p. 219.

95 The major charges not met by the Riccardi were a part of the cost of the garrison at Dryslwyn and the repairs and new works at Aberystwyth (£320). See Morris, *Welsh Wars*, p. 219. Most of the Riccardi payments are found in their enrolled account, E 372/132 m. 1. For the others see E 372/133 m. 28, E 372/134 mm. 1, 2d., E 101/4/21.

96 E 101/352/15. A marginal note states simply "per mercatores," but an entry above this one has the fuller identification "per mercatores de Luka." Thus it is reasonable to link this payment also with the Riccardi.

that the Riccardi loans provided approximately 80 percent of the funds needed. We can also determine how much they received from royal revenues ready at hand, i.e., how much of the king's money bolstered their resources for the war. Since the wardrobe was traveling on the continent with the king when Rhys ap Maredudd broke out in revolt, the Riccardi financing of English arms in 1287 is not buried in a summarized wardrobe account. The merchants' payments and receipts are listed in a separate enrolled account. The only receipts from the king's money charged to them were £823 12s. 10d. from the exchequer. Money extracted from the Jews accounts for £430 of this sum, with a further £300 coming from the Canterbury mint.[97] This indicates that the merchants received from crown resources only about 10 percent of what they provided for the campaign—eloquent testimony to the need for royal bankers.

A later change in the bookkeeping tends to obscure this fact. Their enrolled account was cancelled and in a general reckoning for the wool custom they were given discharges on customs revenue received in 1286-1289; allowances for wages advanced to cavalry and infantry, £1,105 15s. and £6,116 14s. 3d. respectively, were written into this later account.[98] This change is simply a matter of record-keeping; the revenue source to which Riccardi loans were later charged in no way alters the fact that in a critical time the company had loaned funds which the regent would have been hard pressed to find elsewhere.

5. CRUSADE TAXES AND BONDS

We have seen how the massive financial requirements of the campaigns in Wales forced King Edward to tap every available source of money and to rely heavily on advances from his merchants. Two of the mechanisms by which he bolstered his resources and theirs deserve special comment: his seizure of funds stored in England for the crusade, and his negotiation of loans

[97] E 372/132 m. 1.
[98] E 372/134 m. 3.

from the various leading Italian companies operating in England. The Riccardi were closely involved in both cases.

Their papal ties made them logical agents for any action relating to papal crusade taxes. At the time of the first campaign the proceeds of the sexennial tenth for the Holy Land, collected by papal authority in England, lay in various churches for safekeeping. To Edward it must have been a most tempting treasure. He would not even be forced to lay hands on it directly if only he could maneuver the deposits of the crusade money to his bankers. At the beginning of June 1276, a group of magnates meeting at the New Temple, London, had advised the collectors that it would be wise to transfer the deposits to Italian firms for the greater security of the money while the barons and knights were away at war. The king not only gave similar advice, but he suggested that the Riccardi be used as the depositaries, and even offered to guarantee their restitution of the money when the pope or the papal collectors should request it. No doubt his motives were transparent, for the collectors acted upon the advice to deposit with Italian firms but did not accept the king's suggestion to confine the deposits to the Riccardi.[99]

An indication that the pressures of war finance would renew Edward's interest in the crusade tenth came as early as May of 1282, for on the 24th of that month he placed an embargo on the exportation of any of the money from the realm. Then in March of 1283, standing in great need of funds and angry at the clerical procrastination over a grant, Edward ordered the seizure of the money. His audacity netted £29,237 18s. 9-1/2d. of the "old money" (i.e., coins minted before the 1279 recoinage), and £10,558 8s. 7-1/2d. of the "new money."[100] Some of the money was quickly transferred to the Riccardi to bolster their resources. In early May the king directed that, from the tenth seized at Durham and York, that part which was out of the new money should be transferred to the Riccardi.[101] At some other time

[99] Lunt, *Financial Relations*, p. 332. *C.P.R. 1272-1281*, p. 214.
[100] Lunt, *Financial Relations*, p. 336, and *E.H.R.* 32, pp. 52-55.
[101] *C.C.R. 1279-1288*, p. 206.

further deposits of the new money were presumably placed with the merchants, for when Edward decided to restore the tenth, after the war and the urgent financial pressure were nearly over, the Riccardi were ordered to return "the whole of the tenth taken in new money to those from whom it was received."[102] Although the old money could be easily returned–none of it had been spent and much of it was yet in sacks under the original seals–£4,175 10s. 7-1/4d. of the new money had gone for Welsh expenses. At this time the Riccardi sent Edward the letter noted above, describing their difficulties. They were apprehensive about their involvement with the seized money, and prayed that the king would protect them from loss and disgrace. Their fellows in Italy had acknowledged receipt of the money before the pope, and now, though the king wanted this money returned, they had not been repaid the sums they had turned over to him and were not sure if any repayment would be forthcoming.[103] Their fears were groundless, for Edward ordered repayment out of the proceeds of the thirtieth. Thus in the account for this tax it is stated among the expenses that on behalf of the merchants £3,133 2s. 9-1/2d. were repaid at the New Temple, £338 17s. 2d. at Canterbury, £604 0s. 7-3/4d. at Salisbury, and £100 at Chichester.[104]

Papal crusade taxes were useful to the Riccardi, but in understanding how they managed their massive loans it is more important to consider their role as intermediaries between the crown and the entire Italian merchant-banking community in London. During each war they raised no small part of the money advanced to the king by negotiating a series of loans from their fellow-countrymen. In effect, the English government and its bankers combined their credit enabling Edward to tap the resources of a number of the major *societates* operating in England.

[102]E 359/4A m. 4. *C.P.R. 1281-1292*, p. 70.

[103]The original is preserved among the Ancient Correspondence, S C 1, 31 no. 44, in rather bad condition. It appears in calendar form in *C.D.I. 1285-1292*, no. 166.

[104]*Ibid.* Cf. Lunt, *Financial Relations*, pp. 336-337.

The Welsh campaigns were supported by the most advanced financiers of western Europe.

About the time the king was mounting his main drive in the 1277 campaign, Orlandino da Pogio received royal letters obligatory for loans from fifteen companies, totaling 13,150 marks. His instructions were to receive the money or restore the king's bonds.[105] The Riccardi did receive the loans, for their account for the fifteenth of 1275 shows that they repaid the advances from the proceeds of this tax.[106] The list of firms thus repaid, as well as the sums involved, do not correspond exactly with those stated in the letters obligatory, indicating that some of the firms were unwilling or unable to lend the crown the sum stated in the bond. Two firms for which bonds were issued made no loans at all—the Salumbeni, from whom the king wanted 1,400 marks, and a small firm from Siena whose loan was to be only 100 marks. But these refusals were more than balanced by additional loans negotiated with two firms from Cahors and one from Montpellier which brought 1,100 marks, and by additional loans from some firms. The sum repaid by the Riccardi was 17,250 marks, much more than the total of the bonds. But it is unlikely that the payment of interest is responsible for this increase, because the bonds probably included interest in the amount of the loan acknowledged. Moreover, seven firms were repaid exactly the amount of the letter obligatory given them. To explain the higher repayment received by four firms in terms of interest would necessitate accepting the improbable rates of 100 percent for two firms, 66 percent for another, and 60 percent for the fourth. It is more likely that these firms agreed to advance larger loans.[107]

105*C.P.R. 1272-1281*, p. 214. The date is 14 June 1277.

106E 372/123 m. 23d. Liberate Roll 8 Edward I, C 62/56. Ten days after the issue of the letters obligatory Edward wrote to the Riccardi giving them instructions on how the money was to be handled. They were to collect all the funds which they were to send to him in one convenient center—Boston or elsewhere—so that he could have it whenever he wanted. Only one loan of this series is specifically mentioned, but the intent obviously was to centralize a war chest.

107Two Florentines, Hugelino de Vichio and Lotherio Bonaguide, representing the Company of Telgarius de Scala, accepted a bond for 1,000

It is impossible to know what amount of interest is included in this total figure of 17,250 marks (£11,500); the actual Riccardi receipt for war purposes would undoubtedly be a considerably smaller sum. Yet a figure on this order of magnitude represents an important portion of their expenses on the king's behalf and indicates one means by which they were able to provide such large sums through the war and its immediate aftermath.

It was so convenient a procedure that the king had recourse to it again. Within a few weeks after the seriousness of the second war became known Edward turned once again to the Italian firms, acting through his merchants of Lucca. The first transactions took place on the Thursday before St. George (20 April) and on the Sunday and Tuesday following the Ascension (3 and 5 May). The king issued letters to fourteen Italian companies and two groups of merchants from Cahors for loans totaling 11,875 marks. The Riccardi, who received the loans, provided 1,000 marks, as did the Bonsignori, Scotti, Cerchi, Frescobaldi, Scala, Bardi, and Pulci. Smaller amounts were received from the other Italians and from the merchants of Cahors. Repayment would be forthcoming within a year from the following Whitsunday, "which the king promises to do in good faith."[108] By June the campaign was gathering momentum,[109] and it is not surprising to find a second series of bonds being issued to raise further funds. In July the Riccardi received the loans from the firms which had acted several months earlier. Three additional companies also took the king's bonds. This time they totaled 13,000 marks, including the letter for 1,000 marks accepted by the Riccardi themselves. These loans were to be repaid "within a year of Michaelmas next."[110] Finally, a third series of letters obligatory were

marks, but were repaid 2,000 marks. Apparently this was a repayment not only for the 14 June loan but also for a previous loan of 1,000 marks negotiated in February of 1277. At that time the king promised repayment "by the hands of Luke of Lucca and his Fellows" a fortnight after Michaelmas in the fair of Boston. *C.P.R. 1272-1281*, p. 196.

[108]*C.C.R.V.*, pp. 215–216.

[109]See Morris, *Welsh Wars*, pp. 155–157.

[110]*C.C.R.V.*, pp. 230–231.

issued a year later, on 20 June 1283, to nine of the firms. The total of these loans came to £3,900, which sum the king promised to repay at London in the octaves of Michaelmas. This time the Riccardi did not themselves add a loan.[111]

The wardrobe account for 11 and 12 Edward I states that the proceeds of all three series of loans brought £19,633 5s. 10d. to the merchants of Lucca during the second war.[112] This represents well over a quarter of the sums handled by the Riccardi during these war years. But once again the question concerning interest concealed in this sum is not easy to resolve. The receipts from nine firms exactly match the sum of the bonds given them. In the two cases where the recorded receipt falls below the total in the bonds we must conclude that the Riccardi failed to place some of the bonds. Unless this was true in the case of one of the 1,000-mark bonds in favor of the Bardi the rate of interest received by them would have been nearly 72 percent.[113] If interest was paid on these loans–and it is almost inconceivable that it was not–the wardrobe charged itself, through the Riccardi, with inflated receipts.

When the rebellion of Rhys ap Maredudd took the English government by surprise and the Riccardi were expected to supply the funds for a campaign, the regent turned to the now-familiar device of supporting the king's merchants with loans from other Italian firms. The bonds drawn up in late August and early September of 1287 are still preserved among the chancery files in the Public Record office. Many show notations in Italian and the slits which denote cancellation.[114] The bonds indicate that the government hoped to obtain loans from thirteen Italian firms in addition to an advance from the Riccardi (beyond the payments

[111] *Ibid.*, pp. 272–273. Cf. the order for letters patent dated the Friday after Trinity, 1283. C 81/1691 no. 18.

[112] E 372/130 m. 5.

[113] See Whitwell's conclusion, "Italian Bankers and the English Crown," *T.R.H.S.*, n.s. XVII (1903), p. 220. The firm of William Johannis and John Donedeu either did not accept a £100 bond or they received 13 percent interest, a figure by no means too high.

[114] C 202/H/3 nos. 27–53.

the company was then making in the field), as well as an advance by the sheriffs of London and Middlesex on their farm. There can be no doubt that these loans were negotiated for the purpose of war finance, for each specifically states that the money is "for our business in our current expedition in Wales." Each bond also indicates that the Riccardi will receive the money and that repayment will be made through their hands.

Although the enrolled Riccardi account for the war shows that the loan from the sheriffs (£66 13s. 4d.), was duly paid, it does not mention the Italian loans.[115] The wardrobe account gives no help since it is concerned with the king's continental activity. Moreover, the bonds themselves present serious problems of interpretation. The letters obligatory for six firms were enrolled on the Welsh Roll under the date 30 August. We have the original bonds issued the following day to twelve firms, along with two duplicates. Another series of original letters, dated 8 September, went for loans from ten firms. The endorsements also are erratic. Of those dated 31 August, ten carry a note stating that Riccardo Guidiccioni and fellows have later made repayment, but only seven of these show that he attested receipt of the money for the Riccardi. In the series of 8 September there are notations of Riccardi repayment for five of the companies named in the previous bonds and two additional ones, but no endorsements testifying to receipt. Three of the letters in the 31 March series were altered to state a higher sum: that for the Bonsignori was increased from 200 marks to £233 6s. 8d.; that for the Bardi from 175 marks to £250; that for the Pulci and Rembertini from 300 marks to £400. The corrected letters of 31 March for the Bonsignori and the Pulci and Rembertini were repeated under the same date, and still another bond, naming only the Pulci, appears with those dated 8 September. Also among the letters of this date is the corrected bond for the Bardi. The varying numbers of the firms, amounts of the loans, and nature of the endorsements make it hazardous to fix any total for the loans which came to the Riccardi. Do the three series of bonds indicate successive

[115] E 372/132 m. 1.

stages in negotiating a single loan from each firm or rather several cumulative loans?

Some idea of the number of loans and the revenue put at the disposal of the king's bankers appears in a letter patent dated 8 December 1288.[116] The king acknowledged his indebtedness to the merchants of ten companies who had together loaned 5,000 marks and paid it by royal order to Riccardo Guidiccioni and his fellows of the Riccardi. The contribution made by each society to this total is not given, but they were all among the firms for whom bonds were issued during the war, and there can be little doubt of the connection. On the previous day the Riccardi had received a writ of *liberate* for the repayment of 5,000 marks to these ten firms.[117] This evidence indicates that there were probably two series of loans, on 31 August and 8 September, for the 5,000 marks, or £3,333 6s. 8d., is very close both to the total contained in the letters issued to the ten firms on these two dates (£3,250) and to the total in the letters for all firms on these dates (£3,366 13s. 4d.). In addition to the money they collected, the two Riccardi loans would increase the total sum raised for the war chest by £800; but the total figure no doubt contains an element of interest. If the loans brought the king's bankers 5,000 marks, this would mean that about two-fifths of their expenditures during this war came from other Italian firms. The proportion was probably lower, however, because of this concealed interest in the letters. The table on the following page summarizes the information on these loans.

We must often be satisfied with approximations in investigating the role of Italian financiers in the Edwardian conquest of Wales. Yet the limitations of medieval financial documents do not obscure the basic conclusion. The conquest was achieved in no small measure because Edward I could back his military and organizational skill, his drive and determination, with the financial resources of the Riccardi of Lucca and, through them, the resources of the major companies of Italian merchant-bankers operating in

116 *C.P.R. 1281-1292*, pp. 310-311.
117 C 62/65 m. 4.

Company	*30 August*[118]	*31 August*[119]	*8 Sept.*[120]	*Liberate*[121]
Bardi		£250 0 0	£250 0 0	x
Pulci and Rembertini		400 0 0	400 0 0	x
Frescobaldi Albi	£66 13 4	66 13 4	66 13 4	x
Frescobaldi Nigri	66 13 4	66 13 4	66 13 4	x
Scala		66 13 4		
Mozzi		400 0 0	400 0 0	x
Amannati		66 13 4		x
Cerchi Albi	100 0 0	66 13 4	100 0 0	x
Cerchi Nigri	66 13 4	116 13 4	66 13 4	x
Bonsignori		333 6 8		x
Riccardi	400 0 0	400 0 0	400 0 0	
Bettori	66 13 4	66 13 4	66 13 4	x
Rustici			50 0 0	
Total (without Riccardi)	366 13 4	1,900 0 0	1,466 13 4	5,000 marks (£3,333 6s. 8d.)

England. The financial flexibility which the Italians provided translated easily into military power in late thirteenth-century warfare and brought a new element into the age-old conflicts across the Welsh border.[122] Edward I could defeat the traditional Welsh guerilla tactics; he could plan his operations with the assurance that cash in any reasonable amount could be obtained; he could continue a crucial campaign through the winter of 1282-1283; he could hire crack Gascon mercenaries to fight that campaign; he could raise great fortresses to seal his victory, drawing on the labor force of all England. Orlandino da Pogio, Riccardo Guidiccioni, Francesco Malisardi, and their fellows were in all probability unknown to any Welshmen, but it would be hard to overestimate their importance in the ending of Welsh independence.

118*C.C.R.V.*, pp. 310-311.

119C 202/H/3 nos. 28-41. *C.C.R.V.*, pp. 309-310. The original letters for the Pulci and Rembertini and the Bonsignori are duplicated.

120C 202/H/3 nos. 42-53. An incomplete list appears in *C.C.R.V.*, pp. 310-311.

121C 62/65 m. 4.

122See the comment by J. Beverley Smith in *The Bulletin of the Board of Celtic Studies*, XXI, Part II, p. 159 note 5.

Chapter V Arrest and Failure

I. REASONS FOR THE RICCARDI FALL

When Edward ordered the Riccardi to give up the cocket seals on 29 July, 1294,[1] depriving them of the collection of the customs, he was in effect breaking off the relationship which had successfully linked king and banker for more than two decades. Thus the reasons for this rupture and the collapse of the Riccardi about seven years later are of clear importance. These two phenomena were obviously related, and we must investigate their connection as well as the causes behind each.

The Italian scholar Emilio Re has outlined what would seem to be the basic factors in the decline of the company, emphasizing a series of misfortunes which gradually brought ruin.[2] In 1291 Philip IV arrested the Italians in France and extorted large fines from them in return for the right to remain and do business in France. At about the same time substantial papal tax deposits were recalled when the sexennial tenth imposed in 1274 was granted to Edward I, and the tenth for the aid of Sicily was granted to Charles of Anjou. In 1294 the Riccardi were badly hurt by the war measures of the two kings in conflict over Gascony. Edward I seized the wool of all foreign merchants and later arrested the Riccardi and sequestrated their assets, asserting that they owed him more than they could pay; Philip IV similarly

[1] E 159/68 m. 86d.

[2] "La compagnia dei Riccardi in Inghilterra e il suo fallimento alla fine del sec. XIII," *Archivio della Società Romana de Storia Patria*, XXXVII (1914).

moved against the company in France, arresting Riccardi members as bankers to his enemy. A "run on the bank" occurred; internal dissension racked the failing company; papal intervention failed; bankruptcy was only a matter of time.

These are undoubtedly the important elements in the failure of the firm, but they are not all of equal importance, nor can the story of the last years of the Riccardi, from 1291 onward, be told in terms of an unmitigated slide to disaster. These years of crisis fall into two periods, with the events of 1294 forming the watershed in Riccardi affairs. In the years after 1294, having lost the close rapport with Edward I and suffered arrest and confiscations on both sides of the channel, they would have required a near-miracle in order to recover themselves and inspire the necessary confidence of clients.

This is not to underestimate the seriousness of the setbacks of 1291, but we must examine them more closely. The Riccardi share of the levy on Italians in France, nor even the total sum Philip realized from all of the firms, cannot be determined. However, one account sets the figure at 221,000 *livres tournois*.[3] Lacking the French court connections of some of their fellow-countrymen, the Riccardi could not reduce their share through this channel. Yet as cameral merchants they could expect papal support, and it was not long in forthcoming. Nicholas IV twice wrote to Philip on behalf of the several firms which had served the Roman Church advantageously for so long a time, urging that they be freed from any burden.[4] Although we may doubt that the agents of Philip the Fair ceased troubling the Riccardi and other cameral firms because of papal admonitions, the pope's support would put them in a somewhat better bargaining position.

Whatever loss of capital was caused by the French seizures was made more serious by the recall of deposits of papal taxes—the tenth for the conquest of Sicily, and the sexennial crusade tenth

[3] J. R. Strayer, *Studies in Early French Taxation*, p. 17. It must be remembered that the pound of Tours was worth only about one-fifth as much as the pound sterling.

[4] *Registres de Nicholas IV*, II, nos. 7326, 7384.

of 1274. A part of the former tenth was requested from the Riccardi several years before Philip's extortions, the latter in the same year. An unspecified portion of the tenth "persecutione regni Sicilie concesse" was held by the Riccardi in February 1286, when they executed an elaborate instrument of deposit.[5] But at least some of this money had to be returned in 1289 when Nicholas IV granted it to Charles of Anjou. The sums involved are difficult to determine. Some idea of the scale is given by the Bonsignori books, which state that this firm accounted with the Riccardi for about 8,384 gold florins in January of 1289, and that they later received about 5,075 *libre pisani* from the merchants of Lucca in March of 1290.[6] Sums of this size represent only a small part of their total deposits, for in 1295 Boniface VIII asked for no less than 80,000 gold florins from the Riccardi.[7] Thus it is difficult to see how the transactions involving the tenth for Sicily could have seriously embarrassed the merchants before 1295.

The more serious case concerned the money for Edward's proposed crusade. When the English king was granted the proceeds of the tenth for the Holy Land in 1291, the prize of eight years of negotiation, it was only logical that the transfer of deposits held by Italian firms would be effected through the Riccardi, bankers to both pope and king. They were to provide 100,000 marks for the first half of the grant at the feast of the nativity of St. John (24 June) 1291.[8] The money is described as being deposited outside the realm of England and was held by various firms from which the Riccardi would have to collect. Italian financiers had no doubts as to the effect of the withdrawal of so large a sum

[5]Gino Arias prints this in *Studi e Documenti di Storia del Diritto*, pp. 157–166.

[6]*Ibid.*, p. 62.

[7]E 101/601/5 p. 26, letter of 10 October 1295.

[8]A copy of the bull was entered in the "Liber A," E 36/274 fo. 18 m. 57d. It is printed in *Foedera,* I, ii, p. 750. Cf. *Registres de Nicholas IV,* II, no. 6668. The instructions for payment of the second half of the tenth also appear in the "Liber A," E 36/274 fo. 21 mm. 60–61, and are printed in *Foedera, loc. cit.* Cf. Lunt, *Financial Relations*, p. 340 n. 7.

from circulation. We have the assessment by one of the Cerchi: "E ancora crediamo che moneta sara cara uguanno, per lo fatto de' denarii della decima che il papa dae ora novamente al re d'Inghilterra."[9] The amounts due from each of the several firms was a matter of disagreement between the merchants and the papal chamberlain, leading to "grandissimi dibacti." The Riccardi set their share at 13,000 marks, but the papal camera thought they owed 17,600.[10]

Despite the uncertainties in the evidence on the French extortion and the recall of papal taxes, the meaning of these events for the Riccardi seems to be clear at first glance. Within a span of a few years the merchants had lost a large sum of money, reducing their capital at a time when the money market was tight. But we must ask how badly the company was hurt by this blow and to what extent Edward's action in 1294 was influenced by the state of the Riccardi in the several years preceding his move.

It has been suggested that the shadow of impending bankruptcy stretched across the society as early as 1290 and that the Riccardi were literally dependent on royal grants to maintain solvency. When the king could no longer keep his bankers afloat, according to this view, he seized their assets in payment of their debts to him.[11] This interpretation simply will not fit the facts of 1290-1294. The Riccardi account for the period shows that large

[9] Re, *Archivio*, p. 101, citing Emiliano-Guidici Paolo, *Storia politica del municipi italiani,* II, p. 234.

[10] Re, *Archivio*, p. 101. Arias, *Studi*, pp. 70, 72.

[11] This is the view of M. D. O'Sullivan, *Italian Merchant-Bankers in Ireland in the Thirteenth Century*, pp. 71-76. Cf. his "Italian Merchant-Bankers and the Collection of the Customs in Ireland, 1275-1311," *Medieval Studies Presented to Aubrey Gwynn, S.J.*, pp. 175-179. O'Sullivan makes broad and often incorrect generalizations on the basis of the Irish evidence printed in the *C.D.I. 1285-1292, 1293-1301*. The fact that the Riccardi received more from the Irish exchequer than they paid into it, far from indicating a desperate effort to bail out a sinking firm, simply shows that the merchants were being paid out of Irish revenues for advances made elsewhere. The yearly payments of £120 went for expenses of customs collection, and could not in any case have significantly helped a company which operated on the scale of the Riccardi. The merchants did not begin

amounts of money were indeed coming to them, but this is hardly strange for a firm of royal bankers. Moreover, the account clearly indicates that these receipts were in repayment for past Riccardi advances. The merchants had by no means ceased to provide substantial loans. Between August and November of 1293 they advanced £10,000 for household expenses.[12] Then in the opening months of 1294 the king's brother, Edmund, Earl of Lancaster, borrowed 25,031 marks while on a diplomatic mission in Paris.[13] Finally, we have seen the volume of their money-lending to great lords and the dominant position of the company in the export of English wool.[14] In light of this evidence it can not be assumed that the Riccardi were already on the rocks. Quite to the contrary, they appear to have weathered the blows of 1291 and to be functioning normally as royal bankers and important merchants.

Why, then, should Edward in a period of severe crisis break with a firm of bankers who still retained their financial power? No explanation of his action accompanied the writ which deprived them of the customs, but in the orders for sequestration of their goods and debts the official reason given again and again is that the merchants are held to the king in so great a sum that their resources are insufficient to pay.[15] The full particulars of the charges against them were first placed on the pipe roll for 26 Edward I,[16] and were repeated there year after year until 6

to suffer seriously from internal dissentions, once Baroncino had left in 1286, until after 1294. They did not commit a great blunder in calling in deposits of papal taxes; the initiative on such a move rested entirely with the pope.

[12] C 81/7 no. 597. *C.P.R. 1292-1301*, p. 59. E 372/139 m. 6.

[13] S. C 8 file 260 no. 12970. See below, p. 337. The references to this loan in the Riccardi letters indicate that the partners in France provided the money and handled all arrangements. E 101/601/5, p. 26d., letter of 10 October, 1295.

[14] Above, Chapter I Section 2.

[15] See, for example, the order for arrest and confiscation in Ireland. "Quia mercatores de societate mercatorum de Luka nobis in tanta pecunie summa tenentur quod eorum facultates ad solucionem debiti nostri non sufficiunt. . . ." E 159/68 m. 83d.

[16] E 372/143.

Edward II, when they were moved to the Rotulus de Corporibus Comitatum.[17] The list of charges is as follows:

£	s.	d.	
333	6	8	Issues of vacant bishopric of Hereford, May, 3 Edward I
166	13	4	From bishop of London, for service in Wales
20	0	0	Farm of Windsor
2,000	0	0	From Dionisia de Monte Canisio, Ralph de Coggeshale, William Hastings
133	6	8	Received for Roger Moubray
22,812	19	11	"Remanencia compoti" for customs
33	6	8	From Matthew de Multon, scutage for Wales
2,200	0	0	From constable of Bristol, of the 30th
246	13	4	Received "de diversis"
435	5	0	From Philip Willoughby, Gregory Rokesle, Ranulf de Dacre
466	13	4	From same
600	0	0	From same
100	0	0	From same
61	13	4	Owed for Federigo Venture
£29,609	18s.	3d.	

[17]E 372/129 m. 5d. A shorter and quite different list is given on the LTR Memoranda Roll, E 368/70 m. 26. The sheriff of London has been ordered to summon the Riccardi to answer for eight sums totalling more than £7,000. But now, in Michaelmas term of 1298, the merchants are given respite until the coming octave of Hilary 1299. Of these eight sums only three are found on the Pipe Roll lists of charges: the payment from the Bishop of London, the 2,000 marks, and the £20 farm of Windsor. The charges dropped on the Pipe Roll lists include: £4,404, fines from merchants; £666 13s. 4d., from William of Windsor; £27 9s. 8d., surety for Walter of Watford; 500 marks, received from the Archbishop of Canterbury; and 100 marks, listed without explanation.

Many of the items making up the list are of the sort which might appear among the charges put against any fallen medieval financial official. Some are quite old, such as the money received from the keepers of the bishopric of Hereford in 1275, or the fine for service and scutage for Wales, which date to either 1277 or 1282-1283. The £2,200 out of the thirtieth of 1283 should not appear in this list at all. The Riccardi had accounted for this sum along with other receipts from this war levy.[18] The most important charge, though, is obviously the customs money. This can be identified as the remainder left on their account for the customs for 1286-1290, after deductions were made for the "surplus" of expenses in the previous account and the expenses for the 1287 Welsh campaign.[19] The period covered by the account coincides with the years which Edward spent on the continent, years of very heavy Riccardi expenditure in his service. In trying to determine the balance between king and banker in 1294 we might consider it likely that this customs money became partial payment for the more than £103,000 which Edward acknowledged that the Riccardi had paid for him on the continent during these years.[20] Suspicion of this customs charge–and indeed suspicion of much of the entire list–finds ample confirmation in letters close issued nearly twenty years after the king broke with the Riccardi. Passions had cooled by the time Edward ordered the

[18] E 359/4A m. 4.

[19] E 372/134 m. 3. E 352/82 m. 19.

[20] See Chapter II, Section 2. In the 1290-1294 account the merchants were given a block discharge for £54,180 of the king's money they had received during these years "for money in which the king was held to them upon the last account of the merchants at the exchequer." E 372/143 m. 35d. This clearly points to repayment of Gascon expenses. There is no evidence for repayment of the remainder. Even if the merchants finally received them, the profits of the duchy could not eliminate so large a sum in the few years before the collapse of the company. On these revenues, see above, pp. 157-158. In 1295 when the Riccardi discussed the king's obligation to them, they mentioned "the account of Gascony . . . which is around 1,000 marks which he has to give us, and similarly of the currency (*moneta*) of Gascony, as Orlandino knows, he has to satisfy us for 2,000 marks. . . ." E 101/601/5, Letter of 10 October, 1295. The reference to the *moneta* indicates the Gascon mint in which the Riccardi were active.

barons of the exchequer to cease demanding any sum received by the merchants prior to 7 July 1290 (except for customs receipts between the preceding Easter and that date). They had, reads the order, on that day rendered an account with which he was completely satisfied and he had given them an acquittance. The order was first issued 6 December 1305, repeated in January of the following year, and reissued by Edward II in October of 1309.[21] Thus the official list of charges against the Riccardi is false, and expresses the king's anger with the company more than it shows the actual balance of accounts. It is not surprising that at a time of acute crisis Edward should draw up such a list against the merchants who he thought had failed him.

What is surprising is the attitude toward the king found in the Riccardi letters of 1295-1301. Here there are no sulfurous denunciations of a perfidious and ungrateful king. To the contrary, they hopefully noted any softening in his attitude toward the company and frequently expressed the desire to be able once again to establish the old connection. "He must be quite willing to have us return to prosperity and honor, so that we might be able to serve him as we used to; for even if he looks to all the merchants in the world we are certain that he will not find there merchants who will serve him with as great a faith or love, or as willingly as we have served him, and will serve him even more so, if God puts us in the condition of being able to do so."[22] In another letter the Riccardi in Lucca exhort their London partners to handle affairs there wisely, adding "and may God . . . give you the grace to do so that it may be to the honor of Milord the king, to whom God grant life and wealth, and to our safety, and also so that we may return to our former state and serve the king and the other lords as we formerly did."[23]

Yet at the same time the Riccardi acknowledged that they were indebted to the king. Their constant goal in these years was to

[21] *C.C.R. 1302-1307*, pp. 357, 360; *Ibid., 1307-1313*, p. 186. C 54/127 m. 16. E 368/76 mm. 23, 22d.

[22] E 101/601/5, p. 23. Undated fragmentary letter, written after October 1295.

[23] *Ibid.*, p. 27, letter of 10 October 1295.

convince Edward to come to an account with them, to deduct from what they owed him the value of goods and debts he had taken into his hands, to collect as his own the debts yet outstanding, and then to give them terms for the small remainder.[24] In October of 1295 the home office sent to London a rough list of these outstanding debts from which the king could be satisfied. It begins with their estimate of what the king himself owed them. "We think that it is from 40,000 marks upwards. Afterwards he should settle what Milord Edmund owes us, which is around 30,000 marks, and if he should want to review the damages we have had from him, it would make [a total of] 40,000. Now counting this the rest should be easy to obtain."[25] The Riccardi thus thought that 70,000 or 80,000 marks would reduce their debt to manageable proportions. For the rest they listed the sums owed them by various bishops, earls, knights, etc., to a total of 8,800 marks, "without mentioning other debts which are owed to you from 100 to 200 marks." They also noted that the king had in his power the wool and leather of the society worth around 6,000 marks and the debts of two other Lucchesi, Giuntoro Ranieri and Lando Ronsini. Finally, they reminded their partners that there were "many good debts" in Ireland and those the Bonsignori owed them in both England and Ireland. Unfortunately the Riccardi never gave a specific statement of the exact extent of their obligation to Edward, but it is clear that they considered it to be something more than 90,000 marks, or £60,000. This is more than twice the amount of Edward's own charges against them.

[24] *Ibid.*, pp. 26d., 27. Cf. p. 2, letter of 5 December 1297; p. 14d. undated letter; p. 38, letter of 3 November 1301.

[25] Both these sums are actually written as only 40 marks and 30 marks, yet they must be read as a shorthand for this number of thousands of marks. The mention of several specific sums owed to them by the king (1,000 marks and 2,000 marks) show that the royal obligation could hardly be 40 marks. Moreover, in other documents we learn that the bulk of Edmund's debt was made up of 25,031 marks loaned in France, indicating that the figure of 30 marks should be read as 30,000. S C 8 file 260 no. 12970.

In order fully to explain the state of accounts in 1294 we would like to have more evidence. Yet we can suggest a hypothesis which goes far toward explaining the healthy state of the Riccardi in 1291-1294, the debt which they readily acknowledged at the end of this period, and the reasons why Edward broke with them so abruptly in the summer of 1294.

It is possible that the Riccardi treated the proceeds of the sexennial crusade tenth like any other source of royal income in their charge—that when they collected the sums due from the other depositaries they simply added this money to their own funds. According to the general working agreement with Edward I royal revenues in their hands were not transferred to royal officials, but were retained as repayment for past advances and as a cushion against future demands. If this were the case with the sexennial tenth, the Riccardi would not have been seriously undermined by the demands made on them around 1291. Rather, they would have benefited greatly by the calling in of the tax and could easily have continued their normal service to the English crown while conducting the private business of the firm as usual. Edward normally had a standing debt of about £20,000 with his bankers,[26] but if they retained the tax proceeds the balance would have been more than reversed; royal revenues in their hands would exceed the king's debt to them several times over. The crippling blow to their fortunes could then be pinpointed at the outbreak of war between England and France. Edward had turned to his bankers in each of his three previous wars and he undoubtedly expected to do so again in 1294. He stood in gravest need and they held a huge sum of his money. But the situation had changed entirely. The two most important bases of Riccardi activity were split apart by war and the shifting of funds from one country to the other, so important for a firm such as the Riccardi,[27] became impossible. The sudden failure of negotiations over Gascony caught Edward completely by surprise; the

[26] E 101/126/1. E 372/143 m. 35d.

[27] See Re, *Archivio*, p. 106. A passage in the letter of 10 October 1295 shows that their business in England and France was most important to the firm.

requests for sizable funds which we would expect him to present to the Riccardi could have been no less a shock to them. Perhaps they were caught with much of their capital tied up in long-term projects. They had, for example, made large loans to the Bonsignori and Bettori that were not repaid by 1297,[28] and we have seen that when their wool was seized it included the entire year's supply from eleven religious houses.[29] When Boniface recalled their deposits of the papal tenth for Sicily it was the final blow.

We can picture Edward's going into a purple rage upon learning that not only were his bankers unable to finance the coming war with France, but also that the papal tenth, secured after years of negotiation, could not be fully recovered. In one of their letters the Riccardi quoted Edward's declaration that "what he had taken of ours he had taken as from men who had deceived him."[30] A passage in what seems to be the earliest of the extant letters refers to "the great indignation of the king, and also the ill-will which he showed he had towards the company, and which could be seen from his actions."[31] At this point they were prematurely hoping that the royal wrath was cresting.

Some further support for the hypothesis comes from the evidence on the tenth itself. We can see the various firms of Italian merchants paying their shares of the deposits to the Riccardi on behalf of the English king,[32] but proof of the delivery of the money to Edward cannot be found. The painstaking student of the financial relations between English kings and the papacy, William Lunt, thought that the money was paid by the Riccardi, but confessed his doubts in a footnote in which he observed that

[28] E 101/601/5, p. 5, letter of 5 December 1297. The account with the Bettori was finally closed on 1 January 1300, at which time they owed the Riccardi £87 17s. and £916 15s. tournois. But the Lucca Riccardi complained that Edward had taken all the debts secured by exchequer recognizance, apparently without crediting the sums to their obligation to the crown. S C 1, 58, no. 20 B.

[29] See Chapter I, Section 2.

[30] E 101/601/5, p. 4, letter of 5 December 1297.

[31] *Ibid.*, p. 25d., letter of 10 October 1295.

[32] Arias, *Studi*, pp. 58–59.

"payment is not well attested in royal documents." He felt that payment was likely, though, because the papal order to the Riccardi was preserved in the exchequer; the merchants would not have surrendered this document unless delivery of the money had been made.[33] Yet we now know that this mandate could easily have found its way into governmental archives as a result of the seizure of all the Riccardi *libri et scriture*.

If the papal tenth was at the root of Edward's break with the company, then the rough idea of mutual obligations presented by the Riccardi would be explained. The sum of 100,000 marks would not be charged to them in the exchequer records for it was not a source of revenue which came under exchequer jurisdiction. But an indebtedness of this size would match the scale of outstanding debts from which they hoped to repay the king.

2. THE EVENTS OF 1294

There are many gaps in our information about the actual process of Edward's break with his bankers, but the outline of events in 1294 can be quickly told. An order for the arrest of the wool and goods of foreign merchants was issued on 2 June.[34] The wool of the merchants of Lucca was taken by royal officials at the same time as that of other firms,[35] but beyond this we do not know the extent to which the king's relationship with them had deteriorated. The collection of the customs was still in their control, and they were also collecting money owed them without interference.[36] When they were deprived of the customs seals on 29 July, we can be certain that the tie with Edward was broken.[37] Yet the only extant order for the arrest of the merchants themselves came on 28 October and applied only to Ireland. Their

[33] Lunt, *Financial Relations*, p. 341 and note.

[34] E 159/68 m. 82.

[35] *Ibid*., m. 87.

[36] See, for example, the case involving the executors of the late Thomas Bek, Bishop of St. Davids, on 6 July. E 159/67 m. 52.

[37] E 159/68 m. 86d.

goods were to be taken into the king's hands and their arrest effected lest they flee from the king's power without license.[38] We can reasonably assume that the arrest in England was carried out at about the same time under similar instructions. It is clear from the Riccardi letters and government documents that an arrest was carried out in England. In September of 1295, when their seized wool was being sold abroad, Edward ordered that a member of the *societas* should supervise the sale, but specified that it was to be someone resident abroad; none of the Riccardi in England was to be allowed to leave the realm for this purpose.[39] In December Edward had begun to collect their debts for his own use through the exchequer.[40]

Men were at once assigned to collect the Riccardi wool. The sacks which had belonged to the company were gathered in Southampton, Sandwich, London, and Hull, with the carting being done at their expense.[41] In November, when the fleet organized and led by Laurence of Ludlow crossed the Channel, 227 sacks of Riccardi wool were included in the holds of the ships. The overloaded vessel in which Laurence sailed went down, drowning the man who had originated the idea of wool seizures. The Riccardi lost wool worth 25 marks, but this sum was allowed them, and the remainder of their wool was sold for £1046 4s. 11d.[42]

The bulk of their wool, however, had not been shipped with the

38 *Ibid.*, m. 83d. *C.F.R. 1272-1307*, p. 347.

39 *Ibid.*, m. 86d.

40 E 101/601/5, p. 1. E 159/68, m. 83. As late as 21 October the merchants seem to have been receiving money owed them. *Ibid.*, m. 48d.

41 E 159/68 mm. 87, 88d.

42 E. B. Fryde, "Financial Resources of Edward I in the Netherlands, 1294-1298: Main Problems and Some Comparisons with Edward III in 1337-1340," *Revue Belge de Philologie et d'Histoire* 40 pt. 2 (1962), p. 1181, citing E 159/1 m. 25. J. de Sturler, "Deux 'comptes enrôlés' de Robert de Segre, receveur et agent payeur d'Edouard Ier, roi d'Angleterre, aux Pays-Bas (1294-1296)," *Académie royale des sciences, des lettres, et des Beau-arts de Belgique, Brussels, Commission Royale d'Histoire, Bulletin*, 125 (1959), pp. 593-594. He prints E 372/144 m. 31, 31d. On Laurence of Ludlow see Eileen Power, *Wool Trade*, pp. 79, 112-113.

Ludlow fleet, but was sold in 1296-1297 by Elias Russell, citizen of London, and Gilbert de Chesterton, citizen of Stanford, as supervisors to Robert de Segre, king's receiver in the Low Countries. It was Segre who had also accounted for the earlier sale. After packing and shipping costs of £136 11s. 7d. were deducted, the wool brought £4400 14s. 5d.[43] The sales took place in Antwerp and Brabant with a Riccardi-appointed agent being included in each negotiation.

Although a small part of this wool was shipped from Ireland (via London), most of the wool bought by the company in Ireland was apparently transported and sold at a later date. In January of 1296 a supply of 48 sacks 46 nails (along with three lasts of hides) was ordered shipped to Yarmouth and thence to Brabant, but whether this was actually carried out is uncertain.[44] Nearly a year later, in March of 1297, another order concerning Riccardi wool in Ireland directed that it be sent to Sandwich and then on either to Flanders or Brabant.[45] But once the wool arrived in Sandwich it was actually carted to London and shipped out from that port. A large quantity is involved, 195 sarplers of wool plus 4 lasts 8-1/2 dicra of hides.[46]

Chesterton and Russel reported selling twenty-nine sacks of Irish wool from the Riccardi in 1297, but no more than that; and in the spring of 1298 the London customs collectors sold Riccardi Irish wool worth £1,996 12s. 9d.[47] At the price brought by the Irish wool sold by Chesterton and Russel—about £3 a sack—

[43] E 372/146 m. 54.

[44] E 159/69 m. 24d. A sack of wool is an amount weighing 364 English pounds; 52 "nails" make a sack. The "last" is a measure of 200 leather hides. See Baker, *T.A.P.S.* 51 (1961), pp. 7-8. It is possible that the 49 sacks 8 nails of wood and 3 lasts of hides sold under the supervision of Chesterton and Russel, included in their wool sales abroad, represent this Irish shipment sent via London instead of Yarmouth. But the quantities are slightly different and there is no indication in their account that this is Irish wool.

[45] E 159/70 m. 109d. *C.D.I. 1293-1301* no. 384.

[46] E 122/68/3. Sarplers are large bags weighing more than the official sack. The dicra, or dicker, is a unit of ten hides.

[47] E 401/143.

this would mean something like 662 sacks. Yet in July of 1301 the English administration thought there was still more Riccardi wool in Ireland, for they ordered it to be appreciated and sold, the proceeds going to the king's new banking firm, the Frescobaldi of Florence.[48]

Thus it is quite difficult to trace the shipment and sale of all the wool taken from the Riccardi,[49] but from the documented transactions we can see that the king collected £7,460 5s. 5d.[50] The loose ends in the evidence make a larger sum seem certain.

Having examined the wool sales it is interesting to turn once more to the king's estimate of the merchants' obligation to him. The Riccardi could easily have been cleared of the £29,609 charged against them at the exchequer, even if we ignore their own estimates and rely solely on government documents. If we deduct the £18,924 Edward owed them from their final account, and the profits he made from their wool, the charge is at once reduced to about £3,324. At this time Edward's clerks had drawn up a list of debts owed the Riccardi which came to £6,927, without counting the debts of three bishops, five earls, and about a dozen important men in the administration, listed separately without the sums they owed.[51] Even if Edward were unwilling to collect from the men on the second list, considering the political

48 E 368/72 m. 56d.

49 While the Irish wool seems particularly elusive, the records of English wool are not totally reassuring either. A roll of customs particulars from Hull, in such damaged state that no date appears, mentions 249 sacks 6 stone of Riccardi wool shipped from that port. It clearly was being sold for the king's benefit as repayment of the debt of the company, thus dating the roll as after 1294. In the Chesterton and Russel account the quantity of wool shipped from Hull and sold abroad is only 41 sacks 7 stone. Furthermore, an order on the LTR Memoranda Roll for 31–32 Edward I shows that the king granted Gui Ferre 26-1/2 sacks of wool which Baroncino Gualteri owed the society. E 368/74 m. 31.

50 The Receipt Roll for Easter 25 Edward I shows that the London customs officials paid £122 12 s. 0d. into the exchequer for leather belonging to the Riccardi. E 401/141.

51 E 101/126/7. See Chapter I, Section 2. The list can probably be dated between July and October of 1294, i. e., after the king broke with his bankers (as seen in the loss of customs control), but before the death of

gain of ignoring the debts to be greater than the economic gain of extracting the last shilling, the Riccardi resources were more than ample to meet the charge in exchequer records.[52] Moreover, we know that the king did collect debts which appear on neither of these lists, such as the £751 owed by the archdeacon of Lincoln,[53] and recovered further sums from the sale of Riccardi property in Ireland.[54]

The Riccardi lists of debtors and the property of the *societas* in England and Ireland certainly offered a rich field, but how much of his loss did the king actually recover? Taking into account the papal sexennial tenth, how did the books stand when Edward died? Although we cannot know precisely, it seems that Edward had moved quite far toward restoring a balance. The exchequer in England had gone to work on those who owed money to the Riccardi, squeezing about £4,000 out of them by 1307.[55] The Dublin exchequer did its part also, recovering at least £1,084 from Riccardi goods and debts in Ireland.[56] Moreover, Edward had decided that it was politically profitable to pardon various people on the Riccardi list. The Earl of Lancaster, the Earl of Warwick, Roger Mortimer, Stephen de Penchester (constable of Dover and Warden of the Cinque Ports), John de Havering (justiciar of Wales, seneschal of Gascony), and others were allowed to

---

John de Sanford, Archbishop of Dublin, who appears on the list without any such notation as "defunctus" or "nuper defunctus." He died on 2 October 1294.

52 One of the sums contained in the £6,927 is the £2,600 owed by Jacopo Bettori ("Jacobus Bettre"). The Bettori were failing at this time and recovery of all of this debt might have been quite difficult. This would reduce the total of the list of debts to £4,327. But this figure, plus the other sums taken from Riccardi goods and debts, still comes to more than £3,324.

53 E 368/71 m. 53. This was collected in installments between 1296 and 1300.

54 *C.D.I. 1293-1301*, nos. 226, 565, 682.

55 Based on the Receipt Rolls, E 401/138 through 167.

56 The sums were £518 0s. 4d. in 1295, £405 5s. 0d. in 1298, £419 12s. 8d. in 1299. *C.D.I. 1293-1301*, nos. 226, 565, 682 respectively.

write off the loans they had received from the merchants.[57] The total of these obligations came to roughly £1,000, without counting that of the Earl of Lancaster.

If we accept the Riccardi estimates of what Edward owed them at the time of their fall from his favor[58] and their claim that the loans to Edmund of Lancaster should be put on the royal account, then the king ultimately recovered much of the money he was to receive from them for the papal tenth. For if we add to Edward and Edmund's debts the sums recovered by the English and Irish exchequers, the known profits of Riccardi wool sold by the king, and the debts of the politically important which Edward chose to ignore, the total comes to approximately £59,210 out of the proceeds of £66,666 of the sexennial tenth:

£46,666	debts of King and Earl of Lancaster
4,000	debts to Riccardi in England
1,084	debts and property in Ireland
7,460	known wool sales
£59,210	

Yet it hardly need be added that the king's real loss is not to be measured in such a balance sheet. At what was the most critical period of his reign he had lost the services of the firm which had been for two decades a major prop to his financial structure. It was beyond doubt a catastrophe.

In France, as in England, the exact date of the arrest is not

[57] E 368/72 m. 28. *Ibid.*, 73 m. 36d. *Ibid.*, 77 m. 53 d. *C.P.R. 1301-1307*, pp. 116, 468. *C.C.R. 1288-1296*, p. 309. *Ibid.*, *1296-1302*, pp. 58, 249, 251, 431, 536. *Ibid.*, *1302-1307*, pp. 11-12.

[58] It seems entirely reasonable to do so. Their estimate of his obligation is 40,000 marks, or roughly £26,666. In their final account the king owed them £18,924, and to this can be added several sums mentioned in their letters: about 3,000 marks from Gascony; an indeterminate assignment on the dues of the county of Ponthieu; and 3,000 marks from "the affair of Sandwich." This comes to nearly £23,000, with the sum from Ponthieu missing. See below, n. 96.

known. Jordan cites a document ordering the arrest on 8 October 1294,[59] but we have another order, sent to the seneschal of Beaucaire on 13 August, which refers to the arrest as already having taken place.[60] The disruption that Philip's orders caused in the company is reflected in their letters. Explaining why a certain transfer of 541 *livres tournois* was not made, the partners in Lucca confessed that "the only reason why we did not do so is that we had great fear and trepidation of the people of the king of France, because of the prohibition which was made to us by them that, under pain of our bodies (*core*) and possessions, we should not pay any money for you over there. . . ."[61]

Philip's orders to the seneschal of Beaucaire instructed him to search their books diligently for any evidence of payments made for the king of England within the last year. If none were found, their books and writings were to be returned and public proclamation made in the fairs that debts owed them were to be paid. We may suspect that Philip had no doubts about the outcome of such a search. The document shows, moreover, that as in England arrest meant a loss of their vital business records. The suspension of their debt collection probably indicates that Philip himself was taking these. He seems to have collected a fairly large sum from the Riccardi in one way or another. One account from this period which refers to the Italians in general and the Riccardi in particular shows a payment of 65,000 *livres tournois*.[62] Concerning Riccardi personnel in France at this time we have very little infor-

59 *De Mercatoribus*, p. 28, citing Archives Nationales (Paris), L 278 no. 2.

60 *Histoire Generale de Langueduc*, X, p. 303. The reference was taken from Bigwood, *Annales d'histoire*, 2 (1930), p. 204 n. 3. It appears in calendar form in E. Martin-Chabot, *Archives de la Cour des Comptes, Aides et Finances de Montpellier*, p. 23, no. 114. The order for arrest reads "Nos socios de societate Richardorum de Lucca et eorum bona fecissimus arrestari pro eo quod ipsi regi Anglie gentibusve aut consiliariis suis pro ipso mutua et pagamenta de pluribus peccuniarum summis in regno nostro dicebantur fecisse in nostri gravamen. . . ."

61 E 101/601/5, p. 5d., letter of 5 December 1297.

62 Boutaric, *Notices et Extraits des Manuscrits*, XX, 2e partie, p. 129.

mation beyond the fact that a small branch was maintained in Paris until 1300.[63]

3. STRUGGLE FOR SURVIVAL

Once the company had been undermined by the events of 1294, we can follow their struggle for survival in some detail, drawing mainly on the series of their letters from this period. It was to be a desperate chess match, with two kings and a powerful bishop ranged against them. Edward I and Boniface VIII were touchy creditors whose good will had to be cultivated; Philip IV was an outright enemy.

The condition in which the merchants found themselves was a serious one. A letter from late 1297 summarizes their analysis of the situation. To the London partners, who were complaining that the home branch had not provided enough help, the *socii* in Lucca wrote the following:[64]

> . . . we are well aware of the anger and the troubles that you have had and still have, and we certainly believe that they are much greater than what you have told us. Now if we could show you we would show you and you would see clearly that we have suffered it with you and are suffering it to the very end. . . . However, as you know and as we have written to you in all the letters which we have sent to you, we have been and are in such a state and condition that we have not been able nor are we able to find either friend or relative or lord who might have helped us or wanted to help us. On the contrary, those to whom we have rendered great services and great honors everywhere, and who are in the world only because of God, first of all, and secondly only because of us, and they are now in great condition and great riches—these people have acted the worse towards us, and have tried the hardest to obtain our harm and damage. Now we can say, and do say,

[63] Piton, *Les Lombards,* I, pp. 126, 130, 142, 149.
[64] E 101/601/5, p. 1, letter of 5 December 1297.

> that all of this has befallen us because of the cursed seizure which the king of France has made against us, and then because of the other one over there [i.e., in England], and because of the great debts which you have sent us and which we have not been able to pay, nor are we able to pay. Because of this we have lost all gain everywhere, so that we do not find anyone willing to give us credit of even £10 of Lucca. And similarly, if we want to obtain money by selling our possessions, which are the best and the prettiest which we have, we cannot find anyone who will give us money for them . . . and if we do find some buyer willing to do such a trade they ask for security, and you have heard above how easily we can find it . . . nor can we find a way out unless we pay, but we cannot pay, either the whole or in part. Therefore all our affairs are lost, for we cannot utilize any of our accounts nor ask for money from those who owe us. But those people to whom we owe money want to be paid, and they bring against us all the actions (*processi*) they can find. . . . Whence the griefs have been so many, and from so many parts, that we are dying from them and do not know what to do, nor shall we ever find an escape until God delivers us of this and peace is made between the kings and we return in the favor of our lord [i.e., Edward I]. We hope in God that all of this will be accomplished, and that it will happen soon, with His help.

Parts of this catalogue of woes are recited in nearly all of the Riccardi letters. It is clear that a "run on the bank" occurred after their arrest on both sides of the Channel in 1294. They complained that "because of these two adversities everyone to whom we owed money ran to us and wanted to be paid, and because of this we were held very tight everywhere."[65] The scar-

[65] *Ibid.*, p. 25d., letter of 10 October 1295. This is reflected in the exchequer plea rolls by the sudden increase in the number of instances in which an attorney is named against the Riccardi in a plea of debt. In any year previous to 1294 there might be a few such cases. See for example E 13/8, 9, 12, 13. But in the three years after the break with Edward I the number of instances jumps to 20, 15, and 9. E 13/20, 21, 22 respectively.

city of money and the impossibility of finding the credit which was the lifestream of a company caused great distress. When the London Riccardi commented on the great market for wools, the response from Lucca was that this market was no surprise; what amazed them was that any money was available at all.[66] A few years later they declared: "It seems that money has disappeared."[67] But the most revealing indication of their enfeebled credit concerned the great money markets of the Champagne fairs. "We are in such bad shape that at the fairs of Champagne, where used to be all our gain and that of all merchants, and where we used to have credit and could borrow 100,000 and 200,000 *livres tournois* and even more, we are now reduced to such a point that if we wanted 100 *livres tournois* we could not find them. . . . "[68]

Things were indeed going badly in France as well as in Italy and England. "And if you refer to our debts [to be collected] in France, we can tell you that they could not recover enough money to get out of the debts which they themselves have over there up to now. They have purchased many woolen cloths and very expensive ones, from which, up to now, we have not gotten 1,000 gold florins, since in Puglia there is a great quantity of them and they are sold very slowly."[69] The members of the French branches of the company lived in fear during these years. "We are very wary with the people of the king of France, for all they need is the slightest reason to jump against us and destroy us completely."[70] When an old promissory letter from Edward I was lost, one of the Riccardi agents, apparently stationed in Flanders, was thought to have brought it to Paris. But he hotly denied this, assuring the home office that "even if it had been given to him to be brought to Paris, he would not have brought it for any reason, for fear that it would be found on him by the people of the king of France."[71]

[66] E 101/601/5, p. 2d., letter of 5 December 1297.

[67] *Ibid.*, letter p. 31d. (probably 1301).

[68] *Ibid.*, p. 25, letter of 10 October 1295.

[69] *Ibid.*

[70] *Ibid.*, p. 1, letter of 5 December 1297.

[71] *Ibid.*, p. 4d., letter of 5 December 1297.

With the enmity of two kings directed against them—each for his own reasons—as a result of the war, the Riccardi longingly awaited an Anglo-French accord as a first step toward recovery. "You should know that we are well aware and admit that we will be able to do much for you once the truce is made, and we will be able to send and recover a certain amount of money to you to give to the king. . . ."[72] They were certain that once peace was made their efforts at the papal court would also be more productive.[73] But when Edward and Philip did arrange a series of truces, beginning in 1297, there was no improvement in the state of the merchants.

The general Riccardi plan was simple and consistent throughout these years. They were confident that their assets were sufficient to meet their debts and that they could recover if only they could get their creditors to collect from their debtors. Boniface was to be satisfied partly from the debts of prelates, who were particularly susceptible to pressure from the Holy See. The Colonna cardinals are specifically mentioned in this regard. The Riccardi had enjoyed good relations with this powerful family, writing of the two cardinals Jacopo and Pietro as good friends and lords to the *societas*. Thus the conflict between Boniface and the Colonna caused them much concern, and they reported the course of the quarrel to London, but they were hopeful that a reconciliation would be effected and that the pope would be able to collect what the Colonna owed them, "which is a large amount," deducting this from their debt to the *curia*.[74]

Yet they counted on the reduction of this debt mainly by assigning to Boniface their possessions and money seized by Philip the Fair. As we have seen, they hoped to repay Edward largely by deducting his own obligations and those of his brother, with the remainder coming from sums owed the society in England and Ireland. In implementing the plan they would work through all their friends in the various courts, but they placed

[72] *Ibid.*, p. 25, letter of 10 October 1295.

[73] *Ibid.*, p. 2, letter of 5 December 1297.

[74] *Ibid.*, p. 4d., letter of 5 December, 1297; p. 11, letter of 1300 (?).

great emphasis on obtaining papal support in dealing with the two kings. When their troubles began in 1294 they could not foresee that the future would bring *Clericis laicos, Unam Sanctam*, and "the crime of Anagni."

In order to bring papal influence into the balance on their behalf in England or France, they had first to reach agreement with Boniface. In the end this proved an impossible task.

The opening round, however, went to the Riccardi. In what seems to be the earliest letter of the series we learn that two cardinals[75] sent to England on other business spoke to the king about the affairs of the company. In order to please them and the pope, Edward agreed to commit the accounting to Antony Bek, Bishop of Durham. This was a cause of celebration among the London partners whose praise of the bishop is reflected in a letter from Lucca describing him as "a very wise man and upright," a "special lord of our company," who would "know and see clearly that truly our company cannot satisfy the desire and wishes of milord the king, which are ours also, because of what has happened to us. . . . " They were prepared to strengthen his clarity of vision. In the rough list of outstanding debts in England, included in this letter, they noted that his obligation stood at 800 marks, "if you think you should mention it to him."[76] But all their efforts and all the goodwill of Bek brought them no discernible relief.

Moreover, the financial needs of the papacy put an obvious

[75] These were probably the cardinals of Albano and Palestrina who, in the parliament summoned in August of 1295 at Westminster, harangued Edward in Latin on the blessedness of peace. See C. M. Frazer, *A History of Antony Bek*, p. 65.

[76] E 101/601/5, p. 26d., letter of 10 October, 1295. In what seems to be a later letter the Lucca Riccardi say they are writing to Bek "asking him and beseeching him that our affairs should be recommended to him and that, by God, it should please him to recognize the truth, and to have it known to the King, concerning our inability to do the will of the King and to carry out his intentions, for the reasons which we tell him. Since the King has entrusted our affair to him, as far as money is concerned, he should keep in mind this one time the great love which he has always had towards the company." *Ibid.*, p. 23d.

limit on the patience Boniface would show to the Riccardi: it was only his interest in recovering what they owed him which seems to have prompted the help he gave them. When a demand for 300,000 gold florins was made on the depositaries of the *decima*, the Riccardi share was set at 40,000.[77] In a panic the merchants sent Labro Volpelli to the curia where, as their letter describes it, the following scene took place:

> Labro arrived at the curia and went to the pope and threw himself at his feet and said, "Holy Father, you know our condition and our affairs as well as we do. Both in France and England we do not have the power to give a penny; but you know what the king of France holds of our money against God and reason, so that we ask you by God to send someone there and ask for the money as if it were yours, and take it, and you will have it right away. Similarly, we have to receive much money from prelates; take this and pay yourself of what we owe you." Therefore the pope took compassion on us and granted us grace, as you will learn later.

The self-interest in this display of grace is clear in their summary of his reply. Boniface "thought that if he pushed us and came against us our affairs would go very badly and the church therefore would not be paid, but would be in worse shape."[78] Thus he agreed to send a clerk to Philip, asking for delivery of the Riccardi money which actually was money belonging to the church. The Riccardi hoped that a surplus might even be recovered, so that funds could be transferred to England, and that the pope would provide "good letters and strong" so that proceedings against their debtors would be effective.[79]

The aura of grace was quickly dispelled. "Know that, starting a month ago, the pope has started this new thing with us . . . be-

[77] The letter does not specify which of the several papal tenths is involved here.

[78] This was also his attitude towards the failing Bonsignori in 1298. See Edouard Jordan, "La faillite des Bonsignori," *Melanges Paul Fabre*, p. 418.

[79] E 101/601/5, pp. 26, 26d., letter of 10 October 1295.

cause of the expenses he incurs for King Charles. . . . " Once again the Lucca *socii* shuddered upon receipt of a request, this time for a written obligation concerning the tenth for Sicilian affairs. A sum of 80,000 gold florins was expected as the Riccardi share, with 20,000 to be paid within two months. They answered that they "could not be able to pay for anything in the world . . . even if he hangs us all by the throat." Reiterating their plea concerning their French assets, they argued that Boniface should take the 10,000 *livres tournois* Philip had evidently agreed to give, collecting from the well-known Musciatto. The merchants recited a long list of debtors, urged the pope to send general letters for collection "at our expense, through us," and promised repayment not only of the 80,000 florins, but of their entire debt in this fashion. Boniface would hear nothing of it and arrested the two representatives of the firm who were in Anagni (Lagna). A third, Riccardo Guidiccioni, was more fortunate. Being ill, he had gone to the baths at Viterbo where he heard of the arrest and slipped back to Lucca. There Boniface had sealed the Riccardi house and everything in it.[80]

They quickly sent Stefano Buzolini to the pope "with very good and humble letters from us, both to the pope and the cardinals." Ambassadors were also dispatched by the commune of Lucca, and the merchants breathed more easily. Somehow they reduced the papal ire and even won Boniface over to a partial implementation of their plan. A letter was sent to England recommending the Riccardi and their affairs to Edward in lavish, but very general, terms.[81] Some collection of Riccardi money for the pope in France also continued, for in February of 1297 an order for delivery of 20,000 *livres tournois* went to the firm of the Franzesi. The money had been received "as is said, by you from our dearest son in Christ, Philip, Illustrius King of the French, for the Riccardi Company of Lucca. . . . "[82]

[80] E 101/601/5, p. 28d., letter of 10 October 1295. The two Riccardi agents were Bonino Riccardi and Sir Nicolao Chiavari.

[81] *Foedera,* I, ii, p. 835. This seems to be the letter referred to in the Riccardi letter of 5 August 1296.

[82] *Registres de Boniface* VIII, nos. 2326, 2329.

The papal letter to Edward made little dent in his resolve not to come to a formal account with his former bankers. Nor does it seem that any more positive result came from the mission of the priest of Santa Felicita, sent by the pope two years later. The Lucca Riccardi anxiously asked what answer Edward gave this cleric about the affairs of the company;[83] although we do not have Edward's answer, it could hardly have been what the merchants wanted. Persistently the Riccardi approached their old friends and clients, urging them to speak to the king on their behalf. The instructions from Lucca reminded the Riccardi in London not to relent. "We also ask you, as urgently as we can, to do your best, day and night, to get in touch with all our lords and friends over there whom you think to be closest to the king, and to ask them to beseech the king for us, so that he should calculate as having been paid what he has taken from us, and similarly the other things which we have said . . . so that at his return there you may settle everything with him."[84] On another occasion they wrote "good and beautiful letters, with many prayers and recommendations" to Edmund, the king's brother, the Bishop of Durham, the Earl of Lincoln, the treasurer, and Robert Tibetot.[85]

The copies of the letters carried to London no doubt pleased the Riccardi there, but they were greatly disappointed by what they considered a lost opportunity. When Walter Langton, the treasurer, went abroad in 1296-1297, seeking alliances against the French, they expected to learn that careful instructions and perhaps one of the partners would be sped to the Low Countries. It was most important to influence "Messer Gualtieri da Langatone" since "the fate of our affairs will be what he will want." Yet no one was sent. After weakly countering criticism by the assertion that they were never really certain he was there, the Lucca partners admitted the real reason for inaction: " . . . even if

[83] E 101/601/5, pp. 2, 44, letters of 5 December 1297 and 21 April 1298.

[84] E 101/601/5, p. 2, letter of 5 December 1297. Edward was then on the continent.

[85] *Ibid.*, undated letter, p. 23d.

we had known for certain that he stayed over there, still the fear and fright that we have that the king of France might hang us is so much the more reason why we have not had the courage to go there."[86]

But when either Langton or members of his party came as far as Rome, the Lucca Riccardi reported that they were anxiously awaiting him, hoping to arrange a meeting between the English treasurer and the pope which would help their relations with both England and Rome. They assured the men in London that he would be honored in every way possible. "Would it please God that we had the means, as we have the goodwill."[87]

Several years later the bishop of Vicenza thought that he had obtained a promise from Boniface to send to the kings of England and France the letters they sought. But nothing came of it, despite the fact that the attempt was costing them much money.[88] They next cornered a brother of a certain cardinal and informed him of the unfulfilled promises. Since he had been summoned by the pope they were optimistic about his ability to help them, for they knew that Boniface "has such a disposition that none can talk to him unless it is at his will."[89] But again, there was no result.

About a year later hopes turned to the coming of English ambassadors to Lucca en route to Rome. The plan was to send Labro and several companions with them to present a united front at the curia, although how the envoys were to be won over completely is not explained. Either the visit did not materialize, or it was unproductive, for no further mention is made of the plan.[90]

[86] *Ibid.*, p. 1d., letter of 5 December 1297.

[87] *Ibid.*, p. 46d., undated letter. See G. P. Cuttino, "Bishop Langton's Mission for Edward I, 1296-1297," *Studies in British History* XI no. 2 (1941), p.. 150.

[88] E 101/601/5, p. 17d., undated letter.

[89] E 101/601/5, p. 17d., undated letter. The cardinal might have been the brother of Sir Pietro da Piperno, but the letter is unclear.

[90] *Ibid.*, p. 44, letter of 21 April, 1298. Two later efforts of this sort might be noted. When the merchants learned that the bishop of Pustori was going to Rome, they arranged to see him first, giving him a letter explain-

In trying to come to terms with Edward, the Riccardi were most anxious to obtain a deduction for the loans they had made to his brother, the Earl of Lancaster. As we have seen, this basically involved the sum of 25,031 marks advanced while Edmund was in France "por les besoignes nostre seignur le Rey."[91] In characteristic fashion, the merchants not only approached Edmund himself, but also worked through such friends as Otto de Grandson, Antony Bek, the Count of Savoy, and the Earl of Lincoln.[92] Lincoln seemed a particularly useful contact "as a man who is very grieved when the affairs of 'messer Aimondo' do not go well." But a special appeal went to Edmund's wife, Blanche of Artois, Queen of Navarre. The partners in Lucca congratulated their London associates and were pleased with her show of good will:

> Concerning the conversation which you had with the Queen of Navarre about the money which her husband owes us, and your asking her to act in such a way with the king so that he would count this money in his own account, you did very well and we are happy. Now you say that the king had promised her to do so, but that when he heard our name mentioned, as you say, he got very upset and did not want to do any of this, saying that what he had taken which belonged to us he had taken as from men who had deceived him. . . . We are very happy about her good will . . . but the urging is good so long as she is there, so that we ask you by God to be as eager as you can be in this, so that this affair might be completed.[93]

---

ing their objectives. But despite his good will, matters of finance were not his forte—"he said that he did not understand well those things"—so a member of the firm went along to coach him. Letter of 4 December 1300. A year later the bishops of Durham and "Chester" (i.e. Walter Langton, bishop of Coventry and Lichfield), were expected in Lucca, presumably on their way to Rome. The Lucca partners assured London that they would be honored as much as possible. Letter of 3 November 1301.

91 S C 8, file 260, no. 12970.

92 E 101/601/5, p. 14d., undated letter.

93 *Ibid.*, p. 4, letter of 5 December 1297. The Riccardi in France were to send a full list of particulars on Edmund's debt so that Blanche could agree with the company on the sum owed before she spoke to the king again.

Another objective in England was the return of their books and records, seized by Edward when they were arrested. These were badly needed both in London and Lucca for recovering outstanding debts and determining the individual obligations of members. Thus the letters often discuss the urgency of regaining them. "We urge you as strongly as we can, as we have asked you in many letters, to try to get back your books somehow. . . because we have the greatest need of them and we cannot carry on any business nor arrange our bookkeeping if we do not have them.[94]

When papal influence was not forthcoming they realized that a price would have to be paid. It seems that in 1296 or 1297 £500 was the amount requested. This the Riccardi could not pay. In November of 1301 a letter from Lucca backed their decision not to spend a large sum, "for to lessen our possessions is our death." They would hope in God, await grace from the pope, and meanwhile bribe with smaller sums "those people to whom a payment is useful."[95]

The Riccardi frequently gave attention to such specific cases, working through any indirect channel available, but at least once they directly tried to obtain a general accounting.[96] An undated

[94] *Ibid.*, pp. 4d., 5, letter of 5 December 1297; p. 15, letter of 5 September 1301; p. 40, letter of 3 November 1301; p. 31d., undated letter.

[95] E 101/601/5, p. 40, letter of 3 November 1301, p. 45, undated letter. The passage in the second letter is not entirely clear due to the damaged condition of the manuscript. The information was apparently transmitted to the Riccardi by Otto de Grandson.

[96] In their letters the Lucca partners frequently urged that several sums be included in any such accounting. One of these is made up of the money which they insisted Edward still owed them from Gascony. They mention 1,000 marks "for the account of Gascony . . . . and similarly [concerning] the currency of Gascony . . . 2,000 marks." E 101/601/5 p. 26d., letter of 10 October, 1295. A second deduction from their obligation to Edward should come from the dues of Ponthieu (*Pontiso*). Edward had given them a promissory letter charged on these taxes until their loans to him were paid. But the letter was somehow lost and the agents in France, Flanders, and England were told to search for it. *Ibid.*, p. 4d., letter of 5 December 1297. Finally there is the "affair of Sandwich (*Sanguisso*)" by which the company lost 3,000 marks. This arose from a dispute between foreign merchants in 1293 when the Riccardi were ordered to buy the

petition addressed to the king and council mentions the obligation of the king's brother, but continues with a broader request that the king "por dieu de sa grace comander que acounte soit ove eaux aussi bien de ceux [25,031 marks] comme de deners en les quieux les ditz marchantz sount tenuz au dit nostre seignur le Rey e que allowe leur soit ceo que il poiront resunableant mestrer que alloue leur deit estre de droit." The petition brought some results, for John Droxford, William de Carlton, John de Kirkby and Hugh Nottingham were appointed to hear the account and notify the king.[97]

This may or may not be the accounting referred to in a second source, the Lord Treasurer's Remembrances Memoranda Roll for 34-35 Edward I. In Easter term of 1307 the barons of the exchequer were informed that Orlandino, Thommasino, and Federigo, "recently merchants of the Riccardi Company of Lucca" ("nuper mercatores de societate Riccardorum de Luca"), had petitioned the king to admit them and their associates to his grace and benevolence and to order that a full account be held concerning their obligations to the king on the day he took their goods and chattels into his hands, and also how much he had recovered since that time. The king was said to have compassion for the state of the merchants and ordered the account so that he and his council could be better informed.[98]

Regardless of the favorable nature of these orders—and regardless of whether they represent royal response to a new petition, or action on the petition previously noted—the result cannot have been dramatic relief for the Riccardi. If any accounting was held before 1301 it did not forestall bankruptcy, if after 1301 it might

---

goods in question and hold them for safekeeping. They were apparently unable to dispose of these themselves and petitioned the king to allow this loss in their account. S C 8 file 260,no. 12959. See Hubert Hall, ed., *Select Cases Concerning the Law Merchant* (Seldon Society XLVI, 1929), pp. xciii–xciv. The letters from Lucca urge that this be put on their account: undated letter, pp. 36d., 26d., letters of 10 October 1295, 3 November 1301.

97 S C 8 file 269, no. 12970.

98 E 368/77 m. 43d.

simply have eased conditions for the surviving members of a firm that had already failed. It is possible that the king changed his mind and that no accounting was in fact held. As to the crucial debts of "Messer Aimondo," in 1306 his heir, Thomas, was pardoned any obligation owed to the Riccardi, or any debts of his father to them, as a reward for his service in the Scottish wars.[99]

As the company failed to make any significant progress toward recovery, and only weakly fended off collapse, internal disintegration became quite evident. Some members were convinced that failure would soon overwhelm the firm and began to look to their own interests. It became difficult to maintain all of the far-flung branches of the firm. Ireland was naturally affected first, being the most distant from Lucca. As noted before, the sole Riccardi agent there probably left in 1301, after a long period of dissatisfaction.[100] But even in France there were problems with personnel. A Benetuccio del Barcanchera was writing one letter after another to Lucca, saying that "he wants to return to Lucca and does not want to stay there any longer, because he can be of no use to us there in recovering our debts, and he cannot get the money without the letter from the pope, and because of other affairs which demand his presence in Lucca, and the expenses there are very great, and if he remains his affairs will be damaged, and his father has told him this too. . . . "[101]

In other instances the self-interest of company agents was even more apparent. The partners who remained loyal to their oath bitterly condemned those who were not and blamed much of their trouble on the dissensions. They were certain that a united front would reduce the boldness of enemies and encourage friends to renewed effort. Adiuto Rosciompelli and his sons and a certain Adoardo and his brother were named as culprits in one letter to London. "When these two shall want the wealth and honor of the company we are sure, as we are sure of the fact that death will come to us, that we would be in good shape, both we

[99] *C.P.R. 1301-1307*, p. 468. E 368/77 m. 53.

[100] See Chapter I, Section 1. Cf. E 101/601/5, p. 16, letter of 5 September 1301.

[101] E 101/601/5, p. 16.

and they. And when the end will come, if we shall be in bad shape, they will not be in good [shape] either."[102] This theme of disunity and treachery is returned to again and again. "We are well aware," they wrote, "that over there there are several men from our own country, and our own flesh and blood, who have done and are doing the worst they can. We know them well and they are doing things we shall never forget. . . . Now may God through His mercy no longer look at our sins and may He have it in His heart and will that those who have to pay up the company pay up, and that we may be of one heart and will as we used to be."[103]

Under these circumstances the difficult task of determining the obligations owed by each partner and factor to the firm became nearly impossible. One of the earliest Riccardi letters contains requests for this information and mentions "the four who have to see and place a charge (*imposta*) upon each companion of how much he has to give." These men probably represented the authority of the commune, but had a limited period in which to act, and apparently lacked any means of enforcing restitution on the basis of their findings.[104] The commission of "the four" seems to have expired before anything could be accomplished, for after Labro was elected one of the priors of the companies, apparently in 1298, a new body of three *arbitri* was named to examine the Riccardi accounts. These are probably the arbiters who appear throughout the remaining period of time covered by the letters.[105] Yet the same inability to enforce any decisions they might reach made an appeal to the papal court a necessary corrective to the continuing discord. Labro, Enrico da Pogio, and Riccardino Gottori obtained papal support in June of 1300. Boniface issued a letter in favor of his "dear sons" of the Riccardi. Before prescribing a solution this document outlined the problem, noting that many partners were acting in bad faith, using company funds

[102] *Ibid.*, p. 17.

[103] *Ibid.*, p. 11, letter of 1300 (?).

[104] *Ibid.*, p. 29. For the parallel case of the Bonsignori see Jordan, *Melanges Paul Fabre*, p. 417.

[105] E 101/601/5, pp. 18, 14, 38–39.

for private purposes. Considering that the company owed so great a sum to the church, the pope felt that this was a reasonable matter for his intervention. When the arbiters had reached a decision, it was to be put into effect under the direction of the bishop of Pistoia who was to use ecclesiastic censure and call upon the secular arm if necessary.[106] Whether this formidable array of coercive power was ever brought to bear before the failure of the company is very doubtful. It could hardly have saved the Riccardi, who were hurt beyond repair in 1300, though it might have distributed the burden of the failure more equitably among the members of the society.

They had apparently placed high hopes on this mission led by Labro who, despite his illness, had been keeping up the morale of his fellows. The mission had been delayed while he recovered.[107]

It is against such a background that we must see the mission of Labro, Enrico, and Riccardino in 1300. Their success in gaining papal backing against dissidents should not obscure their larger goals. The old basic plan was once more urged on the pope: papal letters were to be sent to England helping the Riccardi regain their former state; Boniface was to be satisfied by collecting from the king of France, the Colonna, and the clergy, or—if he would not do this—executors were to be named to recover Riccardi debts from which the church would then be paid. At this time complaints from London were brushed aside with the assurance that "with the aid of God we shall briefly send you good news." In fact, they wrote, "if we do not answer all the things you asked

[106]The pope states that some partners "minus fideliter se gerentes et ad dissipationem omnimodam societatis asperantes ipsius, quasdam de pecunia societates ejusdam quantitates non modicas timere subtraxerunt, eas propriis ipsorum usibus applicando, ipsique, in suo prave intentionis proposito nequitur obfirmati, quantitates ipsas prefate societate restituere contradicunt. . . ." At the same time the Riccardi obtained a second favor from Boniface. To enable them to raise money by selling their goods it was necessary to reassure wary buyers who knew of their indebtedness to the Holy See. A second letter made provision for these assurances. *Registres de Boniface VIII* nos. 3623, 3630. Both are dated 8 June 1300.

[107]E 101/601/5, p. 18, undated letter.

us do not be surprised, because we are very busy in planning this mission to the curia." To gain their requests Labro and his companions took with them "a certain quantity of money to do with it the will of the pope, even though it is a small quantity in comparison with what we own him."[108] After this effort, the results must have been particularly disappointing. The death of Labro came not long after the failure of his mission, and the company thus lost an important leader.[109] He had been a man with high hopes and grand plans for the recovery of the *societas*. Before his mission to Rome the Lucca partners wrote to London that "he is very cheerful and has no doubt that he will be able to obtain from [the pope] those letters and that embassy which he wants to have. Having obtained this he wants to go there [i.e., London] as quickly as possible, and if he goes we are certain that, as you say, the king will see him with pleasure and will give him grace. Of this we are certain and this is one of the greatest plans we have, to have Labro go there. Labro himself has both the talent and the will to advance the honor and the condition of the company and of Lucca. . . ."[110]

Their plans were bringing no relief, but the letters show desperate attempts being made. The Riccardi were hoping to persuade the royal favorite Gui Ferre—their friend "Messer Guido Ferrieri"—to gain Queen Margaret's ear and convince her to ask her brother, Philip the Fair, to give them aid in collecting what was owed them in his realm. Letters should be sent by the King of France to his *baillis* "just as we had at another time at the request of Messer Musciatto."[111] In Rome a Master Bonamore da Corellia was retained, at a fee of 50 gold florins, as procurator at the papal

[108]E 101/601/5, p. 11, undated letter.

[109]*Ibid.*, p. 43, letter of 4 December, 1300.

[110]*Ibid.*, p. 18.

[111]*Ibid.*, p. 4, letter of 5 December 1297. On Gui see Powicke, *Thirteenth Century*, p. 319. The Riccardi often wrote about the means of settling this debt, urging that "Messer Guido Ferieri" and his associates be satisfied "because this is one of those debts we have which we want to pay more willingly and to make good, because of the great good we have received from them." Letter of 5 September 1301.

court. He is described as wise and well-mannered, a great friend of the company who knew all their requests by heart. His connections may have been yet more valuable than his personal abilities. The Lucca partners wrote that "he resides in the house of Cardinal Sir Pietro da Piperno, who is closer to the pope than any other cardinal."[112] But Boniface was interested only in Sicily, and Master Bonamore could report no progress to Lucca. The commune was loyally Guelf, however, and an ambassador from Lucca was at least able to get an audience. But he had much business to discuss and could devote only a little time to the requests of the society.[113]

Affairs in London had meanwhile completely deteriorated. Letters full of biting criticism and anguish over the course of events had given way to silence. The correspondence from Lucca complains of long gaps;[114] in September of 1301 no messenger from London had arrived for six months.[115] By November, the home office was reconciled to abandoning the branch in Ireland.

[112]*Ibid.*, p. 7d., letter of 17 November 1301; and p. 17d., undated letter. The latter shows that he was probably helping the Riccardi before they formally retained his services. They were likewise hoping for aid from Master Geoffrey of Vezzano, a papal tax collector, with whom they had dealt in England. The letters frequently mention their account with "Messer Giuffredi."

[113]*Ibid.*, p. 15, letter of 5 September 1301. When Boniface called for troops to launch his "crusade" against the Colonna, Lucca sent 300 men, both crossbowmen and spearmen. The Riccardi proudly describe them as "the most handsome and best people who went from all of Tuscany, so that the pope was very happy with them and very grateful." *Ibid.*, p. 4, letter of 5 December 1297. They were also hopeful that the success of Charles of Anjou and steadfast loyalty from Lucca would soften the pope's attitude to the company. The Lucca partners write to London: "We understand that Messer Charles was in Florence at the Kalends of November, so that after Florence has been put to order, it will be better if the rest of Tuscany is put to order as well, and is in peace. May it please God that it be so. Therefore because of the news in Tuscany, and because it has for a long time stood firm and steadfast on the side of the church, the pope shows great love for our commune, and does almost everything that the commune asks him as a favor." *Ibid.*, p. 38, letter of 3 November 1301.

[114]*Ibid.*, and undated letter, p. 31d.

[115]*Ibid.*, p. 15, letter of 5 September 1301.

Ghirardo Chimbardi, who alone had apparently represented the society, was given permission to leave, depositing all of the account books and writings, the agreements and letters, in some safe place where they might securely await the return of good times. He was to be most careful, however, to obtain the permission of the Irish treasurer before leaving "so that we shall not have any trouble or indignation from the king, which is something we certainly do not need for anything in the world, and especially now that we are hoping for a reconciliation."[116]

Ideas of reconciliation were merely wishful thinking. We see in one of the last letters in our series that later in that same month the Riccardi in Lucca learned that the London branch had gone bankrupt. Two things are remarkable about this announcement and its reception. It shows, in the first place, the degree to which an international firm had become regionalized by the effects of war and arrest and the subsequent loss of credit and decline. The London branch went under, but we know that Lucca at least struggled on for a while. Second, it is surprising to note how calmly the home office took the news. The response from Lucca mentions grief and sorrow, but is basically concerned with what is to be done to rectify matters. The men in London are admonished to write more often, are told to recover certain sums, are informed of efforts in Rome.

The situation in Lucca was bad enough. We catch a glimpse in late 1301 of the merchants confined to their house as the arbiters, who could not reach a conclusion, were working night and day under a threat of a large fine. "Every day the *seguitore* of the priors, who is a foreign notary, comes to the shop to ask and know whether we are all there, and those who are not found are condemned [i.e., fined]. In such a way the arbiters of our affairs will bring to completion what they have to do."[117] One letter was composed with the Priors literally looking over the writer's shoulder. After the Lucca partners told the London partners once

[116] *Ibid.*, p. 39d., letter of 3 November 1301.
[117] *Ibid.*, p. 10, letter of 17 November 1301.

more to send full financial statements, a final paragraph was added:[118]

> After what we had written up to here the Priors wanted us to tell you that they order you to do what is written above, under penalty of £1,000 for each one. We therefore tell you that you are ordered to do so, both by them and by us.

Yet the Lucca partners, proved masters at loud lamenting, raised no cry of impending doom at this point; much more gloomy letters had been written in 1297. We can only conclude that the failure in London was not seen as the end of the company as a whole, even though the home office survived only as a handful of men who had not yet accepted the inevitable.

The last letter in the series, written on 12 April, 1303, is similar to many composed several years earlier. Doggedly the Riccardi clung to the hope of papal letters, and blamed their failure at the curia on the inability to raise money for this effort. When they sought money, "Everyone says 'I haven't' and those who have more money deny it all the more." Their most pressing fear is that Boniface VIII "will take from us all we have even if we could escape to India. . . . May God help us." They were watching the pope's movements closely and planned to send someone to Viterbo where he was going to stay a few weeks. Likewise, they watched the progress of Edward I's treasurer closely, noting that since he had spent Easter in Genoa or Savona he should appear in Lucca in a few days. "We will call on him recommending our business," they promised, "and we shall honor him at our best, although we cannot do what is suitable and [what] we would like to do. But certainly he will see how much we need." Undoubtedly their hopes had been inflated by the news of the Anglo-French treaty so long awaited. "We enjoyed very much to hear that, God be thanked and praised, and we pray Him to set

[118] *Ibid.*, p. 37, dated 1 November without indication of the year, but probably 1301.

peace between Flanders and the king [of France] and everywhere there is war, amen."[119]

Such hopes were, of course, in vain, but with this letter we have come to the end of our best sources and cannot say when the Lucca *socii* suspended any attempt to meet their creditors' demands. It is possible that such a declaration was never made and that the company merely faded as the members died, their property being confiscated by whatever creditors could most effectively press their claim.

In 1307 Clement V ordered the sequestration of all the goods and debts of the Riccardi in England, suspecting that Adiuto Rosciompelli and his son Vanno held much property in England, Wales, Scotland, and Ireland.[120] But an inquisition taken in 1344 demonstrated that the greater part of the debts owed the church —which together with those of the Bonsignori were estimated at 80,000 florins—had never been recovered.[121]

The pope should have realized that this ground had been well ploughed by the English exchequer. Many debts were collected before Edward's death, and the long memory of the exchequer stretched into the reigns of the second and third Edwards as well. The Pipe Rolls for Edward II contain summons for money owed "of the debts of the merchants of Lucca,"[122] and as late as 4 Edward III a hanaper containing records of the Riccardi debts was kept by the lord treasurer's remembrancer.[123]

Orlandino da Pogio, Federigo Venture, and other Riccardi were in England at least through the first decade of the fourteenth century. Their lot was made somewhat easier when the orders, noted above, freed them from being molested for any receipts

[119]S C 1 58 nos. 20A, B.

[120]*Calendar of Papal Letters* II, 1305-1342, p. 32.

[121]Lunt, *Financial Relations* p. 603.

[122]E.g., E 372/164, London membrane. Collection went on in Ireland at this time as well. See *Historical and Municipal Documents of Ireland, 1172-1320* (Rolls Series, no. 53), pp. 422-425. In 1318 the remembrancer of the Dublin exchequer, Thomas de Warilou, was appointed to sue and levy Riccardi debts in Ireland. *C.F.R. 1307-1319*, p. 372.

[123]E 159/106 m. 145d. Dr. E. B. Fryde supplied this reference.

prior to 7 July 1290. Then in 1309 they were exempted from any pleas or distraints for debt "until they have discharged their debts to the king. . . ."[124] After this we lose all contact with Riccardi personnel.

Throughout the period after 1294 they were presumably still under arrest and certainly out of favor. How difficult the king's officers made life for them does not appear. Although they probably could not leave the realm without license,[125] they were never thrown into prison, with one exception. In 1297-1298 Federigo Venture was held in the Fleet prison because of his failure to pay the king 100 marks as a pledge for a former master moneyer. But Orlandino and Tommasino were able to secure his release by executing a recognizance to the king for the debt.[126]

The conditions of their arrest were not so stringent that they were unable to carry out some transactions by letter.[127] Evidently not all their debts were in the king's hands. But such business as they were able to maintain was usually nothing more than attempted recovery of money owed them, and sometimes the instructions from Lucca are to assign it to the king rather than lose it altogether.[128] In 1302 they retained some control over their London houses and goods, for in December of that year they were permitted to grant the houses in fee simple to Gui Ferre or to satisfy their debt to him in some other way.[129] The fact that letters sent from Lucca between 1295 and 1303 are to be found among exchequer documents indicates that a new

[124]*C.P.R. 1307-1319*, p. 120.

[125]It is evident from their letters that Riccardo Guidiccioni left England, went to Rome, and returned. E 101/601/5, pp. 28d., 24. To do so probably required royal permission if, as suggested above, conditions in England paralleled those in Ireland.

[126]With so much money owing from the company, the fact that so small a sum cast a member into prison is either ironic chance, or perhaps a minor instance of persecution.

[127]E 101/601/5, *passim.*

[128]E.g., *Ibid.*, pp. 3d., 5, letter of 5 December 1297. ". . . and if you should not be able to recover it, we tell you to put it before the people of the king, as we have told you in this letter and make it so that he has it."

[129]*C.P.R. 1301-1307*, p. 13.

seizure of Riccardi records took place in 1303 or later, but on the whole it seems that the merchants were simply being restricted in their movements and transactions, and that any profit which came to governmental attention was siphoned off to the exchequer.

Their standing with the king probably improved over the years, as the memory of the terrible crisis of 1294 became less sharp and painful in the king's mind. Throughout these years the Riccardi had cooperated with the royal administration testifying at the exchequer when needed to unsnarl old accounts, participating in the sale of their wool abroad, assigning to the king debts owed them. Although their loyalty had been no simple matter of free choice, their letters show a constant good will and a consistent desire to regain the king's confidence. The force of Edward's anger—fearful enough at first—may thus have been slowly reduced.

Even so, these were bitter years for the merchants of Lucca. The men who had helped build the company and guide it through times of great prestige and wealth died in bankruptcy and disgrace. In the closing paragraph of the last extant Riccardi letter a partner in Lucca asked for four grey lambskins, "large, well-haired and high," to make a hood, "for I need them in wintertime;" he also begged the London partners to find 50 marks to cover current expenses at the papal court, "because we are unable to find here a person who wants to disburse one gold florin, even if they are friends or relatives."[130] It was a steep fall from the years when they had been royal and papal bankers, had dealt with earls and archbishops, had financed armies, and had maintained an effective and profitable business network across much of Western Europe.

4. LESSONS

Looking at the fate of merchant-bankers who entered government service between the fourteenth and sixteenth centuries it is

130 S C 1, 58, no. 20D.

logical to conclude that however seductive the profits and privileges awaiting king's bankers, the relationship was inevitably fatal for them. In England the Frescobaldi, the Bardi, and the Peruzzi learned this hard lesson in the course of the fourteenth century. On the continent loans to princes likewise proved disastrous to the fifteenth-century Medici and the sixteenth-century Fugger. "It seems," writes de Roover, "that it was a general weakness of what N.S.B. Gras has called 'the financial type of sedentary merchant' to drift from private banking into government finance. Nearly always the results were catastrophic."[131] Financiers repeatedly came to this realization too late. As Sapori noted, "on s'en apercevait toujours trop tard, a l'heur des concordats et des catastrophes, a l'heur des cris, des deceptions, de la rage, quelques instants apres l'enthousiasme de jours heureux."[132]

The dangers which appear in such sharp relief to us today, however, were less evident to the merchant-bankers of the fourteenth century. Perhaps with incurable optimism the leaders of each succeeding firm thought that they could survive where their less skillful or less wily predecessors had failed. Perhaps some companies found themselves holding the proverbial tiger by the tail and simply held on as long as they could. Admittedly it was difficult for merchant-bankers to avoid the dangerous loans to princes. Compulsion aside, the royal courts were major consumers of the luxury goods in which the Italians dealt, as they were sources of investment for firms which may have found themselves with more money than safe outlets in which to invest it.[133]

Had Edward I brazenly ruined his first financiers by excessive demands or by defaulting on his obligations, the warning might have been read more clearly by other Italians. However, the Riccardi failure seems to have resulted from several circumstances, not all of which were directly related to their connection with the English government. The critical seizure of their goods and personnel in France was clearly a blow aimed against the bankers of

[131]*The Medici Bank*, p. 66.

[132]*Le Marchand*, p. XXXV.

[133]De Roover, *The Medici Bank*, pp. 65–66, *Banking in Bruges*, p. 42.

the English king; the investment policy which apparently tied up much of their money at a crucial time was simply an error on the part of Riccardi leadership. On the whole the merchants were treated with fairness by Edward I. Failure came only at the end of more than twenty years of highly satisfactory dealings with the king; it was not triggered by royal perfidy.

If the warnings for Italian merchant-bankers were thus less than crystal clear after the Riccardi collapse, the same could be said of the lessons for the English crown. The historian might insist that the king should have reflected on the fragility of a system that presupposed continued peace and good relations with the king of France and with the pope as well, that presupposed continued free transfer of credit throughout Europe. Merchants who depended on commercial ventures on both sides of the Channel, who lent money to pope as well as English king were vulnerable to a whole host of circumstances beyond Edward's control. This danger was apparently a powerful deterrent limiting Philip the Fair's use of Italians in a system analogous to Edward's.[134]

Reading history backward makes it easy to imagine that we can see the later pattern of king and banker foreshadowed in its first exponents. Yet even after the Riccardi system had collapsed, both king and banker desperately wanted to re-establish the old connection. The merchants' letters document their often-expressed hope of returning to Edward's service.[135] That the king recreated a credit structure based on another Italian *societas* shows his confidence in the utility of such an arrangement. One firm had failed but were the circumstances not unusual? Was there not much to be gained and little risked by trying to re-establish the system with a new group of financiers? Edward and

[134]Strayer, "Italian Bankers and Philip the Fair," *Explorations in Economic History* 7 (1969) p. 118.

[135]E 101/601/5 *passim*. If the letters had been intended for the king's eyes we could write off their statements as nothing more than an attempt to regain solvency through royal favor. But this private correspondence shows that the Riccardi felt no bitterness toward the king, no sense of being forced into a ruinous relationship.

the Riccardi, and all of their respective successors, must have considered the risks greatly offset by the opportunities. English kings striving to support their ambitious policies and Italian merchant-bankers seeking profit and commercial advantage in a foreign land would continue to take the risks for a half-century after the Riccardi failure.

Conclusion

By the reign of Edward I the precocious development of the English government had given the crown broad powers and useful institutions, the growth being especially well marked in the area of finance.[1] A long tradition of painstaking accounting set down in careful records had been established by the exchequer, the first offshoot from the unspecialized royal *curia*. Flexible administration of receipts and expenditures had been secured by household personnel close to the king, first in the chamber and later in the wardrobe. By the time of Edward's reign the problem was one not of audit or administration, but of adequate sources of revenue. Perhaps no government has ever thought that its funds were sufficient for its legitimate needs, but the thirteenth-century English administration faced a genuine crisis. Revenues which had served the Norman and Angevin kings fell far short of adequacy in the changed conditions of the thirteenth century. An expanding government found its costs climbing. The unpaid feudal service of vassals had for some time been giving way to hired armies;[2] salaried and educated officials were likewise replacing a

[1] Two of the most advanced financial administrations in twelfth century Europe could be found in England and Flanders. Comparing their systems Bryce Lyon stressed a fundamental similiarity, but noted also that "In almost every respect the English exchequer of the twelfth century was more advanced than the Flemish *redeninge*." Bryce Lyon and A. E. Verhulst, *Medieval Finance, A Comparison of Financial Institutions in Northwestern Europe*, pp. 80-81.

[2] See the important article by J. O. Prestwich, "War and Finance in the Anglo-Norman State," *T.R.H.S.* 5th Ser., 4 (1954).

less well-trained and less specialized type of administrator. As efficiency increased, more ambitious military and diplomatic policies were carried out. War costs were especially heavy and burdensome. Not only was the machinery of government being elaborated and its sphere of competence enlarged, but at the same time kings and their advisors found that prices were rising, causing further erosion of the customary revenues of the crown such as the shire farms.[3]

Two highly important efforts to secure new revenues had been attempted by Edward's predecessors, but neither effort could be said to have succeeded before his accession. The reaction which generated the Great Charter showed that increased exploitation of feudal revenues (reliefs, wardships, fines, scutage), so thoroughly used by King John, was blocked. Although John's methods were undeniably effective, they helped spark the fires of baronial revolt.[4] Another avenue of approach, the percentage taxes on personal property, was open to Edward I. John had experimented with the idea of these percentage taxes in 1207 (imposing a tax of a thirteenth), and precedents for some type of general taxation could be followed back through the ransom of Richard and the Saladin Tithe to the geld.[5] Yet Henry III had not been able to make lay taxation work. From 1237 to 1269 he was unable to convince "the community" to provide a single tax grant, although he made nine requests. He dealt from a position of serious financial weakness through most of his reign.[6]

[3] J. R. Strayer has noted that by the fourteenth century "the king's oldest and surest revenues were no longer sufficient to meet the expenses of his court and household government even in time of peace." *The English Government at Work, 1327-1336, II, Fiscal Administration*, William A. Morris and Joseph R. Strayer, eds., p. 3.

[4] Sidney Painter, *The Reign of King John*, Chapter IV; J. C. Holt, *Magna Carta*, Chapter II.

[5] Sidney K. Mitchel, *Taxation in Medieval England*, Chapter I.

[6] F. M. Powicke wrote that "Somehow or other, in a rich land, Henry managed to live from hand to mouth, and, if his needs were urgent, to raise loans. The money was undoubtedly there to be had, growing in the fields and on the backs of sheep, if only he could satisfy his magnates that his needs were their needs also. The trouble was that he could so rarely persuade them that this was the case. . . . " *Thirteenth Century*, p. 36.

Edward I took three great steps toward solving the problem of revenue sources. First, he imposed the duty on wool and leather in 1275, tapping the profits of the most important English export trade. Second, because his character and policies inspired confidence in the politically potent groups of the realm, he was able to collect parliamentary taxes on personal property with regularity. Third, he assured liquidity by creating the special relationship with the Riccardi. Despite the increased revenue from the wool custom and taxation, the problem of liquidity remained. Unless he devised some means of anticipating his basically sound revenues in an emergency, unless he could find at all times some means of securing ready cash from his erratic income, he could scarcely act in a decisive and vigorous manner; the conquests, the diplomacy, the impressive program of king's works carried out in the first two decades of the reign would have been impossible.

The impact of the Riccardi can thus be seen in the flexibility Edward achieved, a flexibility which would have been the envy of his father or grandfather. "These arrangements," M. M. and E. B. Fryde have observed, "reveal medieval public credit at its best and most useful. They were advantageous to both parties, endured for a long time and contributed to the financial stability of an efficient government."[7] For twenty-two years the Italian firm was vitally important in guaranteeing the supply of ready money the king needed to carry out his plans. These were not years free from financial strains, but the crippling problems which had plagued John and Henry III were notably avoided; the credit facilities of the Riccardi made the first half of the reign a resounding financial success. It cannot be mere coincidence that these two decades were the most productive years of the reign, bringing general peace and stability in the realm, an important diplomatic role abroad, the great statutes which shaped English law for centuries, and the campaigns which resulted in the conquest of Wales. Nor can it be mere coincidence that the period of greatest emergency in the reign coincided with the years after 1294 when Edward no longer had the services of the Riccardi and

[7] *Cambridge Economic History*, III, p. 437.

could not yet depend fully on their successors, the Frescobaldi of Florence.[8] These would have been severely trying times even if the merchants of Lucca had not been crippled; but the severity of Edward's difficulties and the high-handed nature of his response might have been considerably modified. The great crisis of the reign would have been of a different order had Edward been able to count on the financiers who had served him so well in all the major enterprises of the past twenty-two years.

It is further witness to the importance of the Riccardi that Edward began to establish the same type of special relationship with the Frescobaldi in the late 1290's. Despite the collapse of one Italian firm, the credit facilities they had been able to provide were sufficiently needed to warrant another attempt. In fact the relationship between Edward I and the Riccardi initiated a period of roughly eighty years during which "systematic borrowing [was] a regular method of supplementing royal resources in emergencies and of stabilizing royal finances at all times." Through the first half of the fourteenth century English kings were able to find sufficient credit resources to smooth the erratic curve of incidence of royal revenues. The weakening and collapse of these credit arrangements constituted a significant factor in the problems of the late medieval English monarchy.[9]

Whether or not this skillful use of an Italian *societas* was the product of Edward's own mind is an unanswerable question; we have no minutes of early council meetings, no diary or memoirs to reveal the thoughts of Edward or Robert Burnell, his chancellor and virtual prime minister. But if we make the reasonable assumption that Edward at least had a hand in the process, accepting and implementing what he may not personally have conceived, we gain a new perspective on his kingship. Reading a man's bankbook hardly opens windows into his soul, but how he

[8] *Ibid.*, p. 457. E. B. Fryde notes that between 1294 and 1298 Edward could not find a substitute for the Riccardi. While the Frescobaldi began to lend money in 1296, during the following two critical years they could provide only about £7000 on the continent, where the needs were for much more than this.

[9] *Ibid.*, p. 451.

makes and spends money is one important indicator of his aims and priorities.

In his interpretation of Edward's character Sir F. M. Powicke drew upon his vast knowledge of thirteenth-century England to avoid earlier extreme views. Edward was not the great and providential hero of Stubb's vision who with self-conscious, paternal benevolence took "the nation" into partnership with the crown; nor was he the "dour scheming autocrat" who appeared in T. F. Tout's conception of an "English Philip the Fair," "the organizer of despotism and not . . . the pioneer of constitutionalism." Powicke stressed that Edward was simply a man of his age, living "intensely in conformity with the ideas and tendencies of his time."[10] The financial evidence considered in this study reinforces the doubt that Edward's aims were those of an incipient tyrant; his financial system would not in any case have provided the economic base for autocratic rule. Medieval political theory here coincided with political fact: the king must act with consent. Money to repay Italian loans came mainly from the wool custom and the taxes on moveables, both of which required consultation with the king's subjects.

Yet Edward's credit structure alone, if other evidence were lacking, relieves him of the heavy burden of mere conventionality. It is not necessary to transform Edward into an "anti-feudal" proto-Victorian parliamentarian nor an "anti-constitutional" proto-Stuart tyrant in order to see that he was bringing the mèdieval English monarchy to the height of its power, completing the work of William the Conqueror, Henry I, and Henry II, while basically working within the evolving framework of rights and obligations which we formalize with the name "constitu-

[10] *Thirteenth Century*, pp. 227 ff, and *King Henry III and the Lord Edward*, Chapter XVI, especially pp. 724-25. Cf. his "King Edward I in Fact and Fiction," *Fritz Saxl, 1890-1948, A Volume of Memorial Essays from his Friends in England*, ed. D. J. Gordon. T. F. Tout, *The Place of Edward II in English History*, p. 32. Geoffrey Templeman, "Edward I and the Historians," *Cambridge Historical Journal* 10 (1950). V. H. Galbraith, "Good Kings and Bad Kings in Medieval English History," *History* 112 (1945).

tion." In securing funds adequate to his designs by means acceptable to the politically potent—the "community of the realm"—no less than in his great statutes or his military or administrative innovations, Edward showed originality and imagination. The financial evidence fits what we know of the king from other quarters. Although precedents for many of Edward's policies could be found in the reigns of his father or grandfather, although few of his measures were new creations *ex nihilo*, what is striking is the way in which he used old materials to create a new and much stronger structure. The scope and effectiveness of Edward's financial measures were peculiar to his reign. King John had experimented with customs duties on a significant scale; Henry III had occasionally collected sizable tax grants on lay and clerical moveable property and knew how useful was the ready cash of the Italian *societates*; but Edward I fused these components in an essentially new system which solved the problem of royal finance. As a corrective to earlier extreme views it is essential to see Edward as in some sense a "conventional man in an age of change."[11] But the desire to read the man and the reign in terms of his own age must not preclude a recognition of Edward's highly creative role as a medieval state-builder. The Riccardi system was not the least significant of the tools Edward used.

Successful financial mechanisms were, in fact, crucial to the emerging secular state in England as elsewhere. In a seminal article J. R. Strayer has analyzed the political aspect of the general tendency towards secularization that was so pronounced in thirteenth-century Europe. He argues that the shift in the primary loyalties of Europeans from the Church to lay governments owed much more to the drive of efficient secular rulers for a practical monopoly of political power than to general economic changes or a greater degree of "worldliness."[12] Frequent taxation would have given the financial component of the efficiency and power lay rulers were seeking, but, as M. M. and E. B. Fryde have ob-

[11] Powicke, *Thirteenth Century*, p. 230.

[12] "The Laicization of French and English Society in the Thirteenth Century," *Speculum* 15 (1940), reprinted as Chapter 16 of his *Medieval Statecraft and the Perspectives of History*.

served, "to tax their subjects was one of the hardest things for medieval governments." Taxation was still considered quite extraordinary, if not closely akin to outright robbery. "At this stage," they continue, "regular borrowing from important financiers helped to tide the more important states over the difficult period of fiscal reform during which western society was adjusting itself to the painful necessity of taxation."[13]

England under Edward I clearly shows the culmination of the growth of royal power which had been a theme of English history for several centuries. In those massive castles which still stand in Wales we can see ample testimony to the stark power behind English kingship; in the faded ink of writ and statute we can read the intentions and accomplishments of a great legislator, and sense the increased impact of a government touching the lives of more Englishmen than ever before. The *Quo Warranto* proceedings and *Circumspecte Agatis* show the high claims of this royal power to function as the dominant power, allowing and limiting other jurisdictions by royal act.[14] The dramatic humbling of the Earls and Hereford and Gloucester in 1292 demonstrated the assertion of royal dignity even at the expense of the mightiest lords of the march.[15] When Edward I and London met in headlong collision the result was a loss of the city franchise and thirteen years of rule by royal wardens.[16]

Royal power of this strength required sound finances. Whatever other qualities of Edward's kingship went into the formula of his success, solving the problem of revenues was one key element. The story of the first half of the reign would read quite differently without the Riccardi. In their significant addition to the financial strength of the crown we can measure the importance of the Riccardi to Edward I and to the growth of the English state.

[13] M. M. and E. B. Fryde, *Cambridge Economic History*, III, p. 433.

[14] See Strayer, *Speculum* 15 (1940), pp. 78-9. F. M. Powicke, *Thirteenth Century*, p. 227. Donald W. Sutherland, *Quo Warranto Proceedings in the Reign of Edward I*, Chapter 10.

[15] J. E. Morris, *Welsh Wars*, pp. 224-37. Michael Altschul, *A Baronial Family in Medieval England: The Clares, 1217-1314*, pp. 145-153.

[16] Gwyn Williams, *Medieval London*, Chapter IX.

Bibliography

MANUSCRIPT SOURCES PUBLIC RECORD OFFICE, LONDON

E 359 Accounts of Subsidies, Aids, etc.
E 352 Chancellor's Rolls
C 202 Chancery Files, Tower Series
C 62 Chancery Liberate Rolls
C 47 Chancery Miscellanea
E 122 Customs Accounts
E 101 Exchequer Accounts Various
E 13 Exchequer Plea Rolls
E 143 Extents and Inquisitions
E 403 Issue Rolls
E 159 King's Remembrancer Memoranda Rolls
E 368 Lord Treasurer's Remembrancer Memoranda Rolls
E 372 Pipe Rolls
E 401 Receipt Rolls
E 36/274 Registrum Munimentorum, Liber A.
S C 1 Special Collections, Ancient Correspondence
S C 8 Special Collections, Ancient Petitions

PRINTED SOURCES

Antient Kalendars and Inventories of the Treasury of H. M. Exchequer. ed. Sir F. Palgrave, 3 vols. Record Commission. London. 1836.

Bond, E. A. "Extracts from the Liberate Rolls relative to Loans supplied by Italian Merchants to the Kings of England in the Thirteenth and Fourteenth Centuries," *Archaeologia* XXVIII (1840).

Boutaric, E. *Notices et Extraits des Manuscrits de la Bibliotheque Imperiale.* Vol. 20. Paris, 1862.

Calendar of Close Rolls, 1272-1307. 5 vols. London. 1900-1908.

Calendar of Documents Relating to Ireland, 1252-1301. 3 vols. London. 1877-1881.

Calendar of Fine Rolls, 1272-1307. London. 1911.

Calendar of the Justiciary Rolls or Proceedings in the Court of the Justiciar of Ireland, 1295-1303. Dublin. 1905.

Calendar of Liberate Rolls, 1240-1272. 5 vols. London. 1930-1964.

Calendar of Papal Registers. Papal Letters, 1198-1344. 2 vols. London. 1893, 1895.

Calendar of Patent Rolls, 1232-1313. 9 vols. London. 1893-1913.

Calendar of Various Chancery Rolls (Supplementary Close Rolls, Welsh Rolls, Scutage Rolls), 1277-1326. London. 1912.

Chronica Johannis de Oxenedes. Appendix IV (the special wardrobe account for the war of 1282-1283). Rolls Series. London. 1859.

Documents Illustrative of English History in the 13th and 14th centuries selected from the Records of the Department of the Queen's Remembrancer of the Exchequer. ed. H. Cole. Record Commission. London. 1844.

Foedera, conventiones, litterae et cuiuscumque generis acta publica inter reges Angliae et alios quosvis imperatores, reges, pontifices vel communitates. Thomas Rymer. ed. A. Clarke, F. Holbroke, and J. Caley. 4 vols. in 7. Record Commission. London. 1816-1869.

Historic and Municipal Documents of Ireland, 1172-1320. Rolls Series. London. 1870.

Liber de Antiquis Legibus. Chronica Maiorum et Vicecomitum Londiniarum. Camden Society. London. 1846.

Littere Wallie preserved in Liber A in the Public Record Office. ed. J. G. Edwards. Cardiff. 1940.

Ministers' Accounts for West Wales, 1277–1306, pt. I. ed. M. Rhys. Cymmrodorion Record Series. 1936.

Parliamentary Writs and Writs of Military Summons. ed. F. Palgrave. 2 vols. in 4. Record Commission. London. 1827–1834.

Les Registres de Boniface VIII. ed. G. Digard., M. Faucon, and A. Thomas. 4 vols. Paris. 1884–1939.

The Register of John le Romeyn, Lord Archbishop of York, 1286–1296. Surtees Society. London. 1913.

Les Registres de Martin IV. ed. by the members of the École française de Rome. Paris. 1901.

Les Registres de Nicholas III. ed. S. Vitte. Paris. 1938.

Les Registres de Nicholas IV. ed. E. Langlois. 2 vols. Paris. 1905.

The Register of William Wickwane, Lord Archbishop of York, 1279–1285. Surtees Society. London. 1907.

Rôles Gascons, 1242–1307. ed. X. Francisque-Michel and C. Bémont. Paris. 1885–1906.

Rotuli Hundredorum. 2 vols. Record Commission. London. 1812–1818.

Select Cases concerning the Law Merchant. ed. C. Gross and H. Hall. Selden Society. London. 1908–1932.

Select Cases in the Exchequer of Pleas. ed. H. Jenkinson and B. Formoy. Selden Society, London. 1932.

SECONDARY SOURCES

Altschul, Michael. *A Baronial Family in Medieval England: The Clares, 1217–1314.* Baltimore. 1965.

Arias, G. *Studi e documenti di storia del diritto.* Florence. 1901.

Bautier, Robert-Henri. "Les foires de Champagne: recherches sur une evolution historique," *Bulletin de la Société Jean Bodin, V, La Foire* (1953).

Berlow, Rosalind Kent. "The Development of Business Techniques Used at the Fairs of Champagne from the End of the

Twelfth Century to the Middle of the Thirteenth Century," *Studies in Medieval and Renaissance History* VIII (1971).

Bromberg, B. "The Financial and Administrative Importance of the Knights Hospitallers to the English Crown," *Economic History* IV (1940).

Carus-Wilson, Eleanora. "The Wollen Industry," *Cambridge Economic History of Europe*, II, Chapter VI.

Carus-Wilson, E. and O. Coleman. *England's Export Trade, 1275-1547*. Oxford. 1963.

Craig, Sir J. *The Mint, A History of the London Mint from A.D. 287 to 1948*. Cambridge. 1953.

Crump, C. G. and A. Hughes. "The English Currency Under Edward I," *Economic Journal* V (1895).

Davies, J. C. "The Memoranda Rolls of the Exchequer to 1307," *Studies Presented to Sir Hilary Jenkinson*. London. 1957.

Deighton, H. S. "Clerical Taxation by Consent, 1272-1301," *English Historical Review* 68 (1953).

Denholm-Young, N. *Seignorial Administration in England*. Oxford. 1937.

Dobb, Maurice. *Studies in the Development of Capitalism*. Revised edition. New York. 1963.

Edwards, J. G. "Edward I's Castle-Building in Wales," *Proceedings of the British Academy* XXXII (1946).

Face, R. D. "Techniques of Business in the Trade Between the Fairs of Champagne and the South of Europe in the Twelfth and Thirteenth Centuries," *Economic History Review*, ser. 2 10 (1957-1958).

Feavearyear, Sir A. E. *The Pound Sterling. A History of English Money*. 2nd ed. revised by E. V. Morgan. Oxford. 1963.

Ferris, E. "The Financial Relations of the Knights Templars to the English Crown," *American Historical Review* VIII (1902-1903).

Fliniaux, A. "La faillite des Ammannati de Pistoia et le Saint-Siège," *Revue Historique de Droit Français et Étranger* 4e ser., III (1924).

Fraser, C. M. *A History of Antony Bek, Bishop of Durham, 1283-1311*. Oxford. 1957.

Fryde, E. B., ed. *Book of Prests of the King's Wardrobe for 1294–95, Presented to John Goronwy Edwards*. Oxford. 1962.

——, "The Deposits of Hugh Despenser the Younger with Italian Bankers," *Economic History Review* 2nd ser., 2-3 (1949-1951).

——, "Financial Resources of Edward I in the Netherlands, 1294-98: Main Problems and Some Comparisons with Edward III in 1337-40," *Revue belge de philologie et d'histoire*, 40 pt. 2 (1962).

——, "Loans to the English Crown, 1328-1331," *English Historical Review* LXX (1955).

——, "Materials for the Study of Edward III's Credit Operations, 1327-1348," *Bulletin of the Institute for Historical Research* XXII-XXIII (1949-1950).

——, and M. M. Fryde. "Public Credit, with Special Reference to North-Western Europe," *Cambridge Economic History of Europe*, III, Chapter VII.

Funk-Brentano, F. "Document pour servir à l'histoire des relations de la France avec l'Angleterre et l'Allemagne sous le regne de Philippe le Bel (1294-1297)," *Revue Historique* XXXIX (1889).

Galbraith, V. H. "Good Kings and Bad Kings in Medieval English History" *History* 30 (1945).

Gouron, Marcel. "Alienor de Castile en Guienne (1286-1289)," *Le Moyen Âge* 37 (1927).

Gras, N.S.B. *The Early English Customs System.* Cambridge (Mass.). 1918.

Gras, N.S.B. "Economic Rationalism in the Late Middle Ages." *Speculum* VIII (1933).

Herlihy, David, Robert S. Lopez; and Vsevolod, Siessarev, eds. *Economy, Society and Government in Medieval Italy, Essays in Memory of Robert L. Reynolds*. Kent (Ohio). 1969.

The History of the King's Works. ed. H. M. Colvin. 3 vols. London. 1963.

Johnson, C. "A Financial House in the Fourteenth Century," *Transactions of the St. Albans and Hertfordshire Architectural and Archaeological Society 1 (1901–1902).*

_____. "The System of Account in the Wardrobe of Edward I," *Transactions of the Royal Historical Society* 4th ser., VI (1923).

Jordan, E. "La faillite des Bonsignori," *Mélanges Paul Fabre: Études d'histoire de moyen âge.* Paris. 1902.

_____. *De mercatoribus camarae apostolicae saeculo* XIII. Rennes. 1909.

Laurent, H. "Choix de documents inédits pour servir à l'histoire de l'expansion commerciale des Pays-Bas en France au Moyen Âge (XIIe-XVe siecle)," Academie Royale des sciences, des lettres, et des beaux-arts de Belgique, *Bulletin de la Commission Royale d'Histoire* 98 (1934).

Lloyd, Sir J. E. *A History of Carmarthenshire*. London. 1935.

Lopez, Robert S. "The Trade of Medieval Europe: the South," *Cambridge Economic History of Europe*, II, Chapter V.

Lunt, W. E. *Financial Relations of the Papacy with England to 1327.* Cambridge (Mass). 1939.

_____. *Papal Revenues in the Middle Ages.* 2 vols. New York. 1934.

Lyon, B. D. "Un compte de l'echiquier relatif aux relations d'Edouard Ier d'Angleterre avec le duc Jean II de Brabant," Academie Royale des sciences, des lettres, et des beaux-arts de Belgique, *Bulletin de la Commission Royale d'Histoire* CXX (1955).

Lyon, Bryce, and A. E. Verhulst. *Medieval Finance: a Comparison of Financial Institutions in Northwestern Europe.* Bruges and Providence. 1967.

Madox, Thomas. *History of the Exchequer.* 2nd edition. London. 1759.

Mate, Mavis. "A Mint of Trouble, 1279 to 1307," *Speculum* XLIV (1969).

McFarlane, K. B. "Had Edward I a 'Policy' Towards the Earls?" *History* 50 (1965).

McLaughlin, T. P. "The Teaching of the Canonists on Usury (XII, XIII and XIV Centuries)," *Medieval Studies* 1 (1939).

Miller, E. "The Economic Policies of Governments," *Cambridge Economic History of Europe*, III, Chapter VI.

_____. "The English Economy in the Thirteenth Century: Implications of Recent Research," *Past and Present* 28 (1964).

Mills, M. H. "Adventus Vicecomitum, 1272-1307," *English Historical Review* XXXVIII (1923).

_____. "Exchequer Agenda and Estimate of Revenue, Easter Term 1284," *English Historical Review* XL (1925).

_____. *The Pipe Roll for 1295* (Surrey Membrane). Surrey Record Society, London. 1924.

Mirot, L. *Études Lucquoises.* Paris. 1930.

Mitchell, Sidney K. *Taxation in Medieval England.* New Haven. 1951.

Morris, John E. *The Welsh Wars of Edward the First.* Oxford. 1901.

Morris, W. A. and J. R. Strayer, *The English Government at Work, 1327-1336, II, Fiscal Administration.* Cambridge (Mass.). 1947.

Olsen, Glenn. "Italian Merchants and the Performance of Papal Banking Functions in the Early Thirteenth Century," *Economy, Society and Government in Medieval Italy*, ed. David Herlihy, R. S. Lopez, and Vsevolod Slessarev.

Packard, Sidney R. *The Process of Historical Revision: New Viewpoints in Medieval European History.* Northampton, Mass. 1962.

Painter, Sidney. *The Reign of King John.* Baltimore. 1949. Johns Hopkins Paperback edition, 1966.

_____. *Studies in the History of the English Feudal Barony. The Johns Hopkins University Studies in History and Political Science*, LXI no. III. Baltimore. 1943.

Pirenne, Henri. "The Stages in the Social History of Capitalism." *American Historical Review* XIX (1914).

Postan, Michael. "The Trade of Medieval Europe: the North," *Cambridge Economic History of Europe*, II, Chapter IV.

_____. "Italy and the Economic Development of England in the Middle Ages," *Journal of Economic History* XI (1951).

Piton, C. *Les Lombards en France et a Paris.* 2 vols. Paris. 1892-1893.

Power, E. *The Wool Trade in English Medieval History*. Oxford. 1941.

Powicke, F. M. *King Henry III and the Lord Edward*. Oxford. 1947.

———. *The Thirteenth Century, 1212-1307.* Oxford. 1953.

Ramsay, Sir J. H. *A History of the Revenues of the Kings of England, 1066-1399*. 2 vols. Oxford. 1925.

Re, Emilio. "Archivi inglesi e Storia italiana," *Archivio Storico Italiano* serie VI (1913). Vol. I.

———. "La compagnia dei Riccardi in Inghilterra e il suo fallimento alla fine del secolo decimoterzo," *Archivio della Societa Romana di Storia Patria* XXXVII (1914).

Renouard, Y. *Les relations des papes d'Avignon et des compagnies commerciales et bancaires de 1316 a 1378.* Paris. 1941.

Reynolds, R. L. "Origins of modern business enterprise. Medieval Italy," *Journal of Economic History* XII (1952).

Rhodes, W. E. "Edmund, Earl of Lancaster," *English Historical Review* X (1895).

———. "Italian Bankers in England and their loans to Edward I and Edward II," *Historical Essays by Members of Owens College.* Manchester, 1902.

Richardson, H. G., and G. O. Sayles, "Irish Revenue, 1278-1384," *Proceedings of the Royal Irish Academy* 62, Section C (1962).

———. *The Administration of Ireland 1172-1377.* Dublin, 1963.

de Roover, Raymond. "Les doctrines économiques des scolastiques à propos du traité sur l'usure d'Alexandre Lombard," *Revue d'Histoire Ecclesiastique* 59 (1964).

———. *L'Evolution de la Lettre de Change, XIVe-XVIIIe Siecles.* Paris. 1953.

———. *The Medici Bank, Its Organization, Management, Operations and Decline.* New York, 1948.

———. *Money, Banking and Credit in Mediaeval Bruges.* Cambridge (Mass.). 1948.

———. "The Organization of Trade," *Cambridge Economic History of Europe*, III, Chapter II.

———. *The Rise and Decline of the Medici Bank*. Cambridge (Mass.). 1963.

_____. "The story of the Alberti Company of Florence, 1302-1348, as Revealed in Its Account Books," *The Business History Review* XXXII (1958).

Salzman, L. F. *Edward I.* New York. 1968.

Sandys, A. "The Financial and Administrative Importance of the London Temple in the Thirteenth Century," *Essays in Medieval History Presented to Thomas Frederick Tout*. Manchester. 1925.

Sapori, Armando. *Le Marchand Italien au Moyen Age.* Paris. 1952.

Sayous, A. E. "Les operations des banquiers en Italie et aux foires de Champagne pendant le XIIIe siècle," *Revue Historique* CLXX. (1932).

Schaube, A. "Die Wollausführ Englands vom Jahre 1273," *Vierteljahrschrift für Sozial- und Wirtschaftsgeschichte* VI (1908).

Smith, B. J. "The Origins of the Revolt of Rhys Ap Maredudd," *Bulletin of the Board of Celtic Studies*, XXI, pt. II (1965).

Sutherland, Donald W. *Quo Warranto Proceedings in the Reign of Edward I.* Oxford. 1963.

Strayer, J. R. "Italian Bankers and Philip the Fair," *Explorations in Economic History* 7 (1969).

_____. *On the Medieval Origins of the Modern State.* Princeton 1970.

Strayer, J. R., and C. H. Taylor. *Studies in Early French Taxation.* Cambridge (Mass.). 1939.

De Sturler, J. *Les relations politiques et les échanges commerciaux entre le Duche de Brabant et l'Angleterre au moyen âge.* Paris. 1936.

O'Sullivan, M. D. "Italian Merchant Bankers and the Collection of the Customs in Ireland, 1275-1311," *Medieval Studies Presented to Aubrey Gwynn, S. J.* Dublin. 1961.

_____. *Italian Merchant Bankers in Ireland in the Thirteenth Century*. Dublin. 1962.

Sutcliffe, D. "The Financial Condition of the See of Canterbury, 1279-1292, *Speculum* 10 (1935).

Templeman, Geoffrey. "Edward I and the Historians," *Cambridge Historical Journal* 10 (1950).

Tout, T. F. *Chapters in the Administrative History of Medieval England.* 6 vols. Manchester. 1920-1933.

Trabut-Cussac, J. P. "Les coutumes ou droits de douane percus à Bordeaux sur les vins et les marchandises par l'administration anglaise 1252-1307," *Annales du Midi* LXII (1950).

_____. "Le financement de la croisade anglaise de 1270," *Bibliotheque de l'Ecole des chartres* CXIX (1961).

_____. "Itineraire d'Edouard Ier en France, 1286-1289," *Bulletin of the Institute of Historical Research* XXV (1952).

Verlinden, O. "Markets and Fairs," *Cambridge Economic History of Europe* III, Chapter III.

Whitwell, R. J. "English Monasteries and the Wool Trade in the 13th Century," *Vierteljahrschrift für Sozial- und Wirschaftsgeschichte* II (1904).

_____. "Italian Bankers and the English Crown," *Transactions of the Royal Historical Society* n.s. XVII (1903).

Willard, J. F. "The Memoranda Rolls and the Remembrancer in 1282-1350," *Essays in Medieval History Presented to Thomas Frederick Tout.* Manchester. 1925.

_____. *Parliamentary Taxes on Personal Property, 1290-1334.* Cambridge (Mass.). 1934.

Williams, G. A. "London and Edward I," *Transactions of the Royal Historical Society* 5th ser., XI (1961).

_____. *Medieval London, From Commune to Capital.* London. 1963.

Index